Beyond
A Levels

Also available in the *Future of Education From 14+* series:

Access, Participation and Higher Education edited by Annette Hayton and
    Anna Paczuska
Apprenticeship edited by Patrick Ainley and Helen Rainbird
The Baccalaureate edited by Graham Phillips and Tim Pound
New Labour's New Educational Agenda by Ann Hodgson and Ken Spours
Policies, Politics and the Future of Lifelong Learning by Ann Hodgson
Tackling Disaffection and Social Exclusion edited by Annette Hayton
Young People's Perspectives on Education, Training and Employment by
    Lorna Unwin and Jerry Wellington

Available from all good bookshops. To obtain further information, please
contact the publisher at the address below:

Kogan Page Limited
120 Pentonville Road
London N1 9JN
Tel: +44 (0)20 7278 0433
Fax: +44 (0)20 7837 6348
www.kogan-page.co.uk

THE FUTURE OF EDUCATION FROM 14+

Beyond A Levels

Curriculum 2000 and
the Reform of 14–19 Qualifications

**Ann Hodgson and
Ken Spours**

**KOGAN
PAGE**

London and Sterling, VA

First published in Great Britain and the United States in 2003 by Kogan Page Limited

120 Pentonville Road
London N1 9JN
UK
www.kogan-page.co.uk

22883 Quicksilver Drive
Sterling VA 20166–2012
USA

ISBN 0 7494 3672 7 (paperback)
     0 7494 3979 3 (hardback)

British Library Cataloguing in Publication Data

A CIP record for this book is available from the British Library.

Library of Congress Cataloging-in-Publication Data

Hodgson, Ann, 1953-
  Beyond A levels : curriculum 2000 and the reform of 14--19 qualifications / Ann Hodgson and Ken Spours.
     p. cm.
Includes bibliographical references and index.
  ISBN 0-7494-3672-7 (Paperback) -- ISBN 0-7494-3979-3 (Hardback)
  1. Education, Secondary--Great Britain--Curricula. 2. A-level examinations--Great Britain. I. Spours, Ken. II. Title.
  LB1629.5.G7H63 2003
  373.19'0941--dc21

                              2003005433

Typeset by Saxon Graphics Ltd, Derby
Printed and bound in Great Britain by Clays Ltd, St Ives plc

Contents

Foreword

There is wide agreement that 14–19 curriculum and qualifications in England, including A levels, are in need of reform; and there is growing support for the view that this reform needs to be structural and rather than a modification of existing arrangements. This is a rare situation in the history of any education system. Most countries' academic upper-secondary qualifications are sacrosanct, resistant to change and often enshrined in the constitution. In England, the A level was until recently the 'gold standard' of the educational currency, supported by powerful interests that a reforming government crossed at its peril. *Curriculum 2000* has changed all that. Few reforms in English education have generated so much controversy, and few have had such a radicalizing effect on educational opinion. The problems with examinations, the burdens on students and the controversies over key skills have filled columns of newsprint and launched several official inquiries. They have placed the reform of 14–19 qualifications firmly on the policy agenda.

Ann Hodgson and Ken Spours are respected and influential commentators who for many years have studied the twists and turns of policy and practice in 14–19 education. In collaboration with colleagues in Scotland, Wales and other European countries they have compared English developments with those elsewhere. Since 1999 they have led the Institute of Education/Nuffield Foundation research project on *Broadening the Advanced Level Curriculum* which has studied the progress of *Curriculum 2000* across all sectors of 14–19 education, from the preparatory phase into the third year of implementation. The project has collected data from all the main stakeholder groups using a variety of qualitative and quantitative approaches. Together with linked smaller studies, it provides a rich evidence base for this book.

At one level, then, this book is a well-documented account – and sure to become the definitive study – of the early impact of an important and controversial reform. But it is more than this. The book can also be read as a case study of a global phenomenon: the unification of upper-secondary education and training. *Curriculum 2000* may appear to be a specifically English response to idiosyncratically English problems; but it is also an example, however partial and ambivalent, of a wider cross-national drive to 'unify' the upper-secondary level of education systems and to bring academic and vocational learning closer together. Furthermore, it has faced the same challenges as unification programmes elsewhere: how to develop flexible curriculum pathways without creating an overload of assessment; how to raise the standing of vocational learning while avoiding its colonization by academic values and cultures; how to identify, deliver and assess the generic skills that young people need; and how to engage disaffected young people. These issues are as relevant in Scotland, Sweden, France or Australia as they are in England, even if the design of 'unifying' policies and their impact on education systems are mediated by very different political and institutional circumstances in each country.

A good case study illuminates the context in which the phenomenon is studied, as well as the phenomenon itself. At a third level, therefore, this book is a study of the English 14–19 education system and how this system responds to attempts to reform it. It is written with the deliberate intention to help this system to develop a 'policy memory' and a capacity for 'system thinking'. The past lack of these capacities has led to a cyclical pattern of policy-making in 14–19 education and training – every few years the same policies are recycled and rebadged, and fail to solve the same problems that therefore keep recurring. Hodgson and Spours aim to break this cycle by helping us to learn, not only from the failures of *Curriculum 2000*, but also from its successes and from the good practice that it has nurtured. They argue that *Curriculum 2000* is potentially a stage towards a more durable reform and a more unified 14+ curriculum and qualifications system, but that to realize this potential – to achieve genuine progress and not just another turn of the cycle – we have to understand the English education system and the dynamics of change in this system. One way to do this is to learn the lessons of earlier reform attempts such as *Curriculum 2000*.

At a fourth level, the book can be read as a reasoned manifesto for a new model of 14–19 education. In their last chapter Hodgson and Spours outline proposals for an English Baccalaureate system based on Diplomas offering varying possibilities for specialization around a common core at different levels from Entry to Advanced 2. This model builds on the strengths of the English system, such as choice, specialization and institutional innovation, and on the achievements of *Curriculum 2000*, notably its modularity and its introduction of a new level of study between GCSE and A level. But it also learns from its mistakes. In particular, Hodgson and Spours argue that 'any future reform process needs to be long-term, open and transparent, and to involve stakeholders from its inception to its implementation' (p161).

And just such a reform process may now be unfolding, inaugurated by the government's publication of *14–19: opportunity and excellence* early in 2003, by its appointment of a Working Group under Mike Tomlinson to explore strategic directions for change in 14–19 education, and by wider developments such as the annual Review of 14–19 Education being established by the Nuffield Foundation that funded the research underpinning this book. These developments themselves reflect the influence of Hodgson and Spours, and of the IoE/Nuffield project, on the 14–19 policy process. This book will contribute further to the reform process, by not only proposing new ideas for reform, but also by providing the evidence and analysis on which these ideas are based and by promoting the policy memory and system thinking necessary for effective change.

Professor David Raffe
University of Edinburgh

Acknowledgements

First and foremost we wish to acknowledge the support and resources we have received from The Nuffield Foundation for the Institute of Education/ Nuffield Research Project *Broadening the Advanced Level Curriculum,* which provides much of the evidence for this book. In particular, we would like to thank Anne Sofer and Catrin Roberts for their enthusiasm and for their interest in this research. We also wish to recognize the excellent work of the Research Officer on the project, Chris Savory, particularly in relation to the research for Chapters 2 and 5 and that of Martyn Waring, which contributed to Chapter 7. In addition, we would like to thank Stephanie Fox for her support throughout the project.

Over the last three years we have worked with education practitioners in different parts of the country, notably in the 50 schools and colleges which made up the sample for our research, together with colleagues from South Gloucestershire, Surrey, Essex and Lancashire LEAs. We want to thank these teachers, lecturers and learners for their time, commitment and professionalism. The qualitative research in which they participated has been an invaluable source of evidence and challenged much of our previous thinking in the area.

We are also very grateful to colleagues from the DfES, QCA, UCAS, LSDA and the education professional associations who have shared with us their data and their ideas on *Curriculum 2000*. Their research and writing in this field have provided us with invaluable evidence to compare with our own. In addition, we want to thank ministers and political advisers who have, from time to time, been prepared to give us some of the inside story.

While we take full responsibility for the final text, we are indebted to those who took time to comment in detail on drafts of some of the chapters. Our thanks go to Annie Cullen, John Dunford, Kathryn Ecclestone, Maggie Greenwood, Jeremy Higham, Tom Leney, Geoff Lucas, Alison Matthews, Tim Oates, David Raffe, Chris Savory, Gordon Stobart, Alison Wolf and David Yeomans.

Finally, we want to thank our long-suffering families who never quite believe us when we say that next term will be easier. We are really grateful for their ongoing support and understanding.

Introduction

In November we received in the post what we thought was a PhD thesis: it turned out to be one month's press cuttings on *Curriculum 2000* collected and analysed by the Qualifications and Curriculum Authority (QCA). This document, which was at least seven centimetres thick, demonstrated the continued newsworthiness of A levels, two years after the introduction of reforms to the advanced level curriculum. Two main themes emerged from the thousands of words contained in this document – either *Curriculum 2000* has been a disaster and we should never have messed about with A levels, or let's now finally get on with a new system such as a Baccalaureate.

This book, which is the first to be published on *Curriculum 2000*, tries to explain why the reform of advanced level qualifications has been so controversial by telling a story arising from three years of research. In our view, the book provides a much more textured picture than that portrayed in the media. We recognize that A levels did need reforming, that there are both strengths and weaknesses in *Curriculum 2000* and that we need to use the experience of these reforms to help us move forward to a new and better system.

There are three reasons why we have chosen the title *Beyond A Levels*. The first is that having been around for over 50 years, A levels look immovable yet, at the same time, there have been constant attempts to reform them. Is it possible to move beyond A levels? The second is that *Curriculum 2000* was seen by the new Labour Government as the most far-reaching attempt to date to reform A levels. However, what our research suggests is that the old system has been destabilized, but a new system has not yet been born. So have we moved beyond A levels? Third, if we think it is time to move beyond A levels, then what kind of new system should be put in their place and what features, if any, should be drawn from the past. So, what lies beyond A levels?

To be able to answer these questions requires a sense of the past and its relation to the present. In particular, it requires a sense of 'policy memory'

– what has worked, what has not and how reforms are always part of a wider context. Policy-makers – ministers and their civil servants in particular – are notorious for wanting their own new ideas and initiatives and are often not around long enough to have any sense of 'policy memory', so they are unable to benefit from 'policy learning'. They often suffer from what might be termed 'policy amnesia'. Practitioners, on the other hand, who are usually around a lot longer than politicians, do have a sense of policy memory because of their ongoing efforts to mediate national reforms to make them work at grassroots level.

We start this book, therefore, with a sense of history and set *Curriculum 2000* in its wider context in order to understand why this reform took place and why it took the form it did. This historical and system analysis also helps us to understand where the strengths and weaknesses of the reform originate.

The complex picture we provide is based on several dimensions of research, mainly undertaken over the last three years. Our major source of data is the 50 schools and colleges that formed our research sites in the IoE/Nuffield Research Project *Broadening the Advanced Level Curriculum,* triangulated with quantitative data from national agencies such as the DfES, UCAS, OFSTED, LSDA and QCA. In all cases, we have attempted to capture a range of voices, including managers and classroom teachers and, above all, learners. We think it is the last who have provided the most authentic and balanced account of the strengths and weaknesses of the reforms. Our research also draws on collaborative work with teacher professional associations and colleagues in several LEAs, discussions with other researchers and interviews with key national policy-makers.

The first two chapters in the book provide a framework for understanding the reforms and judging their effectiveness over time. We ask the question, 'Should *Curriculum 2000* be seen as yet another attempt to modernize A levels or should it be seen as a vital step in their replacement?' We attempt to answer this question in the final chapter. Chapter 3 starts the process of analysing the impact of the reforms by examining learner programmes as a whole and assessing how far *Curriculum 2000* is broadening the advanced level curriculum. Chapters 4, 5 and 6 discuss the contribution to this process of the main qualifications components of the reforms – the AS/2, the AVCE and key skills. Chapter 7 reverts back to contextual issues by looking at how three particular levers – the UCAS tariff, funding mechanisms and inspection – are being used to shape what we characterize as a voluntarist reform. This chapter also provides new information on the relationship between *Curriculum 2000* and the universities which, in the opinion of many, are seen as a vital influence in determining the success of the reforms.

Chapter 8, the final chapter, provides our overall assessment to date of the strengths and weaknesses of *Curriculum 2000*. In our view, the reforms have brought about limited breadth and quantitative gains, for example larger programmes of study, more qualifications outcomes and improved A level grades. At the same time, there have been qualitative losses and new forms of division – the decline of enrichment activity, very variable learner programmes, problems with the quality of learning and teaching in what has become an over-assessed, rushed and content-heavy curriculum. This judgement begs the question, 'Where next?'

A background theme running throughout the book, but which comes to the fore in the final chapter, is the long-standing debate about the need for a more unified and inclusive curriculum and qualifications system from 14+. This debate has raged for more than a decade since the publication of *A British Baccalaureate* in 1990, but has never been fully embraced by government because of a continuing anxiety about replacing A levels. The vision of a more unified and inclusive system now appears, at last, to be on the Government's agenda. While *Curriculum 2000* has undoubtedly been a painful experience, it provides us with vital lessons on what learners and teachers see as valuable, what should be taken forward and built upon in the next stage of reform and how to conduct the reform process. In this sense *Curriculum 2000* has been a difficult but useful apprenticeship.

In its recent response to the Green Paper on 14–19 education, the Government has signalled its willingness to consider a long-term approach towards replacing A levels with a Baccalaureate-style system. In this context, we offer some ideas about the architecture of such a system based upon several years of debate within the education profession and informed by the principles of inclusion, high standards and social justice. The vision we offer is an *English Baccalaureate System from 14+* which moves not only beyond A levels, but also beyond the highly regarded International Baccalaureate, because of its ability to include all learners from entry level upwards in all contexts, including both full-time and work-based learning. Finally, the most vital lesson to be learnt from *Curriculum 2000* is the need to conduct the next reform process in a gradual, consensual and managed way. This type of approach, which we term 'strategic gradualism', will allow us to build on the strengths of the English system – its flexibility, choice, specialization and teacher innovation – while at the same time addressing its major weaknesses – voluntarism, division and marginalized vocational education.

1

The importance of 'policy memory' and 'system thinking' for curriculum and qualifications reform in England

We believe that there is little chance of fully understanding the current or future nature of curriculum and qualifications reform without an appreciation of its wider historical and system context. The purpose of this chapter is to provide such a framework of understanding.

Our central argument is that recent history shows a consistent and considerable reluctance by all shades of government over the last 15 years to reform the upper secondary or 14–19 curriculum in a decisive and coherent manner. In our view, as this book will testify, this also includes the most recent attempt known as *Curriculum 2000*. At the centre of this reluctance has been the unwillingness of the Conservatives to reform A levels and the fear of New Labour to be seen to be doing so. Instead, what governments have done is to make changes to curriculum and qualifications in a piecemeal, divisive and permissive manner in order to respond to wider social and economic factors and, in particular, rises in full-time participation in post-compulsory education over the last decade or so. What our historical analysis will show is that the main reform effort to date has focused not on a systematic approach to curriculum and qualifications, but to organizational and regulatory frameworks within an education market. The formation of the new Learning and Skills Council (DfEE, 1999a) is the latest manifestation of this particular policy trend.

Recent events, notably the 'crisis' of the A level examinations in 2002 suggest to us that this approach has run its course. The Government now stands at a crossroads in its second term of office. The Green Paper, *14–19 Education: Extending Opportunities, Raising Standards* (DfES, 2002a), which we will see was simply an extension of the policy of post-16 voluntarism carried into the 14–19 phase, has, in important respects, been rejected by the education profession (see Chapter 8). There are signs that, in response to the A level crisis, the views of the teaching profession and the appointment of a new ministerial team, the Government now feels able to embark upon a more radical and long-term transformation of curriculum and qualifications for the 14–19 phase of education (DfES, 2003).

It is the purpose of this chapter to develop the concepts of 'policy memory' and 'system thinking' to support professional understanding of the possibilities and pitfalls in 14–19 curriculum and qualifications reform. By 'policy memory' (Higham *et al,* 2002) we are referring to the ability of those involved in the policy process to understand where mistakes were made and what good practice deserves to be incorporated from the past into the current reform effort. By 'system thinking' (Hodgson and Spours, 1997a) we refer not only to the historical dimension already outlined above, but also to the relationship between curriculum and qualifications reform and wider economic and social trends, together with education and training system factors that 'shape' these reforms. System thinking is about appreciating that curriculum and qualifications reform cannot be undertaken in isolation from powerful shaping factors such as funding, performance tables and teacher supply.

In order to provide a conceptual framework comprising historical analysis, system thinking and policy memory, we begin by setting out a brief account of the main social, economic and wider education and training trends since the late 1970s, which builds on and updates our previous analysis (Hodgson and Spours, 1997b, 1999a). We then lay out the key national qualifications and curriculum policy responses to these trends to provide a basis for discussion of the relationship between reform in this area and its wider education and training system context. Within these national policy developments we also discuss the role of local and institutional actions. Together, these three factors form the historical and analytical framework within which we locate the recent *Curriculum 2000* advanced level qualification reforms and the new 14–19 education and training policy agenda.

Factors shaping curriculum and qualifications reform – a system perspective

There are a number of important factors which, over the past 25 years, have played a shaping role in curriculum and qualifications reform in this country. Some of these have been present throughout the whole period (eg labour market and participation trends) while others, which are the result of direct education and training policy intervention (eg performance tables and higher education expansion), have only had an impact at certain periods. We will outline these major factors briefly here and then discuss their effects more fully at different stages of the curriculum and qualifications reform process in the following section of this chapter.

Participation and achievement trends

Arguably the most important background factor throughout the whole period from the late 1970s to the present has been changes in the youth labour market and the related increase in full-time post-16 participation. The same period has seen a general rise in social and educational aspirations, but also one of sharp polarization, in which sections of the population have become excluded from this general trend and have not seen education as a viable means of social progress (Oppenheim, 1998; Pearce and Hillman, 1998; Social Exclusion Unit, 1999). The late 1980s, under the Conservatives, saw an increase in participation in full-time education from what, in retrospect, could be seen as 'easier to reach' parts of the cohort (ie the middle quartiles of the youth population) (Green and Steedman, 1997). The Labour Government, from 1997 onwards, focused more explicitly on widening participation in education and training to those sections of the cohort who had been left behind in the Conservative expansion and on those who had traditionally not participated in post-compulsory education and training (Hodgson and Spours, 1999a).

In our historical analysis of the effects of participation on curriculum and qualifications reform policy we identify two distinct periods (Hodgson and Spours, 2000a). The first was a period of rapid growth in full-time participation in the late 1980s and early 1990s leading to the need for new types of education provision, particularly in the field of post-16 broad vocational qualifications. The second was a period of slower participation growth, from the mid-1990s, which caused the Government to think again about the type of qualifications and courses that would encourage more learners to stay on and to achieve from 14+.

From the late 1980s and underpinning this wider participation trend, there have been rises in educational achievement which have led to demands for more full-time post-compulsory education, including higher education. However, this improvement has followed a similar pattern to trends in participation, and the annual percentage increases of learners achieving 'good GCSE grades' and Level 3 qualifications (A levels and their vocational equivalents) has declined since the mid-1990s. We have termed the relationship between these two sets of trends in participation and achievement 'system slowdown' (Hodgson and Spours, 2000a). This phenomenon has been recognized as providing a challenging context for meeting the national target of 50 per cent participation by 18–30-year-olds in higher education by the 2010 (HEFCE, 2001) and is thus now shaping the debate about curriculum and qualifications reform for 14–19-year-olds, as we will see below.

The market and regulation in education and training

A further key background factor to the debate about curriculum and qualifications reform is the 'marketization' of the education and training system (Ball *et al*, 2000; Green and Lucas, 1999). Both Conservative and Labour governments have supported the concept of an education and training market in which learner demand is intended to drive institutional provision

(DES/ED/WO, 1991; DfEE, 1998). During the Conservative era, particularly the period from the late 1980s and the early 1990s, this policy was pursued through the encouragement of institutional autonomy and increased competition between post-16 providers to attract learners. The Labour Government, on the other hand, has placed greater emphasis on stimulating learner demand (eg Education Maintenance Allowances and Individual Learning Accounts), while at the same time encouraging schools, colleges and training providers to collaborate over the supply of provision which is responsive to learner need (DfEE, 1999a). This can be seen as a 'managed market' approach within a voluntarist framework.

While Conservative and Labour administrations have taken somewhat different approaches to participation and stimulating educational demand, they have pursued a very similar policy over accountability and central control. Both have focused on greater levels of accountability as institutional autonomy has increased and as the education and training system has become more marketized and diverse. Both have also used targets and performance measures linked to international comparison, national inspection systems and funding methodology to mould the behaviour of the education providers. We will see at several points in the book that all of these steering mechanisms have had a strong effect on institutional motivation to implement curriculum and qualifications reform.

Part of the national regulatory agenda accompanying marketization has been the trend towards the 'unification' of national regulatory agencies. The first merger was between the Department for Education and the Employment Department, which became the Department for Education and Employment (DfEE) in 1995. This was followed by the merger of the National Council for Vocational Qualifications (NCVQ) and the Schools Curriculum and Assessment Authority (SCAA) to form the Qualifications and Curriculum Authority (QCA) in 1997. Hard on its heels in the same year came the rationalization of the main eight examining and validating bodies into the three unitary awarding bodies: Edexcel, AQA and OCR. Finally, the funding and organization of all post-16 education and training provision (with the exception of higher education) was brought under a single national body, the Learning and Skills Council (LSC) with its 47 local LSCs, together with a Common Inspection Framework which covers all providers in the LSC sector (OFSTED/ALI, 2000). The overall effect so far of this unified regulatory framework has been to create a more direct relationship between central government policy and its implementation at institutional level.

The changing role of teachers and lecturers

The creation of a market in education and training and the inevitable accompanying central government accountability agenda has not only affected the way that post-16 institutions are managed and organized, but has also had an impact on the role and conditions of service of teachers and lecturers. The increase in participation in full-time post-compulsory education has led to more diverse groups of learners and, in many cases, a growth in class sizes. The number of temporary and part-time contracts has increased while, at the same time, more teacher time is spent on bureaucratic and administrative tasks and there is less time for professional development (Leney *et al,* 1998). Within further education, in particular, a 'new managerial class' has been created to cope with changes in funding and the drive to recruit and retain learners (Green and Lucas, 1999).

Recently, and perhaps unsurprisingly given the factors we have just outlined, there has been widespread concern about the shortage of teachers in all sectors. Moreover, constant and often ill-conceived curriculum and qualifications reforms have meant that practitioners have had to spend their time mediating top-down national reforms (Higham *et al,* 2002) rather than being involved in their shaping and management. The combination of these changes in the role of teachers and lecturers, together with centralist or piecemeal reform, has tended to force the education profession into a defensive and reactive stance.

The significance of changes in Scotland and Wales

Despite the general shift towards the centralized control of education (which we also associate with marketization), in the late 1990s there was also a movement towards the political devolution of Scotland and Wales. Up until this point Wales had been almost entirely part of the English education and training system, while Scotland had enjoyed a degree of administrative autonomy since the late 1970s. Increasingly, both Scotland and Wales are now reforming their education systems along different lines from England (Scottish Office, 1994; Welsh Department of Education and Training, 2002). This will allow 'home international comparisons' to be made within the UK in addition to those with other national systems beyond the UK. We will speculate that these comparisons will stimulate debate for more radical change within England as both Scotland and Wales move more firmly to more planned and collaborative systems with a stronger and inclusive curriculum ethos.

Four broad phases of curriculum and qualifications reform policy

In this section we outline an historical and analytical framework to explain the development of curriculum and qualifications policy over the last 25 years. We take the late 1970s as our starting point because it is widely recognized that what has proved to be a constant period of post-14 curriculum and qualifications reform began at this point as a result of intensified economic crisis (the end of the 'long boom'), the growth of youth unemployment and government concerns to create a stronger relationship between education and industry. In this respect, a defining moment was Prime Minister James Callaghan's Ruskin College speech (Callaghan, 1976). Our historical analysis finishes with the publication of the Government's Green Paper, *14–19 Education: Extending Opportunities, Raising Standards* (DfES, 2002a) and its response following the consultation process. The framework we use, which is organized into four broad overlapping historical phases, describes the complex and dynamic relationship between national curriculum and qualifications policy, the wider contextual factors already outlined and local and institutional interpretation and imple-mentation of national reforms.

The New Vocationalism (1976–1986)

We define the period of the New Vocationalism as one that stretches from the mid-1970s through to the mid-1980s and the founding of the National Council for Vocational Qualifications (NCVQ). What characterizes this period is a series of initiatives for the young unemployed (eg the Youth Opportunities Programme and then the Youth Training Scheme) which were eventually accompanied by a range of pre-vocational qualifications and awards, such as the Certificate of Extended Education (CEE), the Certificate of Pre-vocational Education (CPVE) and City and Guilds 365. In addition, the Government introduced the Technical and Vocational Education Initiative (TVEI) to encourage the growth of a more vocational, applied and technical approach to the full-time 14–19 curriculum in schools and colleges.

There were two landmark policy developments in the era of the New Vocationalism. The first was the publication of *A Basis for Choice* (FEU, 1979) which proposed a rationalization of the disparate unemployment initiatives within a single 'framework of preparation', which eventually resulted in the creation of CPVE. The second was the publication of the *New Training Initiative* (NTI) (MSC, 1981), which spawned the Youth Training Scheme. The NTI could also be seen as setting out a new agenda for thinking about the design of qualifications through its argument for outcomes-based standards of a new type. This was eventually to lead to the development of NVQs in the late 1980s.

The factors shaping these developments were found principally outside the education and training system, while radically affecting curriculum and qualification debates within it. Foremost among these was the economic recession and the rise in youth unemployment. The main way in which these economic factors affected the education and training response was that they gave rise to a perceived need for the development of generic or transferable skills to prepare young people for changing labour markets, as well as to cope with youth unemployment. While *A Basis for Choice* proposed a single curriculum framework, what actually emerged was a plethora of initiatives and new awards subsequently dubbed the 'qualifications jungle' (Pratley, 1988). These initiatives were essentially aimed at those who could not gain O or A levels and who could not immediately gain entry to a shrinking youth labour market or apprenticeship.

However, the New Vocationalism was not simply seen as an alternative curriculum for some. By the mid-1980s, and often articulated through TVEI with its role in relation to full-time learners, there was a strong call from a mixture of academics and politicians for a more applied and vocationally-relevant curriculum for all learners (Broadfoot, 1986; Pring, 1986; Pring *et al*, 1988). What had started as a narrow form of vocationalism in the early 1980s was turning into a wave of 'bottom-up' curriculum innovation by the end of the decade.

The period of the New Vocationalism was essentially driven by the Manpower Services Commission (MSC) and the Employment Department (ED) rather than by the Department of Education and Science (DES). It has also been seen as representing a movement to greater centralized control of the education and training agenda and, in particular, of the curriculum, with critics arguing that it represented an imposition of social control (Ranson, 1985), a divisive approach to education and training (Cohen, 1984; Green, 1986) and an emphasis on vocationalism in the absence of jobs for young people (Finn, 1987).

The major impact of the era of the New Vocationalism on curriculum and qualifications reform was fourfold:

1. It marked the beginnings of an attempt to 'massify' post-compulsory education and training, albeit in a controversial way.
2. There was a move to a more applied curriculum with a greater emphasis on more active teaching and learning styles.
3. It marked the beginnings of a move away from terminal examinations and towards the use of continuous assessment and an outcomes-based curriculum.
4. Towards the end of the 1980s, the New Vocationalism moved from an association with the proliferation of qualifications to a policy of rationalizing vocational qualifications within a national framework.

A national two-track qualifications system (1986–1991)

While vocationalization of the curriculum was still prevalent in the late 1980s, it was only in 1986, with the founding of the NCVQ, that a national system of vocational qualifications began to be developed. This could be seen as the beginning of the creation of a national two-track qualifications system – academic and vocational – to replace the piecemeal vocational qualifications and vocational initiatives that characterized the previous era. Interestingly, while this period represented a concerted move towards the formation of a more centrally controlled national curriculum and qualifications system (eg the National Curriculum, GCSE and NVQs), it was also a period of intense local innovation and curriculum development (Hodgson and Spours, 1997b). In fact, in our view, this was the most experimental period for curriculum and qualifications development of the last 25 years, though its scope was limited. The underlying assumption of this period was that a minority of learners would continue to participate in full-time post-compulsory education and the rest would be on training programmes or in the workplace. Training and Enterprise Councils (TECs) were also established during this period to stimulate the growth of work-based training, to oversee government training programmes and initiatives for the unemployed, and to encourage a viable and competitive enterprise culture. As we discuss below, many of the local and institutional curriculum initiatives during this period, on the other hand, were, wittingly or unwittingly, attempts to cater for those young people who wished to stay on in full-time education, but for whom there was a very limited range of national qualifications available.

Five key national curriculum and qualifications policy developments took place during this era:

1. The General Certificate of Secondary Education (GCSE) was introduced as a common 16+ examination to replace the O level and the Certificate of Secondary Education (CSE).
2. A National Curriculum was created for 5–16-year-olds with standard attainment tests (SATs) at the ages of 7, 11 and 14 and related to GCSE from 14+.
3. A national system of competence-based vocational qualifications – known as National Vocational Qualifications (NVQs) – and based on occupational standards was started by NCVQ in 1986.
4. There was a review of A level qualifications led by Professor Higginson, which culminated in a report (DES, 1988) that was instantly rejected by the Conservative Government.
5. There was a series of reports and recommendations for the development of core skills, not only in vocational qualifications but also in A levels (eg HMI, 1989; NCC, 1990).

Throughout this period there was also an increasing attempt to ensure that national agencies responsible for curriculum and qualifications – National Curriculum Council (NCC) NCVQ, DES, ED and the Joint Board of awarding bodies – worked more closely together (DE/DES, 1986).

At the same time, these national developments were matched by a range of local curriculum and qualifications innovations which were primarily designed to meet the needs of an increasing number of young people staying on in full-time education and to motivate those learners who were in danger of dropping out of the system before the end of their period of compulsory education. These local developments principally focused on the introduction of more applied and work-based learning into the full-time education curriculum, experimentation with different teaching and learning styles and modes of assessment, and modularization and unitization of the curriculum.

While it was mainly individual teachers, schools, colleges and local education authorities who led these initiatives, they were supported by examination and validating bodies, national government agencies, such as the Further Education Unit (FEU), and funding sources, such as TVEI Extension. Some notable examples of this experimentation can be seen in the development of the Wessex A level Project (Rainbow, 1993) and the development of Y-models combining BTEC National and A levels in the first year of study (Richardson *et al,* 1993). It could be argued that these initiatives increasingly challenged the national government drive for a divided qualifications system and could also be seen to inspire the development of a more unified approach to curriculum and qualifications which emerged in a variety of reports and policy documents from 1990 onwards.

We would argue that factors beyond the education and training system played a less obvious role in shaping government policy on curriculum and qualifications in this phase, in comparison with the previous one. A notable exception to this was an increasing focus on international comparisons of education and training systems (eg NEDO/MSC, 1984; OECD, 1985), which highlighted the need to increase participation in education and training beyond 16 and the role of qualifications outcomes in relation to this policy aim.

The major shaping influences in the late 1980s thus became ones internal to the education and training system, as government sought to make it more coherent and national in character. This could be seen as a further move towards central government control of education and training, though considerable space was still available for local or mediating national organizations to play a role in curriculum and qualifications reform (Higham *et al,* 2002; Hodgson and Spours, 1997b).

A national triple-track qualifications system (1991–2000)

From the publication of the White Paper, *Education and Training for the 21st Century* (DES/ED/WO, 1991), however, this position changed. Not only did the space for local innovation in curriculum and qualifications reform diminish, but there was a concerted attempt to form a distinctive triple-track qualifications system in order not to dilute the academic track (ie A levels) while catering for the increasing numbers of 16–19-year-olds participating in full-time education (Hodgson and Spours, 1997b). The curriculum and qualifications effects of the 1991 White Paper would be felt for the rest of decade, until the introduction of New Labour's *Curriculum 2000* reforms with their stress on 'linkages' rather than distinctions between the three qualifications tracks (Raffe *et al,* 1998).

The main national curriculum and qualifications development during this period was the creation of a third qualifications track, in addition to A levels and NVQs, based on the introduction of the General National Vocational Qualification (GNVQ). This new broad vocational qualification had some of the design features of NVQs, but was aimed at 16–19-year-olds in full-time education, many of whom could not or did not want to take A levels. At the same time, the academic track was made more exclusive with restrictions on assessed coursework in GCSE and A levels and the tiering of GCSE examination papers (Spours, 1993). These measures could be seen to allow for an expansion of participation in post-14 education and training while preserving lines of distinctiveness and division between different curriculum and qualifications routes. The main way of preserving differences between the three tracks was based on highly distinctive approaches to assessment. The academic track was dominated by external examinations, the broad vocational track was dominated by course-work assessment, and NVQs by observation of the mastery of competences in the workplace.

This formalized triple-track system broadened what had been a national vocational qualifications system by bringing into the framework broad vocational and academic qualifications. More explicit qualifications levels, spanning these three qualifications tracks, were introduced. In addition, a limited alignment of Advanced GNVQ and A level subjects was created to support the concept of parity of esteem within a divided system.

This phase saw a rapid push to more centralized control of the curriculum and qualifications at 14+ based, as we have seen, primarily on assessment policy. In this national context the room for curriculum and assessment innovation at the local level rapidly declined and much of the experimentation of the late 1980s was effectively stifled. The focus for teachers, lecturers and curriculum developers at the local level shifted to the implementation of national curriculum and qualifications reforms, such as GNVQs, and to the process-based and progression-related elements of TVEI Extension such as recording of achievement, individual action planning, careers education and guidance and work-related learning. One way of viewing this shift of innovation at the local and institutional level is as an attempt to mediate for the newly participating full-time post-16 learners the new national curriculum and qualifications system with its tightly bound assessment regime.

The main national shaping influence of this phase was the policy to rapidly expand education and training participation but at lower unit costs. This was achieved through the implementation of the Further and Higher Education (FHE) Act in 1992. This Act took forward the proposals in the 1991 White Paper and attempted to create a market in initial post-compulsory education through the incorporation of further education colleges and the setting up of the Further Education Funding Council (FEFC). This took colleges out of the control of local education authorities (LEAs), which still retained responsibility for school sixth forms. These moves immediately increased competition between the newly incorporated further education colleges and the school sixth forms over provision for 16–19-year-olds and particularly over A levels and GNVQs. The period also saw the rapid growth of small sixth forms in schools that used the 1988 Education Reform Act (ERA) to opt out of LEA control and to take on Grant Maintained (GM) status with all the national government funding benefits that this decision brought with it.

One effect of this more marketized system was the duplication of post-16 provision with similar full-time programmes of study for 16–19-year-olds being offered in both schools and colleges. GNVQs, unlike earlier traditional vocational qualifications, had been designed specifically to be offered in both schools and colleges. It is interesting to note that the majority of students who followed Advanced Level GNVQ programmes saw this new qualification as a means of entry to higher education rather than to the workplace (FEDA/IoE/Nuffield Foundation, 1997).

International comparisons continued to play an important role during this period, particularly in relation to the development of national targets. National Targets for Education and Training (NTETs), which had been called for by the Confederation for British Industry in the early 1990s (CBI, 1993), were subsequently adopted by the government. There were targets for participation, work-based training and qualifications achievements at levels 2, 3 and 4. While the NTETs were clearly intended to enshrine objectives that all education and training providers saw as important and would strive to achieve, they were not widely known about in the school sector, remaining largely the preserve of TECs, and were not key drivers for either schools or colleges. Of much greater importance for these institutions were the performance indicators based on GCSEs and A levels, which they had to publish in their prospectuses in order to provide parents and prospective learners with detailed information on their examination performance. These, together with increasing national and local media attention on performance at GCSE and A level and the publication in the national and local press of 'league tables' of schools and colleges ranked by examination results, further fuelled competition between schools and colleges for high achieving 16–19-year-olds.

The 1992 FHE Act also abolished the binary divide between polytechnics and universities and effectively allowed all higher education institutions the opportunity to rethink their mission and markets for recruitment. All those offering undergraduate programmes, however, were actively engaged in recruiting the increasing number of 16–19-year-olds who were staying on in full-time education during this period. As a result, the new GNVQ qualifications were quite rapidly accepted as entry qualifications to many degree-level courses by many of the new post-1992 universities.

While the whole of the period from 1991 to 2000 can be seen as one of increased participation and expansion in post-compulsory education, albeit, as we have stated earlier in this chapter, with a slowdown in the participation of full-time younger learners from 1994 onwards, national policy on participation took on a somewhat different flavour from 1997 with the move from a Conservative to a New Labour government. The hallmark of the new administration was a focus on widening rather than simply increasing participation in post-compulsory education (Hodgson and Spours, 1999a). Key documents, such as the Kennedy Report (Kennedy, 1997), the Dearing Higher Education Report (NCIHE, 1997), the Fryer Report (Fryer, 1997) and the new government's own Green Paper response to these, *The Learning Age* (DfEE, 1998), made it plain that expanding participation in education and training needed to involve the whole population if the Government's social justice as well as economic goals were to be achieved.

However, as we shall see below, this expansion had to take place without compromising standards, particularly in relation to A levels. This meant that some of the more radical aspects of the curriculum and qualifications reform agenda that were signalled in the Labour Party's own pre-election policy document, *Aiming Higher: Labour's Proposals for reform of the 14–19 Curriculum* (Labour Party, 1996) were relegated in importance (Hodgson and Spours, 1999a).

A 'standards-based linkages' approach to qualifications reform (1996–2002)

This section looks at a new phase of curriculum and qualifications reform brought in by New Labour. We term this phase a standards-based linkages qualifications approach[1] because of the growing emphasis on providing 'bridges' between the three qualifications tracks to encourage participation, progression and more mixing of general and vocational study (Hodgson and Spours, 1999a, 1999b). This phase of qualifications development can be seen to emerge from the Dearing Review of Qualifications for 16–19-year-olds (Dearing, 1996) and also from New Labour's subsequent reform proposals (DfEE, DENI/WO, 1997). However, this approach has its roots not only in the triple-track qualifications system but also in the unification debates that took place from the early 1990s.

Debates about a unified system

Throughout the first part of the 1990s, Labour Party policy, initially on post-16 and subsequently on post-14 qualifications reform, became closely aligned with the unification debate. In 1990, *A British Baccalaureate*, published by the Institute of Public Policy Research (Finegold *et al*, 1990), proposed a single modular qualification – the British Baccalaureate – to replace A levels and vocational qualifications and to be awarded at 18 or 19. This concept of a modular qualifications system leading to a unified form of certification was based on initiatives that took place during the innovative phase of curriculum and qualifications development during the late 1980s discussed earlier. There were also some international influences – notably the modular Scottish Action Plan and, to a lesser extent, the International Baccalaureate. However, the British Baccalaureate was different from the International Baccalaureate because it proposed a multi-level unified award involving both academic and vocational learning.

During the early 1990s, the debate on the reform of post-14 qualifications involved both critique and proposals for an alternative approach. Some of the critique focused on the Government's formation of a more formalized triple-track system. However, most of the debate centred on criticisms of the role and function of NVQs and the newly introduced GNVQs (Hodkinson and Mattinson, 1994; Hyland, 1994; Smithers' 1993). The alternative approaches to reform were dominated by proposals for a unified 14+ curriculum and qualifications system (see Chapter 8).

The Dearing Review and *Aiming Higher*

Following the 1991 White Paper, the Conservative Government had not intended further immediate reform for post-compulsory qualifications. However, by the mid-1990s it was becoming clear that the ambitious achievement targets outlined by NACETT would not be reached without further changes. The problems with the cost-effectiveness of different post-16 qualifications were also highlighted in the Audit Commission/OFSTED report, *Unfinished Business* (1993). At the same time, OFSTED and FEFC inspection reports on the implementation of GNVQs were critical of the new qualifications, particularly their assessment regime, their bureaucracy and their initial low completion rates (FEFC, 1994; OFSTED, 1994, 1996a). As a result of these pressures, in 1995 Sir Ron Dearing was asked to conduct a review of Qualifications for 16–19-year-olds. At the same time, both GNVQs and NVQs were subjected to review by John Capey and Gordon Beaumont, respectively.

In his review, Sir Ron Dearing focused not only on A levels but also used the findings from the Beaumont and Capey Reports (Beaumont, 1995; Capey, 1996) to make recommendations for changes to vocational qualifications. He argued that further reform of qualifications for 16–19-year-olds was justified on the grounds that the academic/vocational divide was inhibiting learner progress, that there were high levels of non-completion, that problems of basic literacy and numeracy existed for all but the highest achievers and that the qualifications system was complex and lacked clarity (Dearing, 1996). While his report made a total of 198 recommendations, the main and most influential qualifications proposals were:

- to establish a 'lateral AS' as a halfway stage to a full A level;
- to reform the Advanced GNVQ into a smaller and more manageable vocational qualification that was more aligned with A levels;
- to create an AS in what were to become the three main key skills (Communication, Application of Number and IT);

- to consider the development of a certificate and a diploma at advanced level to secure greater breadth of study; and
- to create a more accessible and clearer national qualifications framework with a new entry level and a common grading system between A levels and broad vocational qualifications.

The Dearing approach to reform envisaged a system of qualifications tracks in which learners took 'distinctive' courses with a clear identity but which, at the same time, provided an opportunity to change direction and to combine elements of academic and vocational study. What in effect he was proposing was a triple-tracked system, but with 'linkages' between each of the three tracks. However, Dearing's reform agenda was not simply confined to qualifications: he also addressed problems of organizational complexity and quality assurance. His proposals included the merger of the Schools Curriculum and Assessment Authority (SCAA) and the NCVQ to create a single regulatory body with oversight of the linked qualifications system and the further rationalization of awarding bodies. He also thought it necessary to see the phasing out of Youth Training (YT) in the work-based route and its replacement by National Traineeships at a level below that of the newly created Modern Apprenticeships. In this sense, the Dearing reforms can be seen as wide-ranging but without embracing many of the key proposals made by the 'unifiers', and possibly as heading off the need for more radical reform.

Dearing's proposals have to be analysed in the wider political context (Young, 1997). His review took place in the last years of the Major Government with the political prospect of a new Labour administration looming over the horizon and his brief was constrained. Above all, Dearing was a pragmatist and sought to produce a report that would be acceptable to the Conservatives but would also provide a workable legacy for a new Labour Government. Dearing went with the grain of a voluntarist approach to post-compulsory education (for example, his proposed overarching diplomas and certificates were optional) and with an emphasis on 'parity of esteem' between separate qualifications types rather than a more unified curriculum and qualifications system for all.

In May 1996, his report was published, a week after the launch of New Labour's own document *Aiming Higher* (Labour Party, 1996) but development work continued up until the general election in May 1997. *Aiming Higher*, on the other hand, could be seen as the adoption by the Labour Party of many of the reform proposals of the unifiers. It proposed the development by an incoming Labour Government of a unified and modular 14–19 curriculum and qualifications framework in two stages, spanning two Parliaments (Labour Party, 1996).

Qualifying for Success, Curriculum 2000, and changes to the national qualifications framework

In its 1997 general election manifesto, the Labour Party officially committed itself to three elements of qualifications reform at advanced level.

Responding to long-standing professional pressure for changes to A levels, the new Government recognized that the existing advanced level curriculum was too narrow, particularly when compared with other European countries (DfEE/DENI/WO, 1997). It declared, however, that its priorities would be to 'support broader A levels, upgrade vocational qualifications underpinned by rigorous standards and key skills' (Labour Party, 1997). This represented a considerable reduction of its objectives outlined in *Aiming Higher*: there was no mention of modularization, an Advanced Diploma or a single coherent 14–19 curriculum and qualifications system. The new Labour Government was about to embrace the Dearing Review rather than its own pre-election party document.

In order to secure its own interpretation of Dearing, the Labour Government's immediate response was to put the Dearing reform agenda on hold ostensibly on the grounds that the implementation process had been rushed and time was needed to reappraise the situation (DfEE, 1997a). The Government then launched a further round of review and consultation based on its own policy document, *Qualifying for Success* (DfEE/DENI/WO, 1997). At the same time, it indicated a move in the direction of unification by bringing SCAA and NCVQ together into a single regulatory body – the Qualifications and Curriculum Authority (QCA) – and by rationalizing the major academic and vocational awarding bodies into three leading organizations (DfEE, 1997b, 1997c).

In its *Qualifying for Success* consultation paper on 16–19 qualifications, the newly-elected Labour Government proposed to break A levels into two three-unit blocks (AS and A2) which together formed an A level; to make changes to GNVQs to bring them more into line with A levels, in terms of grading and structure; to introduce a Key Skills Qualification in Communication, Application of Number and IT; and 'to work in the longer term towards an overarching certificate, building on the Dearing proposals for National Certificates and a National Advanced Diploma' (DfEE/DENI/WO, 1997, p23). These proposals were designed to create more common features between advanced level qualifications and to break large qualifications down into smaller blocks that could be more flexibly combined into mixed and broader learner programmes. Some aspects of *Aiming Higher* – its proposals for unitization and for an overarching certificate – became the focus of research rather than of immediate development and implementation. QCA was asked to carry out a consultation on unitization of qualifications for adults (QCA, 1999a) and the regulatory authorities of England, Wales and Northern Ireland were tasked with commissioning independent research on designs for an overarching certificate (QCA/CCEA/ACCAC, 1998).

The *Qualifying for Success* consultation document can thus be seen as taking the linkages aspects of the Dearing Report further but without his emphasis on qualifications distinctiveness. It was greeted with muted support by both academics and practitioners, with many feeling that it had not gone far enough in a unified direction, did not promote accessibility to advanced level and remained voluntarist (AoC, 1997; Institute of Education, 1997; NAHT, 1997).

The new AS/A2, AVCE and Key Skills Qualifications developed as part of the *Qualifying for Success* reform process were introduced in September 2000 and replaced the old linear and modular A levels and Advanced Level GNVQs. These qualifications reforms, which became known as *Curriculum 2000*, are described in more detail in the next chapter.

Apart from the development of the *Qualifying for Success* proposals, the main qualifications reform emphasis in the first Parliament (1997–2001) was confined to further enlargement and rationalization of the National Qualifications Framework (NQF) to include a wider range of qualifications than previously and, arguably, to better secure their public recognition. This new stage of development of the NQF aimed to provide a framework of qualifications that could be easily understood by all learners and end-users. The Government believed that a qualification was more likely to be taken up by learners and recognized by employers and higher education providers if it lay within a clear and trusted framework. Moreover, if all qualifications had to meet accreditation criteria in order to enter the NQF, they could be more easily linked and legitimately compared. The policy on the NQF can be seen, therefore, as another aspect of the standards-based linkages approach to curriculum and qualifications reform (Spours, 2000).

The Green Paper – a 14–19 standards-based linkages approach

The Government's White Paper, *Schools Achieving Success* (DfES, 2001a) and its subsequent Green Paper, *14–19 Education: Extending opportunities, raising standards* (DfES, 2002a), both mark an official recognition of the 14–19 phase of education and training which was originally discussed in Labour's pre-election document, *Aiming Higher*, in 1996. However, the Green Paper did not, in our view, represent a rediscovery of the principles behind this previous document; rather it represented an extension to the 14–19 phase of the Government's existing standards-based linkages approach to qualifications reform from 16+.

The Green Paper was seen by Government as a means of building on the reforms and gains in primary education (notably the purported success of the literacy and numeracy strategy) and modernizing secondary education by making the curriculum more flexible and individualized to increase motivation, achievement and employability. It sought to achieve this 'step change in performance in secondary education' (Morris, 2002) by:

- reducing the level of prescription for 14–16-year-olds at Key Stage 4;
- providing a viable and high status vocational ladder for learners who are not motivated by a more academic subject-based curriculum;
- allowing for personal pacing of learning in the 14–19 phase; and
- encouraging 'education with character' through engagement with a broader curriculum including citizenship and work-related study.

Central to its more flexible concept of 14–19 education is increased collaboration between schools, colleges and workplaces around a broader range of vocational provision and pathways of progression.

The main curriculum and qualifications proposals in the Green Paper were the creation of a smaller core curriculum from 14+ and the introduction of new qualifications. It was proposed that the curriculum from Key Stage 4 would be reduced to a 'core for progression', consisting of English, Mathematics, Science and ICT, in which learners were expected to be examined at Level 2, and a 'core for personal development' including RE, Citizenship, PE and work-related learning. The Green Paper also intended to 'broaden' GCSEs by the introduction of a new range of GCSEs in vocational areas. These were seen as a new rung on the 'vocational ladder' leading into the new AVCEs brought in under *Curriculum 2000* and Modern Apprenticeships. In the longer term, the Green Paper suggested there might be a role for overarching certificates (the proposed Intermediate, Advanced and Higher Matriculation Diplomas) as a framework for securing Literacy/English, Numeracy/Mathematics and ICT at Level 2 and recording engagement with a broader range of experiences such as citizenship, work-related learning and RE.

While there was a limited entitlement for all learners from 14 to 16, in the Green Paper proposals there was an intention that the shape of the curriculum should be determined by schools, colleges and individual learners in consultation with their parents. The document thus took a permissive view of curriculum entitlement for the 14–19 phase and relied on coherence of learning experience being secured through individual guidance and individual learning plans.

As we will see in Chapter 8, in its response to the Green Paper (DfES, 2003), the Government appears to be adopting a much more radical approach to curriculum and qualifications reform which, in our view, takes it beyond the standards-based linkages approach.

Shaping and contextual factors of the standards-based and linkages approach

A major shaping factor in the development of this phase of qualifications and curriculum reform has been the move to rationalize the regulation and governance of the education and training system itself. Following a rapid phase of expansion in participation, the marketization of post-16 provision and the introduction of new qualifications in the early 1990s, a period of system rationalization and consolidation was put in place by successive governments from 1995 onwards. While the formation of the DfEE in the early 1990s could be interpreted as a process of tidying up the bifurcated ministerial arrangements of the 1980s, by the mid-1990s a much wider regulatory agenda was underway. This is one way of interpreting the successive unification of governmental and regulatory agencies.

A second major shaping factor was the Labour Government's obsession with political calculation. Although it saw the regulatory mechanisms in post-16 education and training policy, such as funding and inspection, as 'the most significant and far-reaching reform ever enacted to post-16 learning in this country' (Blunkett, 2000), it did not appear to see curriculum and qualifications reform in the same way. In the latter area it was overwhelmingly guided by caution because it perceived a political sensitivity of the middle classes to changes to A levels and to GCSEs.

International comparisons and the resulting production of national targets for education and training in terms of participation and qualifications outcomes constituted a third shaping factor and played an even more significant role under a Labour Government than they did under the Conservatives. The Conservative focus on Level 3 and intermediate technical skills was replaced under the Labour Government by a greater emphasis on achievement at Level 2 and basic skills for employability, and a new target for participation in higher education (50 per cent of 18–30-year-olds by 2010). Under the current administration, targets have become a major mechanism for driving through change in the public sector as a whole and education is no exception. Performance measures are being introduced at every level of the education and training system. The Government sees this as a *quid pro quo* for more investment – a rejection of what they call a 'something for nothing' approach.

The final shaping factor in this period is, once again, related to participation. From 1996 onwards there has been a slowing down in the rates of growth in participation in full-time post-16 education and in levels of achievement in GCSE and advanced level qualifications (Hodgson and Spours, 2002a). At the same time, there has been an increase in part-time employment among 14–19-year-olds (Hodgson and Spours, 2001a). One of the effects of this more static participation picture and the increasing lure of the part-time labour market is a concern about making greater demands on young people in terms of their programmes of study (Hodgson and Spours, 2000b). There is also evidence that long hours of paid work can adversely affect young people's achievements and educational aspirations (Payne, 2001). This is an issue that the Government is only beginning to recognize as significant in relation to curriculum and qualifications reform within a voluntarist system. A linked issue is the problem of financial support for learners during the 16+ phase (Piatt and Robinson, 2001).

The standards-based linkages phase of curriculum and qualifications reform was, therefore, shaped by four major types of contextual factors – rationalization and regulation of the education system; political caution in relation to sensitive areas of policy; international comparisons and targets; and a static picture in education participation. As we will see in Chapter 2, all these factors have had a major impact on the implementation of the *Curriculum 2000* reforms and, as we discuss later in the book, are likely to continue to affect any proposals arising from the Government's recent Green Paper on 14–19 education and training.

Beyond the Green Paper: towards a more 'unified' approach to curriculum and qualifications reform?

The latter part of 2002 was marked by events that appear to be changing the reform landscape. The A level crisis, which focused on the manipulation of AS and A level examination results, generated such a furore within and beyond the education system that it called into question the whole concept of maintaining the 'gold standard' of A levels. The crisis could thus be seen as heralding the end of an era that has lasted over half a century and, as we argued earlier, has always stood in the way of fundamental and necessary system-wide curriculum and qualifications reform.

A second major event in 2002 was the rejection by important sections of the education profession of much of the thinking and many of the practical proposals outlined in the 14–19 Green Paper. Its utilitarian vision, proposals for learning acceleration, the distinction A level grade, a qualifications system starting only at intermediate level and a flawed model of the matriculation diplomas were roundly criticized (eg, AoC, 2002a; ATL, 2002; HMC, 2002; NAHT, 2002; NATFHE, 2002; NUT, 2002).

A third shaping influence in this same period was the appointment of David Miliband as Minister of Education for School Standards. With a background in educational policy and in Downing Street, the new minister appears to have had sufficient insight to realize that a longer-term transformatory policy had to replace crisis management and incremental short-term change in the area of 14–19 curriculum and qualifications (Miliband, 2002).

Recent speeches by ministers, the Government's response to the Green Paper consultation process, published at the beginning of 2003 (DfES, 2003), taken together with the two Tomlinson Reports (2002a, 2002b) on the A level crisis, arguably pave the way for major shifts in strategic thinking about qualifications and curriculum reform. Most importantly, there is increasing recognition of the limits of public examinations and the need to increase the role of teachers' professional judgement in assessment. The Government also appear to appreciate the limits of voluntarism and political short-termism and the need to move towards a more radical, unified and long-term reform of 14–19 education and training.

Debating qualifications and curriculum reform – reflections on the five phases

The period from the late 1970s to early 2003 has seen almost constant curriculum and qualifications reform as both Conservative and Labour governments have introduced changes to the education and training system to meet social, economic and political pressures for change. We have suggested that this period can be divided into five broad phases of curriculum and qualifications reform policy: the New Vocationalism; an attempted move towards a national two-track qualifications system; a formalized triple-track system; a qualifications system which has some linkages features; and, most recently, the possibility of a new more unified phase. The overall movement is one of system expansion in order to accommodate rising levels of post-16 participation. Throughout the period, the underlying developments and debates have essentially been about whether this expansion was to be based on a more differentiated and divided system or a more unified one. Our analysis suggests that the system is moving in a unified direction, but that the current linkages approach remains a compromise between track-based and unified strategies. We speculate, however, that policies are now tending more towards a unified approach for 14–19 education and training.

The first and overwhelming driving force for curriculum and qualifications development has been educational participation with the role of curriculum and qualifications reform being to stimulate and to direct this trend. GCSE is credited with assisting rises in full-time participation in the late 1980s (Gray *et al,* 1993); GNVQs helped school sixth forms attract and accommodate post-16 learners deemed not able to participate in A levels; while the new AS is aimed at opening up participation in advanced level qualifications. The Labour Government has, however, faced a 'plateauing' in participation trends and is looking for ways of further stimulating education expansion involving both qualifications reform and financial incentives such as Educational Maintenance Allowances. The 14–19 Green Paper can thus be seen as a means of introducing more vocational qualifications into the final two years of compulsory education in the hope that disaffected learners will want to participate in post-compulsory education rather than exiting the system. Similarly, the new Foundation Degrees, with their work-related focus, are seen as a basis for the further expansion of higher education.

Accompanying the rise in full-time participation in education has been the decline in the role of full-time employment for 16–19-year-olds and the marginalization of the role of employers and the work-based route. Despite a major attempt to rejuvenate the apprenticeship system through Modern Apprenticeships, the work-based route still caters for a small minority of learners, with the persistent problem of finding quality employer placements (Unwin, 2002). The problem of developing a high status and high volume work-based route, we would suggest, is one of the major reasons for the Government's 50 per cent higher education target. What this target signifies is that the Government sees the future of the English post-compulsory education and training system as essentially education-based rather than work-based. In this sense it is going down a US rather than a German route to further expansion of education and training and is relying upon the institutions that have already delivered expansion to date, notably further education and sixth form colleges, to deliver further expansion.

A second major trend has been the growing politicization of qualifications policy as governments have had to grapple with 'protecting standards' while undertaking a massification of the education and training system. This really started with the Conservatives who, in the late 1980s, questioned the nature of the education expansion they had unwittingly set in motion. The coining of the term 'the A level gold standard' and the introduction of league tables have fuelled the annual media hand-wringing over year-on-year improvements in GCSE and A level results, which are often portrayed not as rising levels of achievement but as falling education standards. The result has been that all qualifications reforms have been framed directly or indirectly by A levels and the calculation of who can and who cannot take them. This is part of the process we refer to as 'divisive expansion'.

The third major trend has been a movement towards more centralized and unified regulatory frameworks to oversee and to regulate the process of divisive expansion within a voluntarist context. This regulatory framework can be now seen to comprise a unified education ministry (now the DfES); a single regulatory body for curriculum and qualifications (QCA); an expanded National Qualifications Framework; rationalized awarding bodies; a more unified post-16 inspectorate; and a single system of funding and planning (the LSC and its 47 local LSCs). Closer observation of the process of creating unitary structures suggests that they can work in complex ways. Potentially, rather than preserving division and diversity, they lead to further system coordination as they bring different qualifications, organizations and steering mechanisms into coherent alignment. This movement could be seen as producing an irreversible unification logic (Raffe *et al,* 1998).

It can be argued that the Labour Government to date has gone with the flow of these trends. It has renewed efforts for education-led expansion – notably the 50 per cent target for higher education and making vocational qualifications more applied or even 'academic'; it has continued with the politicized Conservative discourse of preserving education standards, including frequent reference to the 'gold standard of A levels'; and has persisted with the policy of voluntarism overlaid by a massive development of regulatory frameworks to reinforce accountability. At the same time, however, there have been new points of departure – the opening up of advanced level study through the AS, the development of more planned approaches to local provision promised by the emerging LSC system, and the more unified approaches to curriculum and qualifications reform implied in the Government's response to the 14–19 Green Paper.

Above all, arguably until this most recent document, Government action has been dominated by short-term political consideration in which it has shown an unwillingness to confront the major barriers of A levels and lack of employer engagement in education and training. Instead, it has focused on a mixture of cautious, piecemeal reform of qualifications together with a full-blooded development of regulatory and accountability frameworks. In doing so, it may be seen as having failed to truly understand lessons from the past and, in particular, the power of qualifications to shape behaviour.

In our view, it has thus shown little capacity for 'policy memory', which, in turn, has diminished its ability to engage in 'policy learning'.

In the following chapters we will trace this policy approach from the Labour Party's election manifesto into practice through the first two years of the *Curriculum 2000* reforms. We will show both the gains and limitations of this approach to policy-making in the area of curriculum and qualifications reform. The final chapter, however, reflecting current policy debates about the 14–19 phase of education, will suggest that it is now possible to detect signs of a new willingness by government to engage with both policy memory and policy learning in order to help it establish a viable, sustainable and systemic reform process for this phase.

Note

1. This term is an elaboration of the concept of 'linked systems' developed in earlier research undertaken as part of a study of unification in education and training in England and Scotland in the mid-1990s (Raffe *et al,* 1998).

2

Understanding and judging
Curriculum 2000

Introduction

In September 2000, 16–19-year-olds in schools and colleges across England, Wales and Northern Ireland embarked on *Curriculum 2000*. This reform of advanced level qualifications, which the previous Secretary of State for Education and Skills, Estelle Morris, described as 'the most complex changes to the examinations system that have ever been undertaken' (Morris, 2001), met with considerable problems in its first year of implementation and was already under review within months of being introduced. By 2002, while some of the more immediate implementation issues appeared to be under control, deeper underlying design problems were becoming more apparent. Some of these, principally those related to A level assessment and grading, led to the highly publicized 'A level crisis' of 2002. Other design issues related to the Key Skills Qualification and the Advanced Vocational Certificate of Education (AVCE) were already being scrutinized. By the end of 2002, therefore, all the major aspects of *Curriculum 2000* were under review. Despite the evident difficulties, however, professional support for the underlying principles of the reforms remained strong (Hargreaves, 2001a; Tomlinson, 2002b).

So how might we characterize and understand *Curriculum 2000* and how does this help us to develop a framework for judging the reforms and their future? Building on the historical analysis contained in Chapter 1, here we provide a framework of analytical and conceptual tools for understanding the reforms. We start by describing briefly what *Curriculum 2000* is and then suggest that these reforms can be conceptualized in two main ways: as a 'modernized and aligned track-based qualifications system' or as a 'stage to a unified and all-through system for lifelong learning'. However, in order to understand how *Curriculum 2000* developed, it is also necessary to look at how schools and colleges shaped the reforms from the planning of their introduction in 1999 through to the second year of their implementation in 2002. The final section of the chapter discusses how we might use this framework of understanding to develop criteria for judging the *Curriculum 2000* reforms as a whole and to suggest how they should be developed in order to become part of a more unified, inclusive and coherent 14–19 curriculum and qualifications system.

This chapter, like others in this book, will draw heavily on research undertaken as part of the Institute of Education/Nuffield Foundation Research Project, *Broadening the Advanced Level Curriculum: Institutional responses to the Qualifying for Success reforms* (see Appendix 1 for details of this project).

The *Curriculum 2000* reforms

The *Curriculum 2000* reforms can be seen to have had four major underlying themes:

1. broadening study at advanced level;
2. introducing greater consistency of standards between and within different types of qualifications;
3. rationalizing the number of subject specifications at advanced level; and
4. improving alignment between general and general vocational qualifications.

There was also an expectation from ministers that under *Curriculum 2000* students should consider studying up to five subjects in the first year of advanced-level study (Blackstone, 1998). These themes are reflected in changes to A levels and General National Vocational Qualifications (GNVQs), the introduction of the new Key Skills Qualification and Advanced Extension Awards (AEAs), and the suggestion that there might, in the future, be an overarching certificate at advanced level.

The AS and A2

Arguably the most important new proposal in *Curriculum 2000* was to split all A levels into two three-unit blocks – Advanced Subsidiary (AS) and A2. Under these arrangements students are able to achieve a three-unit AS in the first year of study and to attain a full A level through completing an A2 in the second year. This relationship between the AS and A2 is referred to as 'semi-hooked', which means that the A2 does not stand as a qualification in its own right and any results attained at AS level count towards the final A level grade. The AS is set at a lower level than the A2, although both are contained within level 3 of the National Qualifications Framework. The main aim of the AS qualification block is to encourage learners to take up a broader range of subjects in the first year of study (eg four or five compared to the two or three under the old A level system). A further aim is to provide a more gradual gradient of progression between

GCSE and A level with the opportunity of gaining a qualification after one year of study. This allows learners both to narrow down the range of subjects they take through to full A level and also to exit the education system at the end of one year of compulsory study if they wish to do so. As part of *Curriculum 2000,* a small number of new 'broadening' subjects were also introduced at AS level only (eg Critical Thinking, Science for Public Understanding) in the hope of encouraging learners to increase the breadth of their advanced level study programmes.

New model GNVQs/Vocational A levels/Advanced Vocational Certificates of Education (AVCEs)

Alongside these changes to A levels, GNVQs were reformed to align them more closely with the new style AS and A levels, to make them more manageable to deliver and to encourage greater consistency of standard within and between general and general vocational qualifications at advanced level. They have also been renamed Vocational A levels or Advanced Vocational Certificates of Education (AVCEs). AVCEs were designed into six-unit or three-unit blocks identical in size to A and AS levels with a common A level A–E grading scheme. AVCEs contain a mixture of external and portfolio assessment. All six units in AVCEs, however, are at A level standard unlike the two-level AS/A2 qualification. In addition, learners can take a 12-unit double award AVCE equivalent to two A levels, as under the old GNVQ system. Key skills, which formed an integral part of the old GNVQ, however, were detached from AVCEs so that they could be achieved through a separate Key Skills Qualification in Communication, Application of Number and IT or freestanding key skills units. The main aims of the reform of broad vocational qualifications were to raise the status of these awards in order to promote 'parity of esteem' between 'vocational' AVCEs and 'academic' A levels and to encourage a wider range of students to mix and match general and general vocational qualifications within their programmes of study.

Key skills

The first New Labour administration had a manifesto commitment to key skills and saw them as part of its raising standards and employability agendas (Labour Party, 1997). To this end, a new Key Skills Qualification was introduced in September 2000 to recognize achievement in the three key skills of Communication, Application of Number and Information Technology. The qualification was offered at levels 1, 2 and 3 in the National Qualifications Framework and was designed so that a learner could take different parts of the qualification at different levels (eg Communications and IT at level 3 and Application of Number at level 2). The so-called 'wider key skills' – Problem Solving, Improving Own

Learning and Performance and Working with Others – did not form part of this qualification on the grounds that they were not externally assessed and, instead, they were developed as separate units of achievement. Opportunities for assessing all six key skills were 'signposted' in the new AVCE and AS/A level qualification specifications. While there was no compulsion for learners to take the new Key Skills Qualification, this was encouraged in all official publicity about the reforms. There was Government exhortation for schools and colleges to offer key skills; sixth form colleges and further education colleges had financial incentives to provide them; and several millions were channelled into a high-profile key skills support programme for schools and colleges, delivered by the Learning and Skills Development Agency (LSDA).

From September 2001, as a result of the first Hargreaves review of *Curriculum 2000* (Hargreaves, 2001a), the Government abandoned the single Key Skills Qualification at level 3 and suggested that all advanced level learners who had not gained level 2 qualifications in English, Mathematics and IT should aim to achieve level 2 key skills units in Communications, Application of Number and IT. All other advanced level learners were encouraged to work towards the achievement of at least one key skill award at level 3.

Advanced Extension Awards (world class tests)

Alongside the reform of A levels and GNVQs and the development of the Key Skills Qualification, as part of the *Curriculum 2000* reforms the Qualifications and Curriculum Authority (QCA) was asked by ministers to design specifications for Advanced Extension Awards (AEAs) to replace S level papers and various university admissions tests and to be bench-marked against international standards. These qualifications, which did not form part of the original *Qualifying for Success* proposals, were to be piloted in the first year of *Curriculum 2000* and introduced more widely at a later date. AEAs were originally mapped against GCE subject criteria and offered in 13 subject areas. The AEA was intended to stretch the most able and to provide end-users, in particular universities, with better differentia-tion at the 'top end'.

An overarching certificate at advanced level

Finally, the *Qualifying for Success* consultation paper suggested that there should be work towards the development of 'an overarching certificate' in the longer term. Having received QCA's summary of responses to the consultation process, the Minister of State at the time, Baroness Tessa Blackstone, agreed to consider the 'implications of introducing overarching certification' (Blackstone, 1998). As a result, QCA with its Welsh and Northern Ireland counterparts, commissioned research in this area, which was reported to the DfEE in 1999 (FEDA/IOE, 1999), but did not become the subject of wider public debate or further development in this form in England and Northern Ireland until its emergence, under the new title of 'Matriculation Diploma', in the Green Paper on 14–19 education published in 2002 (DfES, 2002a). In Wales, however, the overarching certificate proposals contained in this research were used as the basis of discussion for the design of a new Welsh Baccalaureate (WJEC, 2001).

The development of qualifications within the national qualifications framework

While the most visible part of *Curriculum 2000* was the introduction of new qualifications blocks, an important background theme was the development of a single national qualifications framework into which all qualifications outside higher education were intended to fit. The *Qualifying for Success* consultation document thus emphasized the Government's support for the first proposal in the Dearing *Review of Qualifications for 16–19-year-olds* (Dearing, 1996) that there should be a 'National framework of qualifica-tions' with four levels (Entry, Foundation, Intermediate and Advanced) 'supported by the development of rigorous and common quality assurance measures across all qualifications' (DFEE/DENI/WO, 1997, p4).

The *Qualifying for Success* reform process, which by 1998 had become known as *Curriculum 2000,* was therefore more about the introduction and reform of different qualifications than a consideration of the curriculum as such. It is for this reason that some have dubbed it 'Qualifications 2000'. In the next section of the chapter we look at the reasons for this type of devel-opment and why the Government chose to create a complicated 'toolkit' of qualifications rather than to introduce the type of coherent 14–19 curricu-lum and qualifications system proposed by many education organizations during the early 1990s.

Throughout their first two years of implementation, the *Curriculum 2000* reforms as a whole have evolved, in part as the result of institutional responses and in part as the result of two important but unscheduled reviews by David Hargreaves (Chief Executive of QCA) and Mike Tomlinson (previous Chief Inspector of OFSTED). Institutional actions, including those of the learners themselves, have shaped advanced level programmes of study and their role is analysed in more detail later in this chapter. The reviews, in the main, have made changes to the assessment arrangements in *Curriculum 2000* and their role is examined in subsequent chapters.

Two ways of understanding the *Curriculum 2000* reforms

The *Curriculum 2000* reforms can, in our view, be characterized in two ways. From one perspective, these reforms constitute the development of a 'modernized and aligned track-based system' which provides the opportunity for learners to move more flexibly between the three different qualifications tracks (general, general vocational and vocational) and to combine qualifications of different types into a chosen programme of study that meets their needs. This was the essence of the Dearing approach and one that was pursued under *Qualifying for Success* (DfEE/DENI/WO, 1997). From the other perspective, highlighted by *Aiming Higher* (Labour Party, 1996) and other more recent radical proposals (eg AoC, 2002b; Hodgson and Spours, 2002b; JACG, 2002), the reforms can be seen as a preparatory stage in the formation of a more 'unified and all-through system for lifelong learning'. These two perspectives are not necessarily mutually exclusive because it is possible to proceed from the first to the second, but they do imply a different approach to the reform process. Arguably, this is the choice that the Government now faces at the end of the second year of the *Curriculum 2000* reforms and in the context of the consultation and debate around the Green Paper *14–19 Education: Extending opportunities, raising standards* (DfES, 2002a).

The reforms as a modernized and aligned track-based system

As part of a modernized and aligned track-based system, the *Qualifying for Success* proposals can be seen as a way of consolidating the series of changes to the qualifications system that had taken place throughout the late 1980s and early 1990s. This was the Dearing and the New Labour Government view of the reforms. It is clear from our discussions with officials between 1997 and 1999 that the Government, at least in public, did not intend the *Qualifying for Success* reforms to be an explicit stage towards further reform of the system. In the consultation document itself it was stated that these reforms would put an end to 'the damaging cycle of constant piecemeal change that has bedevilled our qualifications system over the past few years' (DfEE/DENI/WO, 1997, p5).

The primary aim of the *Qualifying for Success* proposals was to make all advanced level qualifications more accessible and more equally valued, thus providing learners with greater flexibility to move between the qualifications tracks and to build programmes of study based on different types of qualifications (general, general vocational and vocational). At the same time, however, the issue of 'securing high and consistent standards across all qualifications' (DfEE/DENI/WO, 1997, p5) resulted in an emphasis on including a significant amount of external or 'independent' assessment in all advanced level qualifications, whether or not this was consistent with their purpose and design.

The Government was very keen for political reasons that the reforms should 'build on the best of what has gone before' (DfEE/DENI/WO, 1997, p5). In particular, ministers were eager to retain elements of the old A level system, notably the continued emphasis on depth and specialization of study through a two-year AS/A2 qualification. It was important that amidst all the changes, universities, employers, parents (and the press) could still see that A levels were there. On the other hand, GNVQs, which were seen as lacking in rigour and status, were more radically reformed. The new Advanced Vocational Certificate of Education (AVCE), which replaced GNVQ, was designed so that it could be regarded as another type of A level rather than as a vocational grouped award. Both qualifications, however, were designed in three-unit and six-unit blocks so that qualification blocks of different types could be combined together into broader learner programmes.

Modernization of the qualifications system also indicated a need for the introduction of new qualifications, notably the Key Skills Qualification in Communication, Application of Number and IT and the Advanced Extension Award (AEA). While the first was intended for all advanced level learners 'to meet the concerns of business that too many young people lack these skills when they leave school', the latter was designed to stretch the most able (Blackstone, 1999). The Key Skills Qualification was designed as a freestanding award that could function as a form of common learning and as a link between different programmes of study. It is possible to see the introduction of this qualification as further evidence of alignment between the general and vocational tracks because opportunities for assessment of the key skills were 'signposted' in both AVCE and AS/A2 specifications and they were expected to be taken by all advanced level learners.

While the design, content and assessment of the qualifications that constituted the *Curriculum 2000* reforms ended up being highly regulated, the composition of learners' programmes of study and their recognition and acceptance by employers and higher education providers remained unregulated. The voluntarism that had always characterized post-compulsory education and training in the UK remained. In fact, voluntarism was seen as a virtue, because of the importance placed by policymakers on learner choice in post-compulsory education. As the three Secretaries of State for Education and Employment in England, Wales and Northern Ireland stated in their foreword to *Qualifying for Success* (DfEE/DENI/WO, 1997, p2): 'To encourage lifelong learning, we need qualifications that fit different patterns of learning and that allow learners with different needs to follow programmes that suit them.'

Post-compulsory education could not, in the eyes of ministers, be made in any sense compulsory. What was important was to secure demand for learning and participation in full-time education beyond the legal school-leaving age. Moreover, ministers had little inclination to require universities to recognize *Curriculum 2000* outcomes when no one really knew how institutions might respond to the reforms or which combinations of qualifications students might end up taking. Placing this kind of pressure on higher education would also be politically difficult.

However, it is clear from ministerial statements and correspondence that they expected learners to take four or more subjects in their first year of advanced level study, as well as key skills, in order to broaden and increase the size of advanced level study programmes and to bring them more in line with European competitors. In addition, ministers intended that steering mechanisms, such as funding incentives, inspection and the new UCAS tariff would underpin the take-up of key skills (Blackstone, 1998).

There was thus a hope that advanced level learners would be induced to study more subjects with larger and more balanced programmes of study and would be more inclined to complete their course. If they did leave after one year, they might also have something to show for it, notably in the form of AS levels. The reforms were, therefore, introduced with minimum levels of compulsion, the initial drive being left to a mixture of market mechanisms (the fear of being left behind if everyone was doing it) together with a hope that the professional consensus for reform would provide the initial impulse for schools and colleges to offer a broader range of qualifications for learners.

From this perspective, *Curriculum 2000* essentially revolved around A levels. Modernization meant making A levels more accessible and this was the major discourse carried out with the education profession. As far as the public was concerned, on the other hand, the emphasis was on standards – both retaining A levels and upgrading vocational qualifications. Alignment meant linking all *Curriculum 2000* qualifications to the trusted A level – a conscious process of academic drift. The effects of modernization and alignment – bringing in the new while keeping the old – led to problems of purpose and design for all aspects of *Curriculum 2000* and, in our view, also precipitated the Hargreaves reviews of 2001 and the A level crisis of 2002.

The reforms as a stage to a more unified and all-through system for lifelong learning

From the perspective of those who argued for a more unified and all-through system for lifelong learning, the *Curriculum 2000* reforms were seen as the first stage in the creation of smaller, modular qualification blocks, which could be combined into more coherent and balanced advanced level programmes of study recognized in a future Baccalaureate-style diploma award. In this conception, the newly formed qualification blocks would, in time, lose their individual identity to become components of a new more holistic single set of qualifications. As a step on the way to such a system, unifiers signalled their support for several elements of the *Curriculum 2000* reforms – larger programmes of study, a focus on skills as well as knowledge, more common elements of learning, and the possibility of mixing applied and theoretical study. This explains, in part, the widespread professional support initially given to the idea of a Key Skills Qualification.

However, right from the beginning some of the unifiers were concerned at the continued voluntarist approach to the new reforms and doubted whether learners would choose to take broader programmes of study unless there were strong incentives for them to do so (AoC, 1997; Hodgson and Spours, 2000b; IoE, 1997; NAHT, 1997). There was anxiety too about whether the reforms might create further divisions between learners, with those in general further education colleges and on vocational programmes opting to take lighter programmes than those in schools. This initial concern has, as we shall see in Chapter 3, proved to have some foundation.

Finally, while unifiers might have wished the Government to provide a clear signal about where they thought the *Curriculum 2000* reforms were taking the advanced level system in this country, it was obvious that this kind of statement was not going to be made by a New Labour Government wedded to Third Way politics, voluntarism and policy incrementalism (Hodgson and Spours, 1999a).

The unification perspective on *Curriculum 2000* turned into a waiting game. The unifiers wanted a more overt staged approach to system reform from the beginning, with an explicit end-goal of a unified and inclusive 14–19 curriculum and qualifications system. This was denied them. With the political decision to have a more cautious yet, as we will see, complex and unstable reform, the main concern from a unification perspective was whether the Government's modernized and aligned track-based approach would produce increased breadth of learning and reduce curriculum and qualifications division. What the unifiers did not fully foresee was exactly how the qualifications design and implementation issues, principally around assessment resulting from academic drift, would impact on learners, institutions and the whole direction of the reforms. In this sense, nobody fully predicted in advance the major problems that were to beset *Curriculum 2000* in its first two years.

The institutional shaping of *Curriculum 2000* – the dynamic relationship between design, purpose and implementation

In this section we trace the institutional role in shaping *Curriculum 2000* to cast more light on the relationship between design, purpose and implementation issues. It is the interaction between these two that arguably explains the problems and potential of the reforms. We describe this dynamic in the reform process between 1999 and 2002 and suggest that institutional decision-making went through four broad phases during this period – the phase of engagement (summer/autumn 1999); the phase of realization (spring/summer 2000); the phase of implementation and reflection (autumn 2000/spring 2001); and the phase of review and adjustment (summer 2001/summer 2002). These phases are shown in Table 2.1.

Table 2.1 Factors affecting institutional responses to the *Curriculum 2000* reforms at different phases of the reform process (summer 1999 – autumn 2002)

Factor	From complacency to engagement – what is everyone else doing? (summer – autumn 1999)	Realization – its going to happen! (spring – summer 2000)	Implementation and initial reflection – the painful truth (autumn 2000 – spring 2001)	Review and adjustment – consolidation or even retreat (summer 2001 – autumn 2002)
Institutional curriculum tradition	Important in deciding initial response to the reforms	Strong traditions required to see intentions through to realization	Less important at this point	Reassertion of importance in uncertain national climate
Practical implementation issues	Institutions not fully aware of issues prior to publication of specifications – broad-brush curriculum planning at this stage	Becomes very important following publication of specifications and assessment requirements – more detailed curriculum planning	One of the factors in weighing up the cost-benefits of the reforms	An increasingly important factor as the second year of the reforms reveals the full practical implications of the new system
Qualifications design issues	Initial awareness, but no real grasp of their full significance	Becomes significant as institutions begin the implementation process	Increasing significance as the implications of modularity and external assessment are felt	Highly important both in relation to programme planning and support for the reforms
Government expectations	Broad institutional agreement with government expectations but not with regards to detailed curriculum models (eg 5 AS)	Becomes less important as practical issues become more of a priority – exception to this might be the key skills certificate	Becoming more important as implementation becomes more difficult – concern about lack of clarity	Very important following Ministerial announcement of changes to come and the Hargreaves reviews
Costs of reforms and financial incentives	Costs difficult to calculate at this stage and financial incentives only really applied to general FE colleges and sixth form colleges	Becoming more significant as schools and colleges begin to realize the full cost implications of the reforms	An increasingly important factor in steering institutional decision-making as realization about the costs of the second year of implementation are fully taken on board	Still most important for colleges, but becoming more of an issue for maintained schools (particularly with small sixth forms) starting to plan for changed funding under LSCs

Factor	From complacency to engagement – what is everyone else doing? (summer – autumn 1999)	Realization – its going to happen! (spring – summer 2000)	Implementation and initial reflection – the painful truth (autumn 2000 – spring 2001)	Review and adjustment – consolidation or even retreat (summer 2001 – autumn 2002)
Learner attitudes and actions	Not really known but a 'background noise' – concerns about making more demands on learners	Becomes very significant as learners make their choices about programmes of study	Continues to be significant as the first impact of learner drop-out or reduction of study programmes become apparent	Crucial for curriculum planners as learners vote with their feet – particularly in relation to key skills, AVCEs and the fourth subject
Institutional competition and viability	A very significant factor in framing institutional intentions – schools and colleges seeking competitive advantage	Competitive factor declines as some institutions realize they may need to collaborate to offer attractive curriculum packages	Increasing awareness of viability issues as second year of the reforms and smaller group sizes make an impact	Still a factor but mainly in conjunction with learner actions – less important for larger providers
End-users views	Institutions are unclear how to read end-user views at this point, but concerns about currency of new qualifications with HE	Becomes more significant as institutions attempt to 'sell' programmes to learners	Of major importance as learners make decisions about dropping aspects of programmes and in the run up to applications for HE	Continues to be of great importance, particularly the views of HE providers – employer views largely unknown

From complacency to engagement – what is everyone else doing?

As Table 2.1 indicates, we suggest that from the ministerial announcement of the results of the *Qualifying for Success* consultation in 1998 until summer 1999, there was a 'phase of complacency'. At this point schools and colleges had neither enough information to plan for the reforms nor saw them as high priority among other initiatives. At this point, there was still some suspicion (or even hope in some quarters) that *Curriculum 2000* would simply not happen.

The period from summer to Christmas 1999 could be seen as a 'phase of engagement' with *Curriculum 2000*, when schools and colleges came to the full realization that these reforms were going to be implemented in September 2000 and that they had to market their provision to potential learners and their parents. During this phase schools and colleges responded positively to the reforms, driven by a mixture of educational support and a fear of losing competitive advantage if they did not develop their advanced level curriculum. Even though the reforms were largely voluntary, from our interviews at the time it was clear many in schools and colleges believed in the reforms and also felt that pressure would eventually be applied to them to respond. Their hunch was that 'what is voluntary today might become compulsory tomorrow'. They therefore calculated that it was worth 'getting the pain over and done with'. Moreover, because colleges had additional incentives to implement the reforms in the form of a more directive funding methodology, schools speculated that they might be subjected to a similar regime under the proposed Learning and Skills Council system. Responses were dominated by the desire to do something to respond to the reforms within the parameters of curriculum tradition and institutional competition. No one was really in a position to look ahead or to fully consider the implications of their decision-making. This, as we shall see, proved to be the high watermark of the voluntarist approach to *Curriculum 2000*, before a range of difficult or even negative factors began to take hold later in the reform process.

Realization – it's going to happen!

From the beginning of the spring term 2000 until September 2000 there was what we have termed the 'phase of realization'. This was marked by frenzied activity on the part of schools and colleges to find out all they could about the reforms, to firm up their timetables for the autumn term and to consider the practical implementation issues that needed to be addressed. During this period, learners began to make their intentions clear about the number and type of qualifications they wished to take and schools and colleges began to calculate the delivery and cost requirements of the new qualifications and the full extent of the assessment burden of a more modular curriculum. In certain cases this tempered some of the more ambitious plans schools and colleges had made during the previous phase. In many cases, at this stage, however, competition for high-quality advanced level learners spurred on institutions, particularly smaller sixth forms, to make curriculum offers that they would find hard to sustain in the longer term.

The key factors affecting decision-making during the phase of realization were practical implementation issues, the costs of the reforms and financial incentives, learners' attitudes and actions and, related to these but of lesser importance at this stage, end-user views.

Implementation and initial reflection – the painful truth

The third critical phase, which we have called the 'phase of implementation and reflection', lasted from September 2000 to April 2001, when schools and colleges began to evaluate their initial implementation of the reforms in order to plan for September 2001. As Table 2.1 suggests, this phase saw the intensification of many of the factors present in the previous phase. Some learner resistance to the increased workloads under *Curriculum 2000* began to manifest itself through pressure to drop a qualification – usually the fourth AS – although this was opposed in the majority of schools. As coursework deadlines intensified in the spring term and the rush to cover the AS specifications in preparation for the examinations in the summer term began to make themselves felt, more peripheral aspects of the reforms, such as the Key Skills Qualification, were increasingly seen as an irritating distraction. Learners voted with their feet and, in many instances, refused to go to key skill classes, to sit examinations or to collect material for their portfolios. This had a demoralizing effect on teachers and led those who were responsible for curriculum planning in schools to consider a scaling down of provision in this area for the following year. Those who had decided not to offer key skills in the first year of the reforms did not rush to offer them in September 2001. Meanwhile, those who had little choice about offering key skills, because of the funding incentives attached – general further education colleges and sixth form colleges – began to consider how they might change the way they offered this provision in order to make it more attractive to learners for the following academic year.

During the phase of reflection all the factors that had affected institutional decision-making in the previous phase remained significant. However, there was an intensification of the impact of qualification design issues as the implications of modularity and external assessment began to be felt in practice, rather than simply being the subject of speculation. There was also a re-emergence of the significance of Government expectations at this point, when institutions were coming under pressure to allow students to drop their fourth AS or key skills. Schools and colleges looked in vain to the Government for greater clarity of its future intentions in order to shape programmes for September 2001. Moreover, practical implementation issues and financial factors had to be considered in relation to the A2 aspects of the reforms as well as the AS. This was an exceedingly difficult phase for schools and colleges as the painful truth of the new reform package began to make itself clear.

The phase of review and adjustment – consolidation and retreat

The period from the summer term 2001 to the autumn of 2002 we refer to as the 'phase of review and adjustment'. This was the time spanning the first full set of examinations, with all the problems over timetabling clashes, irate parents, exhausted learners and teachers and concerns about low pass rates in AVCEs and Maths AS, which led to the call for a review of the reforms by the incoming Secretary of State, Estelle Morris. It also encompassed the first year of introduction of the A2 element of the reforms and the implementation of some of the minor adjustments to assessment and key skills resulting from the first report by QCA on the *Curriculum 2000* reforms (Hargreaves, 2001a). While preliminary decisions about the curriculum offer for September 2001 had been made in the previous phase, it was during the very stressful summer term of 2001 that final adjustments were made and these were generally marked by pragmatism and by 'what learners and teachers will wear'. As we will see in subsequent chapters, the real design limitations of *Curriculum 2000* began to be felt. Schools and colleges found the Key Skills Qualification hard to deliver and unpopular, and AVCEs were experiencing high failure rates. The AS/A2, while relatively popular with learners seeking high-grade attainment, was less popular with staff because of the effects of early and constant assessment on teaching and learning.

At this stage of the reform process, institutions (and their learners) responded to increasingly apparent design problems by retreating from many of the initial commitments they had made to *Curriculum 2000*. The reforms at the end of their first two years were not set for take-off; rather, schools and colleges were going through a process of consolidation or even retreat in terms of the up-take of the new qualifications. The patterns of provision set during the phase of review and adjustment, in our view, thus represent the true picture of the extent of the *Curriculum 2000* reforms – a picture that is unlikely to develop further over the next few years given the current balance of factors affecting institutional decision-making. Chapter 3 looks at this picture in more detail.

Curriculum 2000: a basis for judgement

While we agree with Hargreaves (2001b) that it is still early days for the *Curriculum 2000* reforms – to date only one full cohort of students has experienced advanced level programmes made up of the new qualifications blocks – we would not agree that it is too early to try to establish some initial criteria for judging the reforms. Our argument for this early assessment is based on four major premises. The first is that all the major elements of *Curriculum 2000* have experienced difficulties. Second, *Curriculum 2000* has taught us, yet again, that any reform of the qualifications system has to be carefully discussed with all key stakeholders and has to have a workable lead-in time to ensure smooth implementation and support for schools and colleges: hence the need to start the debate about any future changes as soon as possible. Third, and possibly more contentiously, our research evidence at the end of 2001/02 indicated that the *Curriculum 2000* reforms in their current form are unlikely to produce any further major changes to advanced level learners' programmes of study and that we are looking at a fixed but unstable picture. Finally, if there is to be a debate about longer-term reforms to the 14+ curriculum and qualifications system as part of the Green Paper on 14–19 education, initial judgements about what is working and what is not need to be made now in order to inform that debate.

However, the challenge is to decide on the type of criteria we should be using to judge these reforms. Depending on the perspective taken on *Curriculum 2000*, the criteria will, of necessity, be different. In this section we examine what type of criteria might be used to judge the reforms from the two different perspectives we have described above – *Curriculum 2000* as part of a modernized and aligned track-based qualifications system and *Curriculum 2000* as a stage towards a future unified lifelong learning system. We then look at what the relationship is between these two perspectives and how they might be linked in the debate about a longer-term reform of the curriculum and qualifications system from 14+.

Curriculum 2000 *as part of a modernized and aligned track-based qualifications system: criteria for judgement*

Perhaps the fairest way of judging *Curriculum 2000* as part of a modernized and aligned track-based qualifications system is to return to the criteria that the Government itself set for these reforms. There are three significant documents which lay out the Government's aims for *Curriculum 2000*: the *Qualifying for Success* consultation document itself (DfEE/DENI/WO, 1997), Education Minister Tessa Blackstone's letter in response to QCA's advice on the *Qualifying for Success* consultation process (Blackstone, 1998) and her press release on the post-16 curriculum reforms in March 1999 (Blackstone, 1999).

The first of these explicitly provides the following broad aims for the reforms (DfEE/DENI/WO, 1997, pp5–6):

Our aims for advanced level qualifications, and indeed for qualifications in general are to:

- secure high and consistent standards across all qualifications, whether general (academic), general vocational or vocational;
- ensure that these qualifications are equally worthwhile and equally valued and that learners can combine general (academic), general vocational and vocational studies;
- develop a clear, coherent and widely understood qualifications framework, within which learners can choose programmes which meet their needs and take credit for their achievements;
- offer scope for specialization where this is necessary for progression, while encouraging more learners to achieve breadth of knowledge, understanding and skills;
- encourage all learners to attain a high level of Key Skills;
- promote positive attitudes and wider access to lifelong learning, and make a return to learning easier;

- offer clear progression routes into Higher Education, employment and further training; and
- raise and widen levels of participation, retention and achievement.

The spirit of the second – Baroness Blackstone's letter to Sir William Stubbs, Chair of the QCA (Blackstone, 1998) – might be captured in the following quotation:

> The Government's commitment is to support broader A levels and upgraded vocational qualifications, underpinned by rigorous standards and Key Skills. The purpose of the consultation was to consider how we might progress towards achieving a national framework which secured qualifications of a high and consistent standard; which facilitated breadth of learning whilst providing for specialization where appropriate; and which supported wider access and continued learning throughout life.

The major objective emphasized in this document is to broaden young people's programmes of study at advanced level to bring them more in line with European competitors. The recommendation is for 16–19-year-olds to take 'up to five subjects to be taken in the first year of post-16 learning and three in the second, and by combining academic and vocational study where appropriate'. There is also an encouragement for 'as many young people as possible to acquire and develop the key skills which are essential to future employability'. At the same time, while the old system is seen as 'narrow, over-specialized and inflexible', there is a determination 'to ensure that A level standards are safeguarded, and that students who wish to do so can continue to study subjects in depth and to rigorous standards'.

The third document which indicates the Government's aims for the reforms – Baroness Blackstone's press release publicly announcing the qualification reforms in 1999 – again stresses the importance of increasing advanced level students' programmes of study but also focuses on the need to preserve traditional standards and rigour:

> A levels have played an important role in our education system for the last 50 years and they will continue to do so in the future with the same rigour, demands on study and high standards.
>
> We are also committed to upgrading vocational qualifications and enabling young people to combine academic and vocational study. That is why we are introducing an upgraded version of the General National Vocational Qualification, based on extensive piloting. This will be both more rigorous and more manageable for teachers.

In addition, the reforms are seen as part of a larger aim of 'extending choice and raising standards for young people'.

The range of aims in these policy documents can be reduced to three central ones. The first and most prominent was the creation of rigorous and highly regarded qualifications designed to fit within a modernized national qualifications framework. Within a system that was to remain voluntarist, promoting the status of the new and smaller qualifications blocks by the inclusion of external assessment could be seen as the only way to encourage learners to take up the full range of new qualifications and to combine them into broader and more mixed programmes of study. Broadening programmes of study was the second major aim, but the exact shape and extent of these programmes was left in the hands of learners, their institutions and end-users in what remained a marketized and competitive system. Third, there was a wider aim to improve the national education system as a whole by increasing the breadth and size of study programmes at advanced level; by encouraging more learners to acquire key skills; by raising and widening levels of participation, retention and achievement; by the establishment of clear progression routes to higher education and employment; and by instilling positive attitudes to lifelong learning.

It is clear from official documentation that the first aim – the establishment of new high status advanced level qualification blocks in both the academic and vocational tracks of the national qualification framework – was absolutely dominant and was seen as the key to the achievement of the other two aims. Initial criteria for success from this perspective might thus include the widespread uptake of all types of qualifications under *Curriculum 2000* because of the trust and respect attached to them as part of the national qualifications framework.

Curriculum 2000 *as a stage towards a future unified curriculum and qualifications system for lifelong learning: criteria for judgement*

As we have explained in Chapter 1, however, beyond Government and even within sections of it, *Curriculum 2000* was not seen as an end in itself but as a stage towards a future unified curriculum and qualifications system for lifelong learning. For those supporting this position, the criteria for judging the success of the reforms will, of necessity, be somewhat different. As a stage in a reform process, rather than as an end point in themselves, the *Curriculum 2000* reforms will need to be judged in terms of their ability to be moulded and adapted to meet future as well as current demands.

As we have suggested above, those who argue for a more unified curriculum and qualifications system also see *Curriculum 2000*, in its current form, as a set of smaller and more aligned qualification blocks from which some learners at advanced level might build broader and more mixed programmes of study – hence the initial degree of professional consensus underpinning the principles of the reforms. What the 'unifiers' are primarily interested in, however, is how this 'toolkit' of qualification blocks might be adapted in the longer term to form part of a more inclusive and coherent curriculum and qualifications framework for all learners from 14+. In this conception, the individual qualification blocks would lose their status as qualifications in their own right and would become credit-bearing components of new diplomas which would make up a more unified curriculum and qualifications system from 14+.

The criteria by which the unifiers' judge the *Curriculum 2000* reforms are thus in reverse order to those who see *Curriculum 2000* as part of a modernized and aligned track-based qualifications system. The unifiers focus primarily on the effects the reforms are having and will have on the future of the education and training system as a whole, rather than on their place within the current track-based aligned qualifications system. In particular, those who see *Curriculum 2000* as a step toward a more coherent and unified system will be looking for the reforms to produce important systemic changes that lay the basis for a new system. Criteria for success at the initial phases might therefore include an irreversible positive change in learner attitudes towards larger programmes of study, significant, across-the-board increases in institutional capacity to support these programmes, and clear support from end-users for greater breadth of study.

Criteria for judging *Curriculum 2000* over time

In reality, these two perspectives are not mutually exclusive. Both accept the need for smaller and more aligned blocks and broader programmes of study at advanced level, although they have different views of how these might be configured. Virtually no one in the policy community now accepts that *Curriculum 2000* is a stable resting place for the reform of the advanced level curriculum. Apart from the more obvious problems arising in the first two years of the implementation of the reforms, the Green Paper on 14–19 education constitutes a clear indication that *Curriculum 2000* provision, which in the first parliament could be seen simply as an 'island of reform', will now have to relate to 14–19 provision as a whole. Third, and as Chapter 1 indicates, the effect of qualifications reform in the English education system in the past has always produced further momentum for change. The question is whether this search for coherence, which comes from the limitations of rushed and piecemeal reform is inevitable or whether it is possible to create a more carefully planned, gradual and inclusive reform process.

Policy makers and practitioners have different timescales in mind when they look at education reforms. Politicians and those who work to do their bidding are caught up in the imperative of the four-year political cycle and thus work with short- to medium-term timescales. Practitioners, on the other hand, have to work both to pressing short-term goals – making policies work this week, this term, this academic year for those learners who are currently in the system, and to less immediate and more aspirational longer-term goals

– developing a better educational environment and system over time for future cohorts of learners. Although politicians may not automatically feel the need to articulate a longer-term vision of where the advanced level post-16 curriculum is heading as a result of the introduction of *Curriculum 2000*, we would argue that practitioners require such a vision in order to be able to work with confidence towards their longer-term goals. This is why we propose that the progress of this reform is measured over time, moving from what might be expected in the initial stages to what should occur in later years given the Government's aim for *Curriculum 2000* to become an important aspect of a system of lifelong learning and for learners to be able to progress within a more flexible and coherent 14–19 phase (DfES, 2002a).

While certain indicators of 'success', such as initial take-up of the new qualifications, can be measured quantitatively in the short term, indicators such as overall post-16 participation and achievement rates, let alone more qualitative measures such as changes to the shape of the advanced level curriculum or the quality of teaching and learning at advanced level, can only be measured over the medium and longer-terms. It is for this reason that the matrix in Table 2.2 has been framed within a long-term vision – a more unified and inclusive lifelong learning curriculum and qualifications system – and highlights connected and progressive short-, medium- and long-term indicators of a move in this direction.

Elective educational reforms, such as *Curriculum 2000*, which depend not only on the wishes of policy makers at the national level but also on the individual and collective decision-making of providers and learners in different local and institutional contexts, are of their nature complex and evolving. It is for this reason that we suggest the need for an approach to evaluating the reforms that takes into consideration the shaping role of learners and institutions. What the matrix also recognizes is that change cannot be imposed by government without institutional commitment and that institutional commitment without sustained government support will not bring about a reform of the 14+ curriculum and qualifications system that will ultimately affect learner participation, progression and achievement. It is important, therefore, to have an evaluation framework that illustrates the inter-relatedness of changes at the individual learner, institutional and education and training system levels.

Short-term indicators – the first years of implementation

As Table 2.2 indicates, we suggest that if *Curriculum 2000* is to be seen as successful in the short term – and by this we mean the first two years of implementation – then there need to be measurable quantitative gains in terms of learner study programmes at advanced level; a clear demonstration from schools and colleges that they are able to make the operational adjustments required to meet these quantitative gains; and explicit financial and political support from government for these goals.

Table 2.2   Criteria for judging *Curriculum 2000* over time

	Short term (2 years)	Medium term (5 years)	Long term (10 years)
Individual learner	Quantitative increases: • Increase in volume of study and number of subjects being taken • Signs that the new qualifications are becoming accepted by learners • Increased participation in vocational and applied qualifications • No significant negative developments (eg losses to existing breadth of learning) • Initial increases in participation and achievement	Broader curriculum experience and qualitative changes: • Engagement with broader programmes of study (eg involving new subjects and combinations of subjects and qualifications) • New cultural norms for advanced level study more firmly-established without loss of extracurricular activities • Significant increases in participation and achievement at advanced level	New knowledge, skills and attitudes in a new 14–19 phase: • Learners see their participation, achievement and progression in terms of an inclusive and unified 14–19 curriculum and qualifications system • Greater willingness to engage with 'challenges' (eg difficult subjects such as maths and MFL) • More emphasis on managing own learning and developing learning skills for the future • Increased willingness to progress to learning beyond advanced level
Institutions	Individual institutional capacity adjustment: • Ability of individual institutions to organize larger programmes of study and improved subject choice • Institutions building on traditional strengths to make wider range of advanced level provision available • Teachers and departments able to adapt to new assessment requirements • Clear plans for further development of advanced level provision after first two years	Collaborative institutional capacity building: • Significant institutional collaboration beginning to take place to improve offer of advanced level provision • Increased focus on creating learner progression routes (eg between levels 2 and 3) • Greater staff capacity to support pedagogic and organizational change both within their own subject areas and across the advanced level curriculum as a whole (eg skill and learning development, integrated project work, new modes of assessment)	Development of local connective learning systems: • Institutions see themselves as supporting learners in a more connective local learning system • Institutional behaviour shaped by collective local needs rather than institutional self-interest • Clear progression pathways between schools, colleges, the workplace and HE

Table 2.2 *continued*

	Short term (2 years)	Medium term (5 years)	Long term (10 years)
National Education and Training System	System adaptation: • Emphasis on securing initial reform effort • Ensuring that qualifications system is able to adapt without systemic problems (eg strain on examination and awarding body system) • Ensuring initial support for reforms from end-users and key players (eg HE, employers, LSC) • Providing financial support for increase in system capacity • Ensuring that reforms have momentum to move to another phase of development	System building: • Emphasis is on system co-ordination so that *Curriculum 2000* is seen as part of wider 14–19 reform programme • *Curriculum 2000* qualification blocks adapted to fit into a unified 14–19 curriculum and qualifications system • Key players tied into future reforms via inclusion in debate and design of new unified 14–19 curriculum and qualifications system	A new unified 14–19 curriculum and qualifications system: • System becomes curriculum and learning-led rather than qualifications and assessment-led • Government ensures underpinning support for new 14–19 curriculum and qualifications system via funding, inspection, performance measures and local planning mechanisms • All key partners (schools, colleges, employers and HEIs) collaborate to participate in and support new unified 14–19 curriculum and qualifications system

What this means in practice, we would suggest, is that more learners should be entering advanced level study because of the lower level of the AS and all learners should be taking more subjects in their first year with an increased volume of taught time.

In terms of what we call 'institutional capacity adjustment', what this will require is for schools and colleges to be able to timetable, accommodate, resource and staff bigger learner study programmes at advanced level. In the short-term, this would probably mean building on traditional strengths. For example, 11–18 schools, which in the past have offered exclusively A level programmes, would need to develop a wide range of AS levels as well as developing capacity in key skills, while considering the possibility of introducing AVCE programmes over time and where appropriate. Other, larger sixth form colleges, which cater predominantly for 16–19-year-olds, should be able to offer advanced level learners a wide range of both AS and AVCE qualifications as well as opportunities to develop key skills even in the short term. It is also reasonable to expect that institutions would have clear plans not only for consolidating the changes undertaken in the first two years but also for their further development in subsequent years.

The third set of short-term indicators is related to the national education and training system level, the role of government and the reform process. First, government has to show its ability to provide the financial, practical and political support to ensure the smooth implementation of the new qualifications. This demands not only the provision of resources for putting on the new study programmes, but also clear messages to key partners, such as QCA, the awarding bodies, the Learning and Skills Council (LSC), OFSTED/ALI, higher education providers and employers, about their vital role in the successful introduction of the reforms. Moreover, it would be the Government's responsibility to underpin the reforms with a set of funding, qualification, planning and inspection levers which ensure that all the key players – learners, schools, colleges, higher education providers and employers – are incentivized to make the reforms a success. At the system level it is also legitimate to expect that during the first years of implementation the reforms gain a sense of momentum and that they are seen to be heading in the right direction.

Medium-term indicators – preparing for the move to a new system

In the medium term, which we define here as a five-year time-span, we suggest that there should have been significant progress at all three levels – learner, institution and system. Within five years, we would suggest that for individual learners the reforms should feel more like 'curriculum change' rather than simply 'quantitative increases' in the number of qualifications taken. At the institutional level, there would be a move from 'institutional capacity adjustment' to 'institutional capacity building'. Finally, at the national education and training system level, national government and its agencies would be expected to have moved to a focus on 'system coordination' rather than simply 'support for change'.

In practice, what this would mean is that all 16–19-year-olds in full-time education (the majority) would be pursuing broader and more balanced programmes of study comprising a mix of theoretical and applied learning and skills. These programmes would be underpinned by more innovative, creative and supportive forms of pedagogy to promote skill building for progression and the ability to study independently, as well as to increase learner motivation and achievement. In the medium term, therefore, there would be an expectation of annual rises in participation and achievement by 16–19-year-olds.

One of the main criteria for judging the success of *Curriculum 2000* in stimulating more fundamental reform in the medium term will be the extent to which schools and colleges are engaged in institutional capacity building. In order to deliver the broader programmes of study and to develop the innovative approaches to teaching and learning indicated above, there will be a need to build staff capability. It will also be necessary to think in terms of an advanced level curriculum and learner programmes of study rather than the delivery of advanced level qualifications. In many cases, this will mean greater collaboration between schools, colleges and employers to ensure the provision of broad, balanced and motivational learner programmes in any given locality.

At the national education and training system level, in the medium term, there would need to be clear links made between all types of reform of the post-compulsory education and training system, rather than the current division between discussion of changes in the work-based route and those in the full-time education system. It would be important too to ensure that all the key players involved in curriculum and qualifications reform – learners, teachers, lecturers, employers and higher education providers – were involved with government and its agencies (eg QCA, LSC, OFSTED/ALI) in the debates about the design of an inclusive and high achieving 14–19 curriculum and qualifications system. One of the major lessons from the *Curriculum 2000* reforms to date, as we will see in Chapter 7, is ensuring that end-users of the qualifications system, such as higher education providers and employers, are committed to the reform process. We would envisage, therefore, that the further development of *Curriculum 2000* would be taking place within a 14–19 reform process which links different levels of provision together and which would signal the end of *Curriculum 2000* as an 'island of reform' focused purely on advanced level.

Long-term indicators – the successful introduction of a new unified and inclusive curriculum and qualifications system from 14+

Within 10 years of the introduction of the *Curriculum 2000* reforms, we would expect to see all learners participating within a more unified and coherent 14–19 curriculum and qualifications system. The type of system this might be and how it relates to current debates is raised in subsequent chapters and explored in detail in Chapter 8.

At the institutional level this type of system would require a more unified or connective delivery structure involving employers and the workplace as well as schools and colleges. At the national education and training system level the 14–19 curriculum and qualifications system would be underpinned by clear funding, inspection, performance and planning incentives for all those involved – learners, providers and end-users – to ensure that each played their part in supporting the system. At institutional level, over a 10-year time-span, schools and colleges would increasingly see themselves as partners in a more 'unified and inclusive local learning system' involving employers as well as education providers. Each would have a defined role in the delivery of the newly emerging system and there would be clear progression pathways from 14+ involving schools, colleges, employers, training providers and higher education institutions. Finally, in developing an articulated and inclusive 14–19 system, there would not only be the need to ensure that appropriate levers and drivers were put in place for all parties, but also a need to establish ongoing dialogue with higher education providers and employers about changes to their provision in the light of the new system.

What the matrix in Table 2.2 demonstrates, above all, is the amount of development that will be needed at all levels of the education system within the next 10 years if we are to realize the full potential of the *Curriculum 2000* reforms as a stage in the creation of a unified curriculum and qualifications system for lifelong learning. We would argue that the complexity of reform in this area makes it imperative to articulate the vision we have for *Curriculum 2000* now as well as criteria for judging its progress. A clear vision would point the direction forward for learners, teachers, parents, higher education providers and employers who are unsure at present what the *Curriculum 2000* reforms are and where they are going. Criteria for judgment would provide the means of assessing the extent to which current developments in these reforms are moving us in the right direction and what further adjustments are required to ensure that they create a stronger and better curriculum and qualifications system for all learners from 14+ in the future.

The importance of understanding the nature of *Curriculum 2000*

We have characterized *Curriculum 2000* as a process of political compromise – more track-based than unified, focused on qualifications rather than curriculum, and incremental rather than strategic. We see this approach to reform at the root of the problems that have beset the new qualifications. The key question is whether this approach will be repeated in the wider reform of 14–19 education or whether important lessons can be learnt from *Curriculum 2000* at this point.

In this chapter we argue, and in subsequent chapters we demonstrate, that the Government's desire to show that A levels continued to exist and that it was improving standards in vocational and applied qualifications through the extensive use of external assessment, introduced deep-seated problems of design and purpose into the new awards. It is these structural issues, rather than simply problems of implementation, in our view, which precipitated the wave of reviews in the first two years of *Curriculum 2000*. Moreover, the focus on the reform of different types of qualifications rather than on the advanced level curriculum as a whole meant that there was an inability to accurately foresee the implications of these changes for institutional delivery or learners' overall programmes of study. This 'fragmented' approach to reform was significantly to contribute to a climate of unpredictability and instability at both institutional and national levels.

Finally, a policy of incrementalism, in which a vision of more long-term change was deliberately set aside, meant that the reform of advanced level qualifications could be interpreted more as an attempt to modernize an old system rather than laying the basis of a new one. This attempt to blend the old and the new was also to cause problems for practitioners. While teachers and managers tried to make the reforms workable, many realized that they did not constitute a stable resting place. Yet there was no Government vision as to how to proceed. This is the challenge now facing the Government in the debate about 14–19 education. Will it be further tinkering and adjustment, or the careful building of a new system based on some of the real yet less publicized achievements of the advanced level reforms?

The following chapters begin this process of judging the gains and limitations of *Curriculum 2000* both in terms of the main elements of the *Curriculum 2000* reform package – AS/A2s, AVCEs and key skills – and changes to learners' programmes of study.

3

Curriculum 2000 – patterns of change

Curriculum 2000 – researching the extent of change

The *Curriculum 2000* reforms aimed to broaden programmes of study while retaining depth, to make advanced level achievement more accessible and to raise the status of full-time vocational qualifications. This chapter looks at changes to learner programmes brought about by these reforms and assesses how far the aims of *Curriculum 2000* have been achieved following two years of implementation.

In order to make an assessment of the extent of change, the chapter first considers the condition of advanced level programmes of study immediately prior to the reforms. Against this benchmark, we then compare the initial take-up of the new qualifications. An aggregate national picture would, however, not tell the whole story about the way in which schools and colleges have engaged with *Curriculum 2000,* because different types of post-16 providers have responded in their own way to the reforms. This very varied set of institutional responses, which we explore later in the chapter, provides a much more textured picture of how the reforms have been established and what their future might be.

To build these national and institutional pictures, we draw upon data from national surveys undertaken by the Department for Education and Skills (DfES), Universities and Colleges Applications Service (UCAS), the Qualifications and Curriculum Authority (QCA) and the Learning and Skills Development Agency (LSDA) during the past three years, together with qualitative data from the 50 schools and colleges in the Institute of Education/Nuffield Foundation Research Project (see Appendix 1) and site-based research carried out by QCA (QCA, 2002a). The views of teachers and learners on the new advanced level study programmes are also included to reflect the perceptions of actors directly affected by these changes. The chapter concludes by suggesting that the legacy of the first two years of *Curriculum 2000* has been one of 'quantitative gains' but 'qualitative losses' in advanced level learner programmes.

Advanced level provision immediately prior to the *Curriculum 2000* reforms

Participation data on advanced level study in the late-1990s shows that over 40 per cent of 17-year-olds in England, Wales and Northern Ireland were taking advanced level qualifications in full-time education and that most of these were taking A levels (DfES, 2001b).

The Department for Education and Employment (DfEE), in collaboration with the Institute of Education (IOE), undertook a national survey in November 1999 to take a final snapshot of advanced level programmes of study prior to the *Curriculum 2000* reforms (DfEE/IoE, 2000). As Figure 3.1 shows, most learners on advanced level programmes were taking A levels with a significant minority on full-time vocational courses. Of those taking A levels, the vast majority were taking three subjects with only a minority taking more or fewer than three, exclusive of General Studies. This represented a relatively low-volume study programme at advanced level in comparison with other European countries.

The number of taught hours on advanced level programmes of study, prior to *Curriculum 2000*, was also very varied, ranging from a maximum of 23 hours per week for a learner on a four A level programme to about 17 hours per week for an Advanced GNVQ learner. At the most extreme, programmes of study for some learners in some general further education colleges, as a result of the funding regime, consisted of no more than 12 hours of taught time.

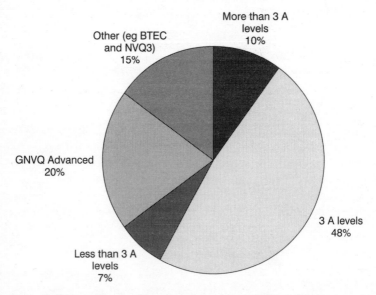

Figure 3.1 Full-time advanced level students by qualification type

Source: DfEE/IoE *Qualifying for Success Reforms* (DfEE/IoE, 2000)

As Figure 3.2 indicates, it was only General Studies that was offered as a broadening activity for the majority of learners in a significant number of institutions. Key skills, over and beyond those studied as part of Advanced GNVQ programmes, were offered to the majority of learners in only 13 per cent of institutions. Information Technology was also a relatively popular form of broadening activity. On the other hand, what the DfEE/IOE survey also showed was that a wider range of broadening activity, including GCSE Maths and English, Special or Step Papers and Sport/PE, was offered to a minority of learners.

Despite the growth in popularity of modular A level syllabuses in the early 1990s, the DfEE/IoE survey found that the extent of modularity was also limited, with only 25 per cent of institutions offering modular syllabuses in a majority of their courses. Modularity thus played a significant role in certain subjects and certain institutions only.

Overall, the data from the DfEE/IoE survey in 1999 painted a picture of advanced level programmes of study that were very variable in size, narrow and traditional. Just over a third of all advanced level learners were following

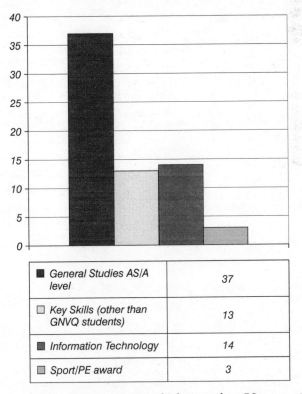

■ General Studies AS/A level	37
▢ Key Skills (other than GNVQ students)	13
▨ Information Technology	14
▨ Sport/PE award	3

Figure 3.2   Proportion of institutions in which more than 50 per cent of advanced level learners were taking additional qualifications in 1999/2000

Source: DfEE/IoE *Qualifying for Success Reforms* (DfEE/IoE, 2000)

vocational programmes of study, which sometimes included key skills, but these programmes were confined largely to certain types of institutions and were often also of low volume. In addition, the A level system looked inefficient, with a significant minority of learners being unable to cope with traditional A levels and having to drop a subject mid-way through their studies. Moreover, learners' experiences of advanced level study varied significantly depending on which qualifications they were taking and the institution in which they chose to study.

Beneath this picture there lay areas of change and progress. A significant minority of learners was on advanced level programmes that included a broadening element. There was also a growing, though still minority, tendency for A level learners to mix both arts and science subjects (QCA, 2002b).

Programmes of study resulting from the first two years of Curriculum 2000

Immediately prior to *Curriculum 2000*, therefore, the system of advanced level qualifications was characterized by three main trends. The first was the dominance of the three A level programme; the second was the growth of vocational programmes of study which now accommodated nearly a third of advanced level learners; and the third was a minority modernizing trend reflected in the growth of modular syllabuses and limited forms of broadening.

In this section we attempt to assess the differences between this picture and the changes brought about by *Curriculum 2000* at the end of the first two years of its implementation. To do this, in addition to the IoE/Nuffield site data, we draw extensively on data from three national surveys undertaken by UCAS (2001) and QCA (2002c, 2002d) together with evaluation reports from QCA (2002b) and OFSTED (2001).

Number of subjects in the first year of study

Survey data suggest that *Curriculum 2000* has significantly increased the size of learner programmes in the first year of study. The majority of advanced level learners started out in September 2000 on programmes of study containing four or more AS levels excluding General Studies. At this early point in the implementation of the reforms, the take-up of four or more subjects was higher among learners on predominantly academic programmes (70 per cent) and lower (59 per cent) if all advanced level learners were taken into consideration (UCAS, 2001). This majority fell back in the second year of the reforms with 66 per cent and 55.5 per cent respectively starting out on programmes of four or more subjects excluding General Studies (QCA, 2002c). What these data suggest is that there has been a retreat in the numbers taking four or more subjects during the first two years of the reforms so that it is now just a bare majority of learners. Nevertheless, the take-up of four or more subjects in the first year of study under *Curriculum 2000* is still considerably higher than the 10 per cent under the old advanced level system.

Number of subjects in the second year of study

The impact of *Curriculum 2000* on second year programmes of study has been less marked. In November 2001, the majority of advanced level learners were taking three A levels in their second year of study – 72 per cent of those on A2 programmes and 60 per cent of all second year learners (QCA, 2002c). This figure is very similar to the proportion of A level students taking three A levels under the old system (see Figure 3.1). In addition, a small minority (12 per cent of all A2 students) took four or more A levels: again broadly the same proportion as under the old advanced level system.

Combination and choice of subjects

One of the reasons for exhorting learners to take more subjects in their first year of advanced level study was to broaden their learning programmes. In its evaluation report of the first year of *Curriculum 2000,* QCA concluded that while the volume of study had changed, the pattern or combination of subjects had not. Learners were inclined to choose complementary subjects leading to full A levels rather than a new pattern of contrasting subjects (QCA, 2002b). Our site visit data and inspection data on learner choices under *Curriculum 2000* also suggest that there has been little significant broadening of the range of subjects taken by individual learners. This is particularly the case for those with lower or average GCSE attainment profiles (OFSTED, 2001).

Changes to the subject composition of programmes of learning can also be inferred from patterns of growth and decline in the take up of particular subjects. Under *Curriculum 2000*, there are some definite subject winners and losers at AS level, with Art and Design, Media Studies, Psychology and General Studies all showing marked increases in examination entries (JCGQ, 2002). At A level, however, the picture is somewhat different with a few subjects showing an increase (eg Computing, Psychology, Media and Expressive Arts). However, there was a decline in A level entries in most subjects and overall the total A level entries declined by nearly 10 per cent between 2000 and 2002.

A prevalent form of behaviour under *Curriculum 2000* has not been new and broader patterns of study but changing and dropping subjects in order to maximize grade achievement. The subjects which teachers thought were dropped in larger numbers than expected at the end of the first year of study, according to the UCAS/QCA survey (QCA, 2002c), were Mathematics, all three Sciences, French and Psychology. This survey also suggested that the subjects more likely than expected to be continued into the second year of study included English Language and Humanities.

Number of taught hours

One of the major aims of *Curriculum 2000* was to increase the amount of taught time in advanced level study to take us closer to the levels found in other European countries. On the surface, this aim has been partially met. However, a closer analysis of the way time has been used in the new system shows a more complex and compromised situation. When compared with the old advanced level system, as we have seen, learners are taking more subjects in their first year of study, leading to an overall increase in weekly taught time of about three hours. However, the average amount of time per subject has been reduced by about 30 minutes per week from 5 to 4.5 hours. Moreover, there is still considerable variation in entitlement and the learners who are most likely to have experienced less of an increase or even a reduction of hours under *Curriculum 2000* are those on predominantly AVCE programmes. The UCAS/QCA survey (QCA, 2002c) suggests that the average amount of time per week given to an AVCE was 5 hours but could, in many cases, be as little as 3 hours 50 minutes. Evidence from the IoE/Nuffield sites suggests that in the majority of cases, these programmes are considerably less well resourced than previous Advanced GNVQ programmes, despite the increased difficulty of the AVCE. The gains in contact are even more compromised when the impact of external testing is taken into account, with the loss of several weeks of teaching time to examinations over the course of an academic year.

AVCEs and mixed study programmes

Another aim of *Curriculum 2000* was to increase the number of learners taking vocational qualifications and mixing academic and vocational courses. The June 2002 UCAS/QCA survey (QCA, 2002d) suggested that about 21.5 per cent of all advanced level learners were taking an AVCE qualification of any size in the first year of study and 16 per cent in the second year. There was also a professional perception in some institutions that participation in broad vocational qualifications had increased, but overall the data suggest a similar picture to that under the old advanced level system.

As a result of *Curriculum 2000*, the total proportion of learners on mixed AVCE and AS level programmes is also around 22 per cent. Most of the learners on mixed study programmes are taking an AVCE alongside a predominantly AS programme, with the most popular AVCEs being ICT, Business and Health and Social Care (QCA, 2002c). Undoubtedly this represents an increase over the old advanced level system, where mixing was a tiny minority pattern.

Key skills

One of the new aspects of *Curriculum 2000* was the introduction of the Key Skills Qualification in Communication, Application of Number and IT. Prior to the reforms, the DfEE/IoE survey (2000) suggested that key skills were offered in a minority of institutions and mainly for students on GNVQ programmes, but that the vast majority of institutions were favourably disposed towards offering some sort of key skills. However, by the second year of *Curriculum 2000* only about half of all first year advanced level learners were taking one or more key skill units and under 40 per cent were working towards key skills accreditation.[1] In learners' second year of study the numbers seeking accreditation were lower still (QCA, 2002d). What these figures suggest is that the level of engagement with key skills has declined over the first two years of *Curriculum 2000* because of difficulties of assessment, delivery and recognition, as well as changes in Government policy following the Hargreaves reviews (Hargreaves, 2001a, 2001b).

Moreover, despite the reputed potential popularity of the wider key skills of Improving Own Learning and Performance and Problem Solving, only a tiny minority of learners were entered for certification in one or more of the wider key skills (4 per cent in Improving Own Learning and Performance and 1 per cent in the other wider key skills) in the second year of the *Curriculum 2000* reforms (QCA, 2002c).

In the final analysis, therefore, key skills remain a paradox – surveys suggest the majority of teachers want their learners to develop them, but now only a minority are actually being offered this opportunity. While the data do suggest that far more learners are doing key skills under *Curriculum 2000* than previously, this is still a long way from the policy goal of key skills for all.

General Studies

As previously stated, General Studies was traditionally used as the main way of broadening advanced level learners' study programmes in the old A level system. The DfEE/IoE survey (DfEE/IoE, 2000) indicated that 37 per cent of schools and colleges offered General Studies to the majority of their learners in 1999/2000, prior to the *Curriculum 2000* reforms. By the end of the second year of the reforms, although it appears that the same number of institutions were offering General Studies under *Curriculum 2000* (QCA, 2002c), A level examination entries for General Studies had fallen significantly in comparison with the position prior to the reforms (JCGQ, 2002). To give a sense of its role under *Curriculum*

2000, virtually the same number of learners were entered for General Studies A level as were entered for Mathematics, whereas under the old system, General Studies had by far the largest number of entries. The AS General Studies fares a little better, having the second highest entry rate after English. Our visits undertaken as part of the IOE/Nuffield Project suggest that General Studies is still a popular award, but that it has shifted its location from being the fourth A level for many to becoming an additional A level for some or, for others, a form of broadening in competition with key skills and some of the new broadening AS levels (eg Critical Thinking).

Enrichment and extra-curricular activities

Under the old A level system, schools and sixth form colleges prided themselves on offering a range of activities and experiences (eg Duke of Edinburgh Award, work experience, sport, music and drama) beyond the main qualifications. These were loosely referred to as 'enrichment'. The DfEE/IoE survey suggested, however, that such activities were taken up by a minority of learners with the possible exception of those in independent schools and some sixth form colleges where enrichment constituted an important element of the curriculum.

There is a widespread perception articulated through national surveys, OFSTED inspection visits and site visits by both the IoE/Nuffield and QCA research teams that the position of enrichment has declined significantly under *Curriculum 2000*. The UCAS/QCA survey (QCA, 2002c) found that a significant minority of institutions (32 per cent) considered that enrichment has declined in the second year of implementation of the new advanced level system. The exception to this is in the further education sector which, following changes to the FEFCE funding methodology in April 2000, was provided with strong financial incentives to offer key skills, tutorials and enrichment of approximately four to five hours per week (FEFC, 1999).

The expectation that students would take key skills appears to have contributed to the decline of the offer and take-up of wider activities, with OFSTED (2001, p15) commenting: 'Where schools have chosen to implement key skills courses and accreditation fully, they have abandoned enrichment programmes altogether to the students' detriment.'

Overall, since the start of *Curriculum 2000*, our site visit data, UCAS survey data (UCAS, 2001) and the QCA site visit data (QCA, 2002a) suggest that the decline in the uptake of enrichment is sharper than the decline in the offer of this provision. The most likely explanation for this is the way the additional timetable demands of *Curriculum 2000* have collided with the continuing popularity of part-time employment for 16–19-year-olds (Elsheikh and Leney, 2002; Fowler *et al*, 2002; QCA, 2002b).

New broadening subjects

A small number of new broadening AS levels has been introduced under *Curriculum 2000*, including Critical Thinking, Science for Public Understanding, Citizenship, World Development, Science and Technology and European Studies. The UCAS survey (UCAS, 2001), undertaken in the first year of *Curriculum 2000*, indicated that the take-up of these broadening qualifications has been insignificant, affecting just over 1 per cent of learners. The most popular of these new broadening subjects is Critical Thinking which, according to interviews undertaken during our site visits, appears to be well regarded by learners and teachers and is thus likely to grow in the future, provided that higher education institutions are prepared to recognize it.

Advanced Extension Awards (AEAs)

AEAs did not form part of the original *Qualifying for Success* proposals in 1997 and only first emerged on the policy agenda in relation to *Curriculum 2000* in the guise of 'world class tests' in the DfEE's letter to schools and colleges about the reforms in March 1999 (DfEE, 1999b). The UCAS/QCA November 2001 survey (QCA, 2002c) reported that only 8 per cent of schools and colleges indicated that they would enter some of their students for an AEA, with a small minority of students in these institutions being entered for the qualification. The current scale of interest in the AEA is illustrated by the following figures – the total number of entries for all AEAs in 2002 was 6,841: this compares with a total of 748,866 entries for A levels in the same year (JCGQ, 2002).

Patterns of participation, achievement and progression

One of the major criticisms of the old advanced level curriculum was that too many learners left post-16 education with few or no qualifications (Audit Commission/OFSTED, 1993; Dearing, 1996). One of the reasons for introducing the two-stage A level under *Curriculum 2000* was to address this problem by providing a qualification (the AS) for learners at the end of their first year of study which was halfway between GCSE and A level. It was felt that this type of award might attract a wider range of learners to advanced level study and, at the same time, provide them with a qualification if they did not feel willing or able to progress to the full A level.

The impact of *Curriculum 2000* on participation rates appears, however, to have been modest, with an increase in the proportion of 16-year-olds on full-time general and broad vocational advanced level courses rising from 43.7 per cent in 1999 to 44.9 per cent in 2000 (DfES, 2001b). This picture of mild growth is supported by QCA research, which found that only 20 per cent of institutions felt that they had experienced an increase in student numbers in the first year of study (QCA, 2002b).

This does not mean, however, that students will remain in study for the full two years of their advanced level programme. Progression to the A2 is not always assured even with a pass at AS. The UCAS survey (2001) showed that nearly 30 per cent of institutions required a particular AS grade to progress to the A2. It is possible, therefore, that greater participation at the age of 16 will not always be translated into greater participation at 17.

While the impact of *Curriculum 2000* on full-time post-16 participation may be very modest, its effect on attainment has been more significant. There are a number of design features of the AS/A level that have the potential to increase levels of achievement in advanced level study. First, these qualifications are modular, allowing learners to build up credit over time and to retake modules to improve grade attainment. Qualifications of this type have been shown in the past to increase achievement rates (OFSTED, 1996b). Second, the AS level is worth 50 per cent of the A level qualification, even though it is set at a lower level, so learners can gain valuable points towards their final A level results by re-sitting AS modules in their second year of study. Finally, the predominant pattern of study under *Curriculum 2000* – four AS levels in the first year and three in the second – gives learners the opportunity to drop subjects in which they are unlikely to do well and to focus on those in which they are most likely to succeed. The combination of all of these factors clearly created the potential for a rise in attainment rates for those on predominantly A level programmes under *Curriculum 2000*.

Indeed, examination results at the end of the first two years of the reforms, shown in Table 3.1, indicate that under *Curriculum 2000* A level results have improved, both in terms of the pass rate and in terms of those achieving the higher grades. As we have already pointed out, however, the number of A level entries has dropped under *Curriculum 2000* reflecting a pattern of learners dropping their weaker subjects at the end of the first year of study. AS attainment, on the other hand, is lower than A level, possibly reflecting the difficulty faced by some learners in taking advanced level examinations effectively after only two terms of teaching. Poor grade attainment in AVCEs,

Table 3.1   Advanced level examination grades in 2001/02

	A	B	C	D	E	U
C.2000 A level (Legacy A level)	20.3 (18.3)	21.6 (19.1)	22.6 (21.4)	18.4 (18.2)	11.2 (12.6)	5.9 (10.4)
AS 2002 (AS 2001)	18.0 (17.0)	18.0 (18.0)	20.1 (20.7)	17.5 (18.0)	12.8 (12.8)	13.5 (13.4)
AVCE (6) 2002	4.3	10.7	19.0	13.8	20.8	21.3

Source: JCGQ, 2002

in the 6-unit award, is even more noticeable and is mirrored by trends in the 12-unit award.[2] The reasons for this are widely recognized – AVCEs are pitched at the full advanced level from the beginning of the course and the assessment regime, modelled on a 'mastery' approach, is less forgiving than the sampling approach used in the AS and A2s.

Overall broadening trends

The effect of *Curriculum 2000* on learners' programmes of study has so far proved to be partial and complex. More subjects are being taken in the first year and more hours being taught, with the greatest change possibly being experienced by the slightly below average advanced level learner who previously took two subjects but who is now taking three or even four. However, the statistics suggest and site visits certainly confirm that those who previously took four A levels under the old system have not had their programmes of study altered to the same extent. Moreover, there is also considerable variability in the size of programmes between those taking predominantly AS/A2 and those taking AVCEs, with the latter potentially losing under the new system.

Gains in the quantity of study are, on the other hand, only one part of the picture. Alongside these gains there have been losses, with the most conspicuous being the reduced uptake of extracurricular or wider activities. *Curriculum 2000* appears, therefore, to have given with one hand and taken away with the other and served different learners in different ways. The reasons for these patterns are explored in more detail in what follows.

Perspectives on the new advanced level programmes under *Curriculum 2000*

The way that learners and teachers perceive and respond to *Curriculum 2000* is undoubtedly important in the first few years of the reforms, because of their power, within a voluntarist system, to shape the new provision. In this section of the chapter we explore briefly their views on the new advanced level programmes before going on to examine in more detail the broader background factors affecting schools' and colleges' responses to these reforms.

Learners' views

So far it appears that learners have neither been the driving force behind the *Curriculum 2000* reforms nor entirely the passive guinea pigs that they have been portrayed as in the national media. Their behaviour in relation to the new programmes of study might be characterized as pragmatic, calculating and stoical as they have responded to the unknown within existing cultural and institutional traditions and contexts. In focus group research undertaken by LSDA, learners commented that they had:

> got used to what you have to do to pass the course. (Tait *et al,* 2002, p57)

Faced with new expectations to study more subjects at advanced level, learners have tended to reflect the prevailing culture of post-16 education rather than to challenge it. What is clear from the IOE/Nuffield Project site interviews is the strength of feeling about the importance of choice and flexibility in post-16 studies, which has been a long-standing feature of the English system. Being able to take four or more subjects was seen by advanced level learners not so much as breadth, but as providing more choice, delaying specialization; providing a 'safety net' in case one subject went wrong and an opportunity to accumulate more qualifications. The modular structure of the new qualifications was also viewed positively, because it allowed the possibility of re-sitting modules of the qualifications to gain a better grade. Learners, therefore, view *Curriculum 2000* as providing flexibility rather than breadth. These features of flexibility have gained widespread learner support and, it appears, have remained the strongest aspect of *Curriculum 2000* throughout its first two years.

What our interviews with learners make clear is that the reason why the study of four subjects for those taking predominantly AS qualifications was so easily established during the first year of *Curriculum 2000* was not primarily down to the insistence of schools or colleges, but because it made sense from the point of view of maximizing their chances and reducing the impact of mistaken choices. In effect, taking four AS levels in the first year of study gave learners more chance of gaining three good A level grades in the second year. Learners did not have to wait for universities to request four subjects: they saw the point in them themselves, although they were irritated that higher education institutions did not support them more overtly.

On the other hand, learners were generally not prepared to experiment and to set new trends in broadening study. Moreover, they were sceptical or even hostile towards prescription. There was a reluctance to choose a contrasting fourth subject (eg those majoring in science did not, on the whole, choose an arts subject). This, we think, reflects their realization that any increase in workload had to be approached with caution and with the exchange value of the qualifications in mind: few progression routes demand a mixed set of qualifications. Learner choice is also, of course, highly constrained by GCSE results. High achievers may have a wide range of GCSE successes to use as a springboard for AS choice, but for many average learners this is not the case. Their good grades at GCSE are likely to reflect their aptitudes in certain curriculum areas rather than in others, and a poor grade in Science GCSE, for example, precludes a whole range of subjects at advanced level. Moreover, given that universities were not demanding a contrasting subject, learners chose on the basis of personal factors such as interest, usefulness to them and a hope that the additional subject might not prove too demanding. As one learner commented:

> I think it *(Curriculum 2000)* hasn't done what it set out to do. It set out to broaden everyone's curriculum, but no one's broadened their curriculum, they've just picked another subject that went with the others they were doing.

Learners were prepared to resist qualifications which they thought had been imposed on them, had little perceived use-value, had little external recognition and added to their already considerable workloads. These were the principal reasons for their rejection of the Key Skills Qualification during the first year of implementation. This comment from a Year 12 learner sums up a very common feeling among *Curriculum 2000* advanced level learners:

> It started off at the beginning of the year with key skills being this new thing and it's gradually gone on and it's got quite negative. Everyone's like, 'Oh God, another key skills lesson to go to'. It got to the point where it's sort of laughable how silly it is, because nobody's going to the lessons, nobody's doing the work for the lessons, everyone's under stress with the AS and GNVQ and things like that and we haven't got the time for it.

Again this view was intensified in the second year of the reforms when the majority of universities demonstrated little support for key skills awards.

Moreover, new evidence from local studies on the role of part-time work in relation to full-time learning suggests that there are clear limits to commitment to higher volumes of study by many learners as they seek to balance their studies with the need and desire to earn money (Elsheikh and Leney, 2002; Fowler *et al*, 2002). It appears that a minority of learners have either cut back or decided not to undertake paid work, so as to be able to cope with increased study workloads, but most appear to have a similar, if not an increased commitment to part-time work in comparison with previous cohorts of advanced level learners.

What has also emerged strongly from the site visits we undertook in the spring and summer terms of 2001 and 2002 as part of the IoE/Nuffield Project, is learners' concerns about the quality of the learning experience in the first year of study under *Curriculum 2000* if they are taking four subjects. Learners on these types of programmes have described the experienced as 'rushed', 'superficial', 'a grind' and 'a bit of a blur'. They have also regretted the lack of time for extracurricular activities:

> I had to have a week off to do work experience and when I come back I was so far behind I couldn't believe it, in just a week, and it took me a month to catch up again. It's awful.
>
> Things like extracurricular activities, they're probably just as useful as an extra subject; universities view extracurricular activities in a different way because they work on different skills you have.

The second year of study under *Curriculum 2000*, however, did not appear to be so onerous from the learners' point of view – since most had dropped their fourth subject.

The learner experience of AVCEs is somewhat different but no less problematical. While learners on predominantly AVCE programmes, the majority of whom were on lower volume study programmes, reported a less rushed learning experience than their fellow students on AS programmes, there was real concern about failure rates and irritation with the detailed evidence required for portfolio completion. These factors appear to have discouraged learners on AVCE programmes from taking other qualifications to broaden their study or to undertake the practical activities that bring this type of learning alive.

Overall, therefore, learners have demonstrated a calculated willingness to go along with the reforms insofar as it is necessary and valuable for them to do so, but they have not been inclined to innovate or to experiment with broader programmes of study. In the current voluntarist climate that surrounds *Curriculum 2000*, it would appear unlikely that this situation will change significantly in the future.

The views of teachers, lecturers and curriculum managers

What emerges strongly from the DfEE/IoE survey (2000) is that schools and colleges broadly supported the principles behind the *Curriculum 2000* reforms. There was widespread support for learners studying more subjects (86 per cent of respondents), for the greater flexibility offered by *Curriculum 2000* (85 per cent) and for integrating key skills in learners' study programmes (76 per cent). There was, however, less support for higher volumes of study (48 per cent) and only minority support for mixing of study (31 per cent).

When discussing teachers' views of the new programmes of study under *Curriculum 2000*, our research suggests that it is important to distinguish between those in the college sector and those in the school sector, since the former have had a somewhat different experience of the reforms to the latter and thus express a different attitude towards them. In addition, it is important to make a distinction between the views of classroom teachers and those of curriculum managers since again these two groups differ to some extent in their responses to the reforms.

It is clear from our site interviews and a survey undertaken by the Institute of Education for the National Association of Teachers in Further and Higher Education (NATFHE) that college lecturers think that *Curriculum 2000* is a problematical reform (Savory *et al*, 2002). So far, it is seen as delivering few benefits, making the curriculum more difficult to deliver, may be undermining learner achievement, and has brought with it a number of organizational problems. Positive comments about the usefulness of modularity suggest that further education lecturers back the basic principles of *Curriculum 2000* but see problems with the actual qualifications and the process of implementation in a sector that has experienced great turbulence during the 1990s. There are three interrelated problems regarding the role of further education colleges in *Curriculum 2000*.

First, the dominance of negative feelings about the reforms may be because further education colleges have not been able to appreciate some of *Curriculum 2000's* more positive effects. These tend to be associated with the greater subject choice and flexibility that can flow from the AS/A level qualifications. However, the emphasis of implementation in general further education colleges has been on the delivery of key skills and AVCEs – the two most problematical aspects of the reforms.

Second, the further education sector's emphasis on key skills and the mixing of general and vocational study has meant a reliance on new qualifications that have rapidly been associated with rejection and problems, as this exasperated college lecturer commented:

> Students almost universally view key skills as an additional and unwarranted burden on already heavy schedules, which it is. The competence-based nature of key skills and its prescriptive criteria mean that the students spend an inordinate amount of time trying to learn how to jump through hoops, instead of the skills they need to develop personally and professionally.

Many learners spurned the Key Skills Qualification during the first year of *Curriculum 2000* and the AVCE was seen as problematic because it was 'too academic' and pitched at the full level 3 standard from the beginning of the programme of study. Our research suggests that many lecturers preferred the Advanced GNVQ, with its emphasis on course-work assessment and flexible learning, or the BTEC National awards, with their emphasis on vocational specificity. As one college lecturer put it:

> Up until now students have gone through vocational qualifications and built up their confidence. This year they have been set up to fail.

Third, further education lecturers saw the majority of their learners as being unable to cope with the demands of *Curriculum 2000*. In many cases, learners choosing to come to further education colleges have lower GCSE and equivalent attainment than those remaining in school sixth forms or attending sixth form colleges. *Curriculum 2000*, with its fuller programmes of study and more external testing, poses particular challenges for this type of learner.

Teachers in schools, as a whole, were slightly less negative about the reforms than college lecturers – nearly 40 per cent of respondents to an IoE/NUT survey on *Curriculum 2000*, for example, agreed or strongly agreed that the reforms would improve post-16 participation (Savory *et al*, 2001a). However, fewer than 20 per cent of respondents in this same survey thought that they had received good or very good staff development opportunities for the introduction of *Curriculum 2000*, which meant that the majority felt that they were not adequately prepared for such a significant reform. In our interviews with learners as part of the IoE/Nuffield site visits, it was clear that they had picked up on teachers' lack of preparedness for the changes. While they were sympathetic to the plight of their teachers, particularly in the first year of reform, they were also aware that teacher lack of preparation was having an adverse effect both on their learning experience and, potentially, on how they were going to perform in AS and AVCE examinations. Teachers too were concerned about learners' abilities to succeed in the new system, with 40 per cent of teachers in the IoE/NUT survey indicating that they thought their learners were doing badly or very badly and only 20 per cent thinking that they were doing well or very well. Clearly these kind of concerns did not make for a positive attitude to the reforms in their first two years of implementation, particularly as teachers' concerns were compounded by organizational issues, such as lack of textbooks, late specifications, examination timetables and accommodation problems. In addition, as we shall see in following chapters, subject teachers had real concerns about the design of all the new qualifications and the impact that they were having on learners' overall experience of the new advanced level curriculum.

Curriculum managers in both schools and colleges were initially much more positive about the *Curriculum 2000* reforms than classroom teachers or lecturers. This is perhaps understandable since they received more preparation for the reforms, on the whole, and were able to see the potential benefits of broader learner programmes of study. However, even this group of professionals began to lose their conviction about the reforms as the problems of the first year of implementation emerged and the complexity of a fully modular two-year programme of study with all its assessment requirements made itself felt.

By the summer of 2002 and the end of the first two years of implementation of *Curriculum 2000*, the views of the teaching profession as a whole can perhaps best be summed up in a quotation from one of the respondents to the IoE/NATFHE survey (Savory *et al*, 2002, p22):

> Theoretically, *Curriculum 2000* is an excellent concept – in practice, it has been a nightmare, both for students and staff.

Institutional responses to the reforms

As we have indicated above, while it is possible to describe broad aggregated national patterns of take-up and experiences of *Curriculum 2000*, different types of institutions have responded differently to the reforms. This view of the reforms is also supported by UCAS and QCA, which have used institutional categories in their national surveys. As a result of these differences, individual learners have encountered rather different configurations of the reforms depending on which institutions exist in their locality and which of these they attend. From our research to date on the IOE/Nuffield Project, we have found six distinctive but overlapping institutional responses to *Curriculum 2000* based on curriculum traditions, patterns of learner recruitment, national funding steers and organizational features (Savory *et al,* 2001b).

Category 1. General further education colleges

General further education colleges can be distinguished from other types of advanced level providers because of their size and diversity of provision, the way they are funded, the relative strength of their vocational provision, the often small size of their advanced level general provision and, possibly most important, the fact that they tend to recruit advanced level learners with relatively lower GCSE or equivalent attainment profiles. As a result of these characteristics, curriculum managers in general further education colleges have tended to see *Curriculum 2000* through the lens of key skills, accreditation at the end of one year of advanced level study, programme flexibility to meet individual learner needs and, in some cases, more mixing and matching of academic and vocational qualifications.

Despite changes in national funding in the second year of *Curriculum 2000*, which reduced the need for colleges to deliver the full Key Skills Qualification, the general further education college response to *Curriculum 2000* is still dominated by key skills. However, in all other respects, the college response to the reforms is less radical than might have been expected from interviews with college staff prior to the introduction of *Curriculum 2000*.

While cross-institutional timetables have been set up in some colleges, there is considerably less mixing of general and vocational study than might have been anticipated. The reasons for this are that only a minority of learners in these institutions are taking four subjects, where mixing is more likely, and those taking AVCEs are tending to take 12-unit courses, which again makes taking a fourth subject unlikely. There are, not surprisingly, a higher proportion of learners undertaking AVCEs in general further education colleges than in other types of institutions but they are, nevertheless, outnumbered by learners undertaking other types of vocational qualifications. Overall, there seems to be a reluctance to force learners into aspects of *Curriculum 2000* other than key skills. General further education colleges thus appear to be following their previous traditions more than might have been expected.

These institutions appear to be organizing their *Curriculum 2000* study programmes along two main lines. On the one hand, there are colleges that have formed or are forming distinct centres for 16–19-year-olds on one site. While making it easier for learners to mix and match general and applied provision, this development may unintentionally cut off *Curriculum 2000*

69

from more specialist vocational provision at level 3. On the other hand, curriculum managers in large multi-site colleges with strong vocational traditions want to remain with a more traditional organizational structure based on vocational areas. In these latter cases, there is a difficulty in providing the type of mixed AS and AVCE packages that *Curriculum 2000* was intended to support. Several of these types of general further education colleges are seriously considering turning their backs on the new AVCE and reverting to the more vocationally relevant tried and tested BTEC Diploma awards.

Category 2. Sixth form colleges

Sixth form colleges constitute a second institutional type based on their relatively high proportion of advanced level learners and, more particularly, the size of their A level cohorts. At the same time, sixth form colleges have been part of the further education sector and, unlike schools, which were funded via local education authorities (LEAs) up until April 2002, they have experienced both the Further Education Funding Council (FEFC) until March 2001 and now the Learning and Skills Council (LSC) funding regimes. National surveys suggest that the distinguishing features of sixth form colleges are that they have a large number of 16–19-year-old learners taking A levels and a wide range of A level subjects on offer (Lumby *et al,* 2002). The provision of broad vocational courses is much more modest than in general further education colleges. Sixth form colleges have relatively low costs for advanced level courses compared with schools because of the efficiency measures they have been placed under since the early 1990s as a result of the FEFC funding mechanism.

These features suggest that sixth form colleges might have been well placed to take advantage of the main strands of the *Curriculum 2000* reforms. However, our research so far suggests that they may not be responding in quite the way expected. This appears to be largely due to the diversity of their learner intake, the organizational and funding constraints they face from having been part of the further education sector and, in some cases, their perception of their position in the market place. Sixth form colleges, therefore, appear to be more of a hybrid than we had anticipated and exhibit features of both general further education colleges and of school sixth forms.

In the four sixth form colleges in our sample, a majority of learners is taking four or more AS subjects and at least one key skill award, the numbers taking AVCEs are just below the national average with more taking the 12- than the 6-unit award, and a small minority of learners are on mixed study programmes. These patterns may be explained by the fact that sixth form colleges have traditionally had high proportions of A level provision and, at the same time, are constrained in their response to a certain degree by the relatively wide ability range of their learner intake.

Category 3. Lower attaining 11–18 comprehensives with predominantly small sixth forms

This institutional category consists of lower attaining (five GCSE A*–C pass rates below 46 per cent) 11–18 comprehensives, most of which have small sixth forms with fewer than 150 learners. Out of our total sample of 50 institutions, 10 schools fall into this category.

Of the two major factors that characterize this type of sixth form, the most influential, in terms of their approach to *Curriculum 2000,* appears to be learners' previous level of attainment at GCSE. Schools with low GCSE attainment scores, on the whole, feed fewer learners through to their sixth forms than those with high attainment at GCSE. This type of attainment profile for the sixth form has meant that GNVQ at Foundation, Intermediate and Advanced levels traditionally featured as an important part of post-16 provision. From our interviews with curriculum managers in these schools, it has emerged that the relatively modest GCSE attainment profiles of many of the learners in the sixth forms led to staff concerns about whether learners would cope with the demands of *Curriculum 2000,* both in terms of the new-style AVCEs and doing more subjects at advanced level. The nature of the intake also affects the culture of these small sixth forms. Often, the sixth form is seen as providing a place of security for 16–19-year-olds who have a range of social or educational difficulties, lack self-confidence and may not wish to travel to learn.

These institutions have thus tended to focus on the progression potential of AS, the possibility of accreditation at the end of the first year of study, and the role of key skills in meeting the basic skill needs of their learners. In the light of the comments made above, it is not surprising that, in comparison with the sample as a whole, relatively fewer learners take four subjects at AS level in these institutions; there is a higher participation rate in AVCEs; there is more mixing of study; and more learners taking key skills than in 11–18 schools as a whole.

This more vocationalized response to *Curriculum 2000* might be explained by the fact that schools with small sixth forms want to attract a range of learners by making a more comprehensive and inclusive post-16 offer. At the same time, however, schools with small sixth forms face significant difficulties in making a confident 'academic' response. The main concerns these institutions appear to face in responding to *Curriculum 2000* are financial viability, the difficulty of providing subject choice, and the ability of lower achieving learners to cope with the increased workloads associated with the reforms.

Category 4. Higher attaining 11–18 comprehensives with large sixth forms

This category of sixth form is defined in terms of the relatively high scores these schools achieve at GCSE (an average of 66 per cent of their learners gain 5 A*–C GCSE grades) combined with their size (5 of the 11 schools in this category in our sample have more than 300 learners in the sixth form and all but one has well over 200). The schools in this category are drawn from a variety of locations including cities, large and small towns and rural areas, but most are in relatively prosperous environments and this may well have an effect on the type of sixth form provision they offer.

In general, schools with high GCSE attainment are more able to feed a large proportion of their Year 11 learners into the sixth form and are more capable of supporting a large and diverse general/academic offer with less need for large-scale vocational provision. They may also be able to attract learners from other schools into their sixth forms and will develop curriculum strategies to encourage this trend. They are thus clearly in a strong position to respond to some of the demands for a broader advanced level curriculum offer underpinning the *Curriculum 2000* reforms.

While these schools were trying to respond positively to planning for the reforms, however, there were criticisms that *Curriculum 2000* could be seen to be lacking coherence and direction. Specifically, there was uncertainty in some of these institutions about how far the reform process was intended to go in the future and anger at the amount of power university admissions tutors appeared to be having in the process. There was a strong sense that the reforms did not go far enough and were a missed opportunity for something much more radical.

These institutions thus tried to offer their learners subject breadth, partly because they believed in it; partly because they thought that their learners could cope with increased workloads; and partly because they thought that it would be necessary to gain at least four AS subjects in order not to be disadvantaged in terms of entry to higher education. At the same time, some of these sixth forms had developed GNVQ provision in the past in order to attract additional learners and, like small school sixth forms, they thus now offer a balance of the 12- and 6-unit AVCEs under *Curriculum 2000*. This enables a relatively high degree of mixed study.

The only area, therefore, where this institutional category is somewhat less ambitious in its approach to *Curriculum 2000* than the sample as a whole is in relation to key skills. This is perhaps not surprising since large school sixth forms, unlike general further education and sixth form colleges, had no funding incentives driving them to offer this type of provision. In addition, this type of higher performing institution is less likely to offer key skills than lower attaining 11–18 comprehensives, because learners are not perceived as needing the type of basic skills their lower attaining counterparts might require and there is no obvious gain to learners in terms of higher education entry.

While the organizational issues for responding to *Curriculum 2000* for large school sixth forms are similar to those of sixth form colleges – ie, limits of accommodation and staffing – there are two important differences. The first is that they received no categorical funding for key skills in the first two years of the reforms and the second is that they face the organizational constraints of being part of an 11–18 institution. Nevertheless, their overall response to the reforms has been ambitious and confident.

Category 5. Middle attaining 11–18 comprehensives

In between these two types of schools it is possible to identify a further category – schools with average GCSE attainment scores (within 3 percentage points of the national average). This group contains schools with a wide variety of sixth form size. It is within this type of institution, as we shall see, that factors other than size and attainment (eg institutional vision, tradition of vocational provision, collaboration with others) may play a part in the institutional response to *Curriculum 2000*.

The key characteristic of these schools is their average attainment profile (between 46 and 52 per cent five A*–C passes at GCSE). However, in our sample, the middle attaining 11–18 schools do not constitute a particularly coherent group. Some have features that tend towards the larger sixth form group and some have characteristics that locate them closer to those with smaller and lower achieving sixth forms. Nevertheless, they exhibit features and responses that are of interest in themselves, not least because they might demonstrate 'national average tendencies'.

Our data show that the middle attaining schools have a slightly lower proportion of learners taking four AS levels than those in large school sixth forms, but a higher proportion taking key skills. The proportion taking AVCEs is lower than in other types of school sixth forms and the proportion mixing study is also lower than in other sixth forms, but higher than in colleges.

In what has been a competitive climate, some institutions are looking to collaborate and this may be coming back onto the agenda after the era of marketization in the early 1990s. Two of the schools in the middle attaining category in our sample, for instance, are part of an existing link with one of the schools in the lower attaining sixth form category. The resulting collaboration appears to have helped all three schools, which would otherwise have struggled to put on a meaningful range of subject choices on their own. Between them, these schools have been able to offer a very wide range of AVCEs as well as AS levels and key skills for all.

This is in very sharp contrast to five of the larger sixth forms with very similar attainment levels who were both more negative about the reforms and more worried about the future. The major affect of collaborative arrangements may, therefore, be to increase the confidence of the contributing institutions so that they can follow the lead of the stronger partner and resist both the organizational and cultural constraints that affect more isolated and smaller institutions. Nevertheless, there are practical difficulties with cooperation between schools that are within a few miles of each other in terms of learner movement, and these should not be underestimated.

Specific institutional factors, such as the leadership role of senior management, can also make a difference to the ways in which a school addresses *Curriculum 2000*. This factor may be more influential in medium-sized middle attaining sixth forms than in others. In small sixth forms, the constraining role of size may exercise too great an influence for the leadership factor to have a significant impact. Conversely, in large high attaining sixth forms, the institutional momentum rather than other factors may be decisive.

It appears that schools in this category have to balance the need to respond positively to *Curriculum 2000*, in order to compete with local sixth form colleges and other schools in their locality, with the organizational constraints of being part of a middle attaining 11–18 school. It may be the case that in the context of balancing, factors other than size and attainment come into play in determining these institutions' responses to *Curriculum 2000*. Examples from our case study institutions suggest that these factors include the ability and desire to collaborate with other institutions and the philosophical stance of the leadership in the institution. This can be seen as a 'centre' effect rather than a 'centre-type' effect.

Category 6. Sixth forms in selective and independent schools

The selective and independent schools in our sample can be grouped together on the grounds that they are all high performing at both GCSE and A level – all institutions attain 99 to 100 per cent five A*–C grades at GCSE and nearly 27 points at A level. Perhaps unsurprisingly, therefore, their approaches to *Curriculum 2000* are virtually identical: learners are taking more subjects – a four-subject norm has been established – and are engaging very little with other major elements of the reform package, such as AVCEs and the Key Skills Qualification.

However, staff in several of the schools in this category commented that they supported the concept of key skills, particularly the wider key skills of Problem Solving, Working with Others and Improving Own Learning and Performance, since these could be encouraged through enrichment activity and reported on UCAS forms. Despite this, all the schools within this category in our sample decided not to engage with the Key Skills Qualification in September 2000 on the grounds of its complexity and its lack of external recognition by selector universities. Given the debacle over key skills in the first year of the reforms (see Chapter 6), it is hardly surprising that this initial response to key skills persisted during the second year of the reforms.

Despite having a cohort of learners who are towards the top end of the ability and attainment scale nationally, these institutions were still concerned about the impact on learners of the expanded curriculum under *Curriculum 2000*. They were mainly worried about the negative effect of the reforms on enrichment activities in areas such as music, drama and voluntary work, which are highly valued and already provide breadth to the existing curriculum in these schools.

For schools in this category, the views of selector universities are seen as a critical factor in determining how far they are prepared to respond to

Curriculum 2000 (Hill, 2001). It was clear that the messages they were picking up was that universities had not significantly changed their entry requirements to reflect the reforms and that it is still important to ensure that learners achieve good A level results in at least three subjects (see Chapter 7). There was little indication that this would undermine a commitment to ask learners to study four subjects, but these schools did not see the need to develop their curriculum offer beyond an extra AS level in Year 12 and possibly more full A levels in Year 13.

Distinctions and similarities

Statistical evidence and discussions with the 50 institutions in our sample suggest that the nature and ability of an institution's learner intake are possibly the most influential factor in how institutions responded to *Curriculum 2000*. Moreover, the historical nature of the intake to a school sixth form or a college will have already shaped its post-compulsory curriculum and ethos and this is unlikely to change dramatically with a non-mandatory reform. The second major factor appears to be funding. These two key factors strongly grouped and divided institutional responses to the reforms.

Our analysis of the six institutional categories used in this report suggests that the first category – general further education colleges – stands out on its own. These institutions are quite distinctive in their approach to the reforms and even in their definitions of who constitutes a *Curriculum 2000* learner.

Close to general further education colleges in some important attitudes and responses to the reforms were, possibly surprisingly, some of the lower attaining 11–18 comprehensives with small sixth forms (Category 3). These two categories of institution share one very important shaping feature: the low attainment profile of their learners. This resulted in fewer learners taking four AS level subjects and more taking key skills. These two categories are, however, divided in terms of funding steers and institutional culture – one offers a place to progress to for the school-weary and the other a relatively sheltered environment for the less confident post-16 learner. For this reason, some small school sixth forms gravitated more towards the next category in our sample, Category 5, the middle attaining 11–18 comprehensives.

While sixth forms in middle attaining 11–18 comprehensives (Category 5), sixth form colleges (Category 2) and higher attaining 11–18 comprehensives with predominantly large sixth forms (Category 4) are reported separately here, they do share some important common characteristics in their responses to *Curriculum 2000*. A majority of the learners in these institutions was taking four subjects; most were taking key skills and a minority was taking AVCE and mixing general and vocational study. What divided these three categories was the degree of their response to the reforms. Higher attaining 11–18 comprehensives with predominantly large sixth forms stood out as taking the most positive overall approach to *Curriculum 2000*, particularly in relation to demands on learners to take more subjects at advanced level. This aligns them quite closely with sixth form colleges, which were also taking a positive approach to the reforms. Where these two types of institutions divided in their response to *Curriculum 2000* was over the provision of key skills. Here funding was undoubtedly the main factor – sixth form colleges were categorically funded to offer key skills, so they were offering them; schools were not funded, so the majority did not offer key skills.

Apart from general further education colleges, the other institutional category that stood out as being markedly different in its response to *Curriculum 2000* was Category 6 – the selective and independent schools. Their response to *Curriculum 2000* could be seen as simple and extreme. On the one hand, they represented the most confident establishment of a four AS norm (and possibly with the highest proportion of learners taking five subjects). On the other hand, they demonstrated virtually no engagement with the vocational or applied aspects of the reforms and thus mixing of study.

What the evidence so far from the IoE/Nuffield Research Project suggests is that learner intake and funding have probably been the two most important factors in determining schools and colleges' responses to the *Curriculum 2000* reforms up to this point. While the effects of funding on curriculum change are self-evident and might well have been predicted, the effects of learner intake are arguably rather more subtle and might not have been so obvious in the minds of policy makers. However, they are explicable and could possibly have been predicted. With the majority of 16-year-olds now progressing into full-time education and attainment rates at GCSE only rising slowly, there are still a considerable number of young people who enter post-compulsory education without the qualifications required to undertake a full advanced level programme of study, particularly with the increased volume of study envisaged under *Curriculum 2000*. It is not surprising, therefore, that those institutions (mainly in Categories 1 and 3), whose intake includes a large proportion of learners with modest GCSE results, have in the past tailored their curriculum offer to meet these learners' needs and will continue to do so. Similarly, at the other end of the scale, those institutions (mainly in Categories 4 and 6), whose intake includes a majority of learners with strong GCSE profiles, have traditionally offered a narrowly academic curriculum and will do the same under the *Curriculum 2000* reforms. Even funding incentives appear to have made little impact on the overall flavour of the curriculum offer in these institutions.

Nevertheless, other factors do have some effect on how institutions respond to curriculum reform of this sort, at least at the margins. Size of institution, as we have seen, undoubtedly still plays an important role and there is some indication that institutional leadership and collaboration can make schools feel more confident in how they respond to national changes such as *Curriculum 2000*.

These differences between the responses of different institutional types to *Curriculum 2000* mean that while full-time advanced level learners are experiencing some common changes as a result of the reforms (eg studying more subjects and having more timetabled time), the effects so far of *Curriculum 2000* both on institutions and on learner programmes have been highly variable. A four-subject norm is probably being secured in most schools and sixth form colleges, but not in general further education colleges. The limited uptake of the AVCEs means that there is much less mixing of study than might have been predicted. Finally, a sizeable proportion of schools, particularly higher attaining ones, are not engaging with key skills. These, and other major variations, are being articulated through different types of post-16 institutions.

These differences can be interpreted not only as institutional ones, but also as a re-articulation of the academic/vocational divide, in which a range of factors – existing social differences (represented through GCSE attainment); different curriculum traditions; the effects of competition between institutions; and the impact of youth labour markets in the form of part-time employment – have reasserted themselves on the emerging shape of the new advanced level curriculum.

The legacy of the first two years – quantitative gains and qualitative losses

How far has *Curriculum 2000* broken the mould of the old advanced level system and to what extent have new patterns and norms been established?

As Table 3.2 indicates, *Curriculum 2000* has significantly broken the mould in relation to the size of learner programmes in the first year of advanced level study. Over 50 per cent of advanced level learners are now taking four subjects (exclusive of General Studies) and they have fuller timetables. These 'gains' take our qualifications system nearer to those of our European partners. However, as this statistic suggests, these quantitative gains have not been realized across the board in terms of different types of institutions or learners. Learners involved in predominantly AVCE programmes may have much lower volumes of study and gain fewer qualifications. This particular pattern is similar to that of the old system but, if anything, the difference is exacerbated because learners taking the old Advanced GNVQ qualifications also took key skills and had a more generous allocation of time for their programmes of study.

Undoubtedly, most advanced level learners are working harder and at an earlier stage in their course than was the case with previous cohorts of learners, on account not only of taking more subjects but also of having

Table 3.2 Degrees of change in different dimensions of breadth in the advanced level curriculum – before and after *Curriculum 2000*

Features of breadth	Old advanced level curriculum	*Curriculum 2000*
Volume of study	Low in comparison with European competitors	Nearer to European competitors
Number of subjects	Between 2 and 3	Between 3 and 4
Spread of subjects	Minority contrasting, mostly complementary	Minority contrasting, mostly complementary
Mixing academic and vocational study	Small minority	Significant minority
Key skills	Primarily offered to students on vocational programmes	Offered to about half of all advanced level learners
General studies	Most common form of breadth and involving a significant minority of institutions	Second most popular form of breadth and involving a significant minority of institutions
Enrichment	Very important in a minority of institutions	Sharply declining role in most institutions
Learning styles and assessment	Diverse with a combination of linear and modular syllabuses and internal and external assessment across a range of awards	More standardized with modular delivery and more external assessment across all awards

high-stake examinations at the end of their first year of study. However, there is little evidence to suggest that these fuller study programmes are significantly broader than those under the old system in terms of contrasting academic subjects. In the absence of clear signals from government or universities, advanced level learners have chosen their four (or in a minority of cases five) subjects in the same kind of way as their predecessors chose their three A levels. Only very occasionally in our research have we come across learners who have deliberately chosen a fourth subject because it contrasted with the first three: most learners have been keen to take up subjects that they enjoy, do well at or want to pursue at a higher level for career purposes.

One area where it appears that there has been some change to advanced level programmes is in relation to mixing general and vocational qualifications. This was hardly evident in the old system but has become a significant minority pattern under *Curriculum 2000,* with most mixing taking place among learners on predominantly academic programmes. Typically, such learners will be taking a 3- or 6-unit AVCE in ICT or Business.

A further gain for *Curriculum 2000* is in the number of learners engaging with key skills. In the old system there was little experience of key skill accreditation beyond GNVQs, although some key skill work was undertaken either through key skills pilots or schemes such as the ASDAN award. Taken overall, just under half of *Curriculum 2000* learners are now involved with key skill accreditation in one form or another. On the other hand, the extent and quality of key skill engagement under *Curriculum*

2000 is highly debatable. Our research shows that most learners and many teachers have very little regard for the type of key skill accreditation introduced under *Curriculum 2000* and would prefer to engage more fully with the wider key skills rather than the main three. Given that the Government set out with an aim of 'key skills for all', the current situation cannot be regarded as a success or as a launching pad for future developments in this area.

In terms of other forms of broadening – new AS broadening subjects, General Studies and extracurricular activities and experiences – *Curriculum 2000* represents at best a static picture, but the common perception is of a net loss. If, in addition, the quality of learning within *Curriculum 2000* programmes is taken into account, particularly in relation to building learning skills for progression, the picture is more depressing still.

The overall position is, therefore, in our view one of quantitative gains and qualitative losses. The quantitative gains are not to be underestimated, because advanced level learners now expect to do more. In this respect, a new norm has just about been established as a result of *Curriculum 2000*. This is an important platform on which to build in the future. On the other hand, the electivism of the system has not changed and learners have not used the new qualifications to 'remedy their weaknesses'. Instead, they prefer to 'build on their strengths', even if this means narrowing their programmes of study. This is the old system logic at work.

In terms of quality of learning, as in the old system, those who are likely to have had the least satisfactory experience in compulsory education have gone on to have the least satisfactory experience at advanced level. Learners on AVCE programmes with an additional Key Skills Qualification have been put through an assessment-driven and bureaucratic experience with a high in-built chance of failure. Those in selective schools, on the other hand, have continued to gain more qualifications and to experience higher volume study programmes. Nevertheless, they too have experienced an assessment-driven qualifications system that may have diminished their enjoyment of sixth form study and made it more difficult to engage with extracurricular activity.

Above all, what all learners have experienced in common under *Curriculum 2000* is more examinations rather than a broader curriculum or a higher quality of learning at advanced level. The picture is not entirely negative, because the modular nature of *Curriculum 2000* allows learners to retake units of learning and thus to gain higher grades in the qualifications they are taking. In this sense, *Curriculum 2000* is a forgiving system and has led to rises in attainment. However, the sheer amount of content to be tackled and assessed has, so far, in our estimation, made *Curriculum 2000* a tedious and uninspiring curriculum that encourages instrumentalism and game-playing to maximize qualification outcome rather than experimentation, creativity and preparation for lifelong learning.

Our findings so far, therefore, suggest that *Curriculum 2000* is making only a partial impact on reforming the advanced level curriculum in this country. Even at this early stage the limited progress of the reforms raises a number of questions as to what might be done to embed more securely a broader and more enjoyable curriculum for all advanced level learners. There is nothing to indicate that the significant differences in institutional approaches to the implementation of *Curriculum 2000* will be ironed out with time. Rather in the current voluntarist climate, these differences are likely to solidify into new and unhelpful divisions. This, we would argue, can only serve to exacerbate the existing differences between the advanced level curriculum experience of different groups of 16–19-year-olds.

Notes

1. This is based on a calculation derived from UCAS/QCA survey data. The percentage total is based on a figure of 52,563 learners being entered for key skill certification out of a total respondent sample of 129,602.
2. Data on the 12-unit award are not included in Table 3.1 because grade achievement is recorded in doubles (eg AA, AB, BB, BC) and thus cannot be easily compared with an A–U scale.

4

Reforming A levels under *Curriculum 2000* – a halfway house?

The difficulty of reforming A levels

Reforming A levels is difficult because they are the dominant qualification in the English qualifications-led education and training system. They have been around for over 50 years, are highly politicized, have been used for selection to university and have been referred to by successive governments as the 'gold standard'. A levels, however, have not remained unchanged over the last half century and have been internally adjusted to meet the needs of new types of learners and to respond to the development of new bodies of knowledge (Young and Leney, 1997). At the same time, the programmes of study that have been formed out of A levels have not changed significantly with most advanced level learners embarking on a three A level programme.

In the light of this history, how should we view the changes that have taken place to A levels under *Curriculum 2000*? Should they be seen as a further adjustment to make A levels more accessible to a wider range of learners or as a more fundamental reform of programmes of study and the structure of the advanced level system?

In this chapter we explore these questions by looking briefly at why the new AS and A level qualifications emerged as they did and how they were experienced during the first two years of their implementation (2000–2002). We also discuss the implications of the Hargreaves and Tomlinson reviews, which were undertaken during this period as a response to the considerable difficulties posed by the new qualifications. Our main argument, based on two years of observing and researching this part of the reform process, is that the new A level arrangements can be seen as a halfway house between the old advanced level system and a potential future new system. The crises that have affected *Curriculum 2000* are, in our view, the result of the desire to preserve A levels while ostensibly establishing a new set of arrangements. We conclude the chapter by assessing the strengths and weaknesses of the AS/A2 within *Curriculum*

2000 and by determining what lessons we can learn from this assessment to inform the debate about a more fundamentally reformed 14–19 curriculum and qualifications system.

The AS/A2 as the latest stage of A level reform

The Advanced Subsidiary (AS) introduced under *Curriculum 2000* was not the first attempt to add a broadening qualification alongside A levels (Kingdon, 1991). The old Advanced Supplementary was introduced in 1987 alongside A levels to encourage students to broaden their programmes of study. By the time that Lord Dearing was conducting his review in 1996, he acknowledged that the take-up of this qualification remained low – for every 15 A levels only one was taken as an Advanced Supplementary (Dearing, 1996). The Advanced Supplementary had failed to take off for a number of reasons. Universities still demanded full A level grades. The old AS was hard work because it had to cover a great deal of core material and felt like taking two-thirds of an A level rather than half. It was difficult to timetable alongside A levels, resulting in few schools offering more than two AS subjects. Finally, the old AS was also outflanked by the changing nature of A levels themselves. The growth area at this time was modular A levels. For all of these reasons, it is justifiable to claim that the Advanced Supplementary did not succeed as a means of broadening because it had to co-exist and compete with the stronger A level.

As we have mentioned earlier in this book, during the late 1980s and early 1990s participation in A level study grew rapidly until in 1995 over one third of 16-year-olds were engaged with this qualification. Many were studying new A level subjects and modular syllabuses were proving increasingly popular. At the same time, the Conservative Government had adopted ambitious national targets, one of which was that by 2001 60 per cent of 21-year-olds should have achieved a level 3 qualification (NACETT, 1994). As more young people attempted A levels, so the problems of failure or wastage rates became more apparent – an issue first highlighted in the early 1990s in the influential report, *Unfinished Business* (Audit Commission/OFSTED, 1993). This was the context for the Dearing review of A levels and other 16–19 qualifications (Dearing, 1996).

Dearing and the 'reformulated AS'

The challenge for Sir Ron Dearing was to maintain the rigour of A levels while making them more efficient by reducing wastage rates. He was aware that a growing number of learners were embarking on A levels without having the capability to complete them successfully. General National Vocational Qualifications (GNVQs), which, arguably, had been introduced to meet the needs of learners with more modest GCSE results, had not proved as popular as the Government had hoped. He argued in his Interim Report (Dearing, 1995) that professional support had been growing throughout the early 1990s for a qualification some way between the GCSE and A level. Here lay the beginnings of the 'reformulated' AS.

This new version of the AS would be 'short and fat' rather than 'long and thin' like the Supplementary AS and, 'instead of covering half an A level syllabus in depth, it would cover the syllabus content in the breadth and depth appropriate for one year's study post-GCSE' (Dearing, 1996, p105). The principal aims of the new AS were to encourage students to take broader programmes in the first year of advanced level study and to provide a qualification for those who did not feel able to complete a full A level. The main issue was to be its weighting and how much value it would contribute towards the full A level. As we will see, this issue emerged as one of the key factors behind the A level crisis in the summer of 2002.

Following the publication of the Dearing Report in March 1996, work on the 198 recommendations was taken forward by four groups: a Joint Committee comprising SCAA and NCVQ committee members, and the DfEE, SCAA and NCVQ themselves. By December 1996, Dearing was able to offer further advice to Gillian Shephard, Secretary of State for Education and Employment, based on the work of this committee over the previous nine months. He confirmed that the new AS would form a constituent sub-set of the full A level course as well as a self-standing qualification in its own right. At this point, Dearing also confirmed that the weighting for the AS, in terms of the total A level grade, would be 40 per cent and 60 per cent for the rest of the A level (later to become known as A2), because the former was intellectually less demanding than the latter. At the same time, however, he argued that in terms of UCAS points, performance tables and national targets, the AS should count as 50 per cent of an A level because it was covering half the content and half of the time of a full A level. The reason for the allocation of 50 per cent UCAS points was to incentivize the take-up of the AS for broadening purposes. SCAA continued its work through to early 1997, focusing primarily on the development of new A level subject criteria and giving consideration to different models of the Subsidiary AS and the A2 (SCAA, 1997). At this time it was envisaged that the new AS/A2 qualifications would be introduced in 1999.

What this brief historical account shows is that the debate about the level and value of the AS in relation to the full A level was present right from its inception. It was generated by the attempt to create new and more accessible advanced level qualifications while still effectively retaining the old A level.

Qualifying for Success *and the development of the new AS/A2 qualifications*

The work of elaborating the Dearing agenda was interrupted by the 1997 general election. While the Labour Party had, in 1996, supported a more radical diploma vision of 14–19 education in its document, *Aiming Higher* (Labour Party, 1996), the Labour manifesto (Labour Party, 1997) referred only to broadening A levels, upgrading vocational qualifications and introducing key skills. New Labour thus largely adopted the Dearing reform agenda for the coming Parliament. The Labour Government's consultation document, *Qualifying for Success* (DfEE/DENI/WO, 1997) was published in November 1997 and, as we have commented earlier, reflected the manifesto commitments much more closely than *Aiming Higher*.

While the Labour administration was minded to adopt the Dearing agenda, it felt that its implementation timescale was too hasty and it stated that it intended 'to move away from the damaging cycle of constant, piecemeal change that has bedevilled our qualifications system for the past few years' (DfEE/DENI/WO, 1997, p5). Following the chaotic first year of *Curriculum 2000*, these words criticizing the outgoing Conservative Government would come back to haunt the new administration.

Qualifying for Success gave the new Labour Government a handle on the qualifications reform process and an opportunity to alter the timescale for their introduction. While some changes would be introduced in 1999 (for example, Progress File and Dearing's recommended Entry Level), the main reforms of the advanced level qualifications blocks were set for September 2000. The Government accepted the Dearing concept of the new AS and A level and its aim to increase participation and efficiency and to promote broadening. The *Qualifying for Success* consultation document specifically asked whether there was support for Dearing's proposal in this area. The QCA report of the consultation found that there was 66 per cent support and recommended its development (QCA, 1998). Moreover, the issue of credit value was clarified with the AS now counting for 50 per cent of the A level grade as well as 50 per cent in terms of UCAS points and in performance tables.

During the *Qualifying for Success* consultation period there was some debate in policy circles about the design of the AS, though in retrospect, few if any serious alternatives to the Subsidiary AS/A level design were put forward. The Government decision to maintain A levels and to postpone movement towards a Baccalaureate seriously narrowed the options for reform. Nevertheless, the Joint Associations Curriculum Group (JACG), a grouping of the main education associations of school and college principals, recommended a 2-unit + 4-unit A level model rather than the proposed 3-unit + 3-unit combination proposal favoured by the Government. The professional associations involved wanted to provide more opportunities to promote subject breadth in the first year of advanced level study and saw benefits in this model from a timetabling and delivery perspective (JACG, 1997). This proposal was rejected, however, on the grounds that two units would be unable to guarantee the necessary coherence of a freestanding AS qualification and that it back-loaded too much work into the second part of the A level course. Scotland's 3-unit approach to Highers was also invoked to support the 3+3 model (QCA, 1998). Our suggestion that a freestanding AS, unhooked from the A2, become part of a new level between GCSE and A level was rejected on the grounds that it meant abandoning A levels.

The other component of the reformed A level was the A2. While the A2 may not have been explicitly designed to be 'harder' than A level, teachers and lecturers we interviewed as part of our research assumed that this part of the A level would be set at a standard higher than the old A level to compensate for the 'easier' AS. Moreover, the A2 element contained a 'synoptic' component that required learners to be examined on material from the whole course – ie, the AS and A2 parts. However, the standard for the A2 was never set and practitioners received conflicting advice from awarding bodies. The design of the AS/A2 was an attempt to balance the characteristics of modular and linear A levels – an issue that particularly exercised Dearing, who remained unconvinced by modular qualifications. The Government was quite happy to go along with this model of the AS/A2 as yet another signal that they were being tough on A level standards.

In all of the discussions we participated in with ministers, civil servants and political advisers during the period 1997–2000, the underlying discourse was the reform of the A level system while maintaining A levels. Nevertheless, there were differences between Dearing and the new Labour Government. While Dearing really wanted A levels, New Labour appeared more concerned to be seen to be wanting them. When it came to A level reform, the new Government was happy to steer a middle course between reformers and sceptics to see how the reforms would evolve. There were also differences of opinion within government about the pace and extent of reform. It is now fairly obvious from all the discussions in which we partici-pated during this period that ministers in the DfEE were more open to ideas about overarching certification and Baccalaureates than was Downing Street, which wanted to keep firmly focused on manifesto pledges. The key to keeping the peace between these strands of opinion and between govern-ment and the profession was to move cautiously in steps and stages but without a stated end goal (Hodgson and Spours, 1999a).

The Government had, nevertheless, a strategic aim for qualifications reform. It saw its first Parliament as putting in place an expanded and reformed national qualifications system comprising smaller and more aligned qualifications which would encourage more mixed programmes of study. Comparability between different qualifications was, therefore, an absolute policy priority. The Government realized that within what was to remain a voluntarist system, the credibility and recognition of new qualifi-cations was key to their take-up and to the promotion of breadth of study.

As the AS/A2 designs were confirmed during 1998 and the policy course set, the focus of debate swung to the conditions for making the reforms a success. In particular, there was concern about whether there were sufficient incentives for students and institutions to broaden their programmes of study (Hodgson *et al,* 1998). There were also worries that the Government's desire to be 'tough on standards' was going to make it more difficult for all advanced level learners to achieve breadth.

The Government was, however, clear in its mind that transparent and recognizable standards were the key to success. Their thinking at this time was summed up by the following statement in a letter from a senior DfEE official:

> The most effective encouragement for institutions will be pressure from students and parents seeking broader programmes of study because they believe that it will help to secure a university place and/or a good job. That ultimately depends on the confidence placed in the standards of the qualifications, by HE and employers.

The underlying assumption was that a particular combination of circumstances would win the day. Professional support for the new AS and the wider reforms, learner competition to obtain a university place and higher education confidence in a tough qualifications standard were seen as sufficient to ensure the take-off of the new AS and broader programmes of study. There would be no compulsion on higher education to recognize these qualifications, since this was expected to flow naturally from their inclusion in the national qualifications framework, and no strong guidance on programmes of study from government to learners, their parents or to the providers. As we will see in Chapter 7, a mild incentive in the form of a reformed UCAS tariff for university entrance, was also put in place.

Rather, ministers hoped that learners would take up to five subjects in the first year and key skills through larger programmes of study (Blackstone, 1998). The details of how this would be organized were left to the newly established Qualifications and Curriculum Authority (QCA), which was asked to produce curriculum guidance for schools and colleges. With these assumptions and in these circumstances, there would be pressure on QCA and on the awarding bodies to create sufficient content in the AS to ensure coherence and to underpin its value as a freestanding qualification. In addition, to make the AS more accessible, specifications (previously known as syllabuses) would emphasize 'coverage' rather than selection of material.

At this stage, little consideration was given to the effects that the design of the AS would have when it formed part of an overall programme of study or part of a full A level. However, this was a concern for QCA. In its advice to government following the *Qualifying for Success* consultation, QCA reflected that broader programmes made up of the proposed 3-unit AS might only be achievable by those 'who currently have the fewest difficulties with advanced level study' (QCA, 1998, p14). QCA implied that other learners (ie, the more marginal advanced level learners) might achieve their broadening by taking key skills and mixing AS with broad vocational qualifications. As we will show, the policy aim of 'broadening

A levels' would turn out to be far harder than anticipated as the prevailing policy assumptions indicated above foundered on the combined effects of design and assessment difficulties together with the detail of practical implementation.

What emerges from this account of the Labour Government's 'take' on Dearing is, first and foremost, their determination to be seen to be being tough on A level standards. At the same time, there were concerns about the accessibility of the new A level and about how many learners would be attracted to using the new AS as a means of broadening their advanced level study. In the final analysis, the Government depended almost entirely on the desire of the education profession for change and the mechanisms of the market to determine the outcome of their policies. It did, however, offer one important incentive to learners to take the AS and that was the 50 per cent weighting in relation to the full A level. We can see here that another step was taken towards both the problems of implementation in the first year of the reforms and the problems of examination results in the second year.

The experience of the AS/A2

While *Curriculum 2000*, as it became known, consisted of the reform of AS/A2, AVCEs and key skills, the development of the AS is widely regarded as the most important aspect of the reforms since it affects the majority of advanced level learners. In this section of chapter we will describe and analyse the experience of the AS/A2 in the first two years of *Curriculum 2000,* with a particular focus on the AS. The story of the other two qualifications is told in subsequent chapters.

The AS within advanced level programmes of study

The Government did not specify the number of AS subjects learners would be expected to take, though as mentioned above, Baroness Blackstone alluded to a desire for learners to take up to five in their first year of study (Blackstone, 1998). The QCA guidance document on *Curriculum 2000* (QCA, 1999b), which was published in the summer of 1999 and thus well after most schools and colleges had already planned and advertised their advanced level offer, simply provided a number of possible curriculum models to support institutional decision-making. The late arrival and tentative nature of this document is testament to the Government's low-key approach to *Curriculum 2000* and its desire, informed by voluntarism, to leave implementation issues up to schools and colleges. What this document stressed was the flexibility that institutions had to design their own programmes of advanced level study using the new qualification blocks. The document outlines no less than eight different possible models for curriculum planning. Final decisions, therefore, were left very much in the hands of schools and colleges and, as we have seen in Chapter 3, institutional traditions, learners' GCSE attainment and, to a lesser extent, funding incentives and institutional competition were the major factors shaping the programmes that study schools and colleges initially provided.

In the event, the predominant pattern nationally has turned out to be four AS subjects in the first year and three A2s in the second year. Institutionally, the pattern was very varied, ranging from 90 per cent of learners taking this type of programme in selective and independent schools to under 40 per cent in general further education colleges (Spours *et al,* 2000). The idea of taking five AS subjects (exclusive of General Studies) in the first year was very quickly rejected by most schools and colleges as being basically unworkable and four has become established as the norm, though, as Chapter 3 points out, a fragile one.

In terms of choice of subjects, the prevailing patterns under the old advanced level system were not significantly challenged. Most learners we interviewed between 2000 and 2002 as part of the IOE/Nuffield Research Project chose their 'additional' subject in the first year of study on the basis of personal interest, progression requirements and the prospect of maximizing grade attainment. Very few actively chose a contrasting fourth subject and, as we have seen, national surveys found that schools and colleges were not overtly encouraging this form of breadth. The only exception could be found in some selective and independent schools, which had their eye on selector universities and medical schools. As we point out in Chapter 7, universities were very unclear what to require of *Curriculum 2000* and stuck, in the main, with the traditional demand of achieving three 'good' A level grades.

Four major delivery problems, all largely unforeseen prior to the implementation of the new qualifications, occurred as a result of the new study programmes under *Curriculum 2000.*

The first was that with a 'free choice' approach to the first year of advanced level study, some learners chose three or four 'essay type' AS subjects and found the combined workload highly stressful, particularly when each of their individual subject teachers made conflicting demands on them. The pressure of a four-subject advanced level study programme with high-stakes examinations at the end of the first year had not been fully thought through by either policy-makers or practitioners. As we shall see, this type of programme proved very difficult for some learners to manage, though many responded by working harder than their predecessors had done in the first year of advanced level study.

The second unanticipated delivery issue with the new qualifications was the positioning of the AS examinations early in the summer term of the first year of study. This proved problematic in practice. Because the A2 was anticipated by practitioners to be more difficult than the traditional A level, in many cases schools and colleges responded by allocating more time to this part of the A level and started teaching the A2 courses straight after the AS summer examinations. This served to create a 'dead zone' at the end of the summer term of the first year of study. Learners, tired from their experience of examinations, were forced to engage immediately with the A2 prior to knowing their AS results and prior, therefore, to making decisions about which subjects they were likely to continue with into the second year. The effective use of this period has been seen as a major problem by all the schools and colleges in our research sample.

Third, there was the complex and esoteric but important issue of 'cashing in' in relation to the AS. This refers to the decision either to accept certification for the three modules constituting the AS part of the A level (cashing in) or to defer taking the credit for these modules in order to re-take individual modules and thus improve the overall grade in the final A level. Learners and teachers were not only given very short timescales by awarding bodies to make these important decisions about cashing in, but were totally unprepared for this type of decision-making, did not fully understand its ramifications and, in some instances, were given unclear or even conflicting advice by awarding bodies and UCAS.

Finally, as we have seen in Chapter 3 the new AS, with its high-stakes assessment in the first year, led to teacher didacticism and learner instrumentalism, as both focused on maximizing grade attainment. One unfortunate side effect of this process was the lack of time and energy devoted to encouraging advanced level learners to develop the skills of independent study required at this level.

The flexibility of a freestanding qualification that provides a 'real' grade and a 'real' accreditation at the end of the first year of study (the AS), but which is also tied to another qualification (the A level), brings with it advantages but also considerable problems. These include complexity, the burden of constant assessment and an erosion of teaching and learning time. No one had fully predicted in advance how difficult the relationship between the AS and A level would prove in practice.

The learner experience of the AS/A2

The research evidence used in this section of the chapter is drawn from the site visits undertaken as part of the IOE/Nuffield Project. The story we tell here, however, is not contradicted by other official evaluations carried out by QCA (2002b), LSDA (Tait *et al,* 2002) and OFSTED (2001). What stands out from this evidence is learners' support for the choice and flexibility afforded by the new AS, but concerns about overload, over-assessment and the uncertain status of the AS.

During the two years of interviews in 2001 and 2002, learners reported to us that they liked the idea of having more subjects from which to choose in the first year of study with the possibility of retaining, dropping or changing subjects in the second year. As one learner commented when asked what his overall assessment of the reforms was:

> I think the extra subject has let me take a subject I wouldn't have taken if I'd had to focus down to three and I think that's been useful because I've enjoyed it and I'm thinking of taking it further and it's also useful to broaden the range of subjects I'm taking.

Learners liked the idea of the fourth subject as a 'safety net' – by this they meant that they could drop a subject and still have the possibility of taking three subjects to A level and applying to a 'good' university. As one learner commented when asked what she would advise next year's Year 12 learners to take:

> I'd say take at least four because you've always got that option to drop one at the end of the first year and still have a qualification and carry on with the rest of the three, so you'd have three A levels and one AS Level.

At the same time, however, it is important to note that the concept of choice and flexibility within *Curriculum 2000* can only be realized in practice in larger institutions. Learners in the smaller sixth forms in our sample complained that their choices were constrained by timetabling difficulties. Choice was also restricted in schools that decided to keep five hours per subject per week for AS levels. This considerably reduced timetabling flexibility, regardless of the size of the school. In addition, in some very large institutions learners' choices were constrained because of the popularity of certain subjects that needed specialist staff, equipment or accommodation. When choice and flexibility are the main (if not only) selling points of a reform, then clearly any institutional constraints on these were seen as a major source of irritation for learners:

> I think it could have been a very good system in theory, but in practice I feel it hasn't been thought out enough. They say it gives you options to get a qualification if you drop something at the end of the year. Well, yes, that's fine, and so you can study more subjects: but you can't, because they can't timetable them.

The AS as a halfway stage in an A level course has been seen in a positive light by learners. Despite the option of leaving the AS examination until the end of the second year, almost all schools and colleges (98 per cent), chose to let students take AS modules in the summer term of the first year. A majority of institutions (59 per cent) also entered learners for some AS modules in the January of the first year (QCA, 2002c). This modular approach, which allows learners to know 'real' examination results at the end of the first year and then gives them the possibility of modular re-sits, has proved popular. This is principally because it gives learners the opportunity to appraise the standard required and to adjust their behaviour accordingly. Even though learners in their first year complain about year-upon-year of examinations, by their second year they realize the benefits of modular assessment for maximizing grade attainment and would not like these opportunities removed. Reflecting on a January AS examination one learner commented:

> It wasn't such a bad pitch because now you actually know what you're going to get if you have to retake it in July. At least you actually know what it is like and that you have to do more revision.

Learners also welcomed the idea of gaining a set of qualifications or 'banking' credit at the end of their first year of study, rather than leaving school with no qualifications or leaving all their examinations until the final year, even though very few actually availed themselves of this opportunity. The AS system is, in these respects, a 'forgiving' one. The downside, however, is that it encourages a new level of instrumentalism where each percentage point is carefully calculated and the chasing of grades has taken precedence over other forms of broadening activity and has affected learners' choice of subject. In the second year there has been a tendency to avoid anything that might compromise achieving the highest possible grades.

The benefits in terms of maximizing A level attainment in the first year of study has been further offset, however, by problems concerning workload and quality of the learning experience. While the learner experience of different subjects varied, with 'essay' and 'practical' subjects being the most demanding in terms of time and mathematics being just plain difficult, the common view of the first year of study from the learner's perspective was that of a rushed, superficial and arduous 10 months driven by examinations:

> It's like an exam factory, because you do your GCSEs, now we're doing AS levels, then we're going to do A levels.

Learners talked about the year as a 'bit of a blur', in which the end-of-year examinations quickly closed in on them. Within the hectic pace of learning there was little time for consolidation, reflection, revision or enrichment activities.

Learners see the experience of the AS as a 'leap' up from GCSE and 'difficult', despite the fact that the new qualification was designed to make the transition between intermediate and advanced levels smoother. This is not principally because of the intellectual demands of the specifications – though maths, science and modern foreign languages were found to be demanding – but more to do with quantity and style of work in what amounts to a 'two-term dash'. Learners have commented on the challenge of carrying out more independent research and juggling with the conflicting demands of a four-subject programme. Moreover, learner workloads have been 'magnified' by the way in which the AS has been delivered. In many institutions there is more than one teacher per subject and the three modules of the AS are often split into separate topics, which makes the AS experience feel like taking a great many subjects rather than four AS levels.

While learners universally report the first year of *Curriculum 2000* programmes to be difficult, some succeed better than others. The higher the GCSE profile, the easier it is for learners to cope with the demands that they face, with some higher achieving students complaining that the AS specifications are 'too bitty', prescriptive and not demanding enough. However, even the highest achievers find that they are stretched to the limit in terms of 'cramming everything in'. When learners were asked to talk about the qualities needed to cope with the first year they mentioned motivation, perseverance and hard work rather than brilliance. Tutors we interviewed in our research reported that the most conscientious learners were often the most stressed, because they felt they could never do every-thing they were being asked to do to a level with which they felt satisfied.

Learners appear to have had a somewhat different experience of the second year of *Curriculum 2000* programmes. Because the majority of learners are taking only three subjects at this point in their programme and because the A2 is a more familiar-looking curriculum for A level teachers, the experience for learners has been much calmer than in the AS. While they may find themselves intellectually stretched by the A2, it is not so rushed as the first year, often because they have started the course in the previous July with a longer run in to the final examinations. By this stage, learners also feel more confident about advanced level study in general because they have already gained up to half of their final A level credit. The learners who feel most pressurized are those who have a significant number of re-sits to take alongside their A2 examinations. Both learners and teachers are concerned about the synoptic component of the A2 because it requires revision of the whole of the advanced level course.

It is undoubtedly true that many of the implementation issues connected with the new qualifications and particularly with the AS (eg late arrival of specifications, changing examination papers and lack of textbooks) adversely affected how learners viewed *Curriculum 2000* in its first year. Learners repeatedly talked about themselves as 'guinea pigs'. However, while the second year of the AS was calmer, it was not necessarily better. As the implementation problems cleared, the underlying design problems of a 3-unit AS being delivered over two terms were more clearly revealed. What appears to be suffering under *Curriculum 2000* is the quality of the learning experience in the first year of study as learners find themselves covering huge amounts of material with little time for consolidation or skill building for the A2. This is one of the consequences of the Government's desire for an externally tested stand-alone qualification at advanced level standard after only two and a bit terms of study.

The teacher perspective on the AS/A2

Successive national surveys either by UCAS/QCA or teacher professional associations and the reviews by Hargreaves and Tomlinson have found that teachers broadly support the principles of *Curriculum 2000*. Having said this, a closer analysis of teachers' views shows them to be more complex and qualified. The evidence for this section of the chapter is largely drawn from two surveys of teachers and lecturers' views (Savory *et al,* 2001a, 2002) together with data from three years of interviews (2000–2002) across the 50 sites that form part of the IoE/Nuffield Project.

What all these sources suggest is that there is strong support for broadening learner programmes of study and for a more inclusive advanced level curriculum. There is, however, far less support for the way in which *Curriculum 2000* has been implemented and the design of the new qualifications blocks. As we will see, teachers in schools and colleges have been particularly critical of the approaches to assessment and its effect on teaching and learning.

An important element of the *Curriculum 2000* reforms was the introduction of modular assessment into all advanced level qualifications. This was a more significant development than many had realized. Prior to the reforms only about a third of all A level courses were modular (DfEE/IoE, 2000), so the majority of A level teachers had no experience of teaching in this way and those who did were used to a different modular model. A survey we carried out for the National Union of Teachers (NUT) during the first year of the reforms found that more A level teachers thought that their subject was suited to a modular approach than those who did not. The only exceptions were Modern Foreign Languages, Art and Design and English (Savory *et al,* 2001a). While in theory the majority of teachers were not against the move to modularity, our site interviews indicated that the way that the new AS specifications have divided subjects into first and second year modules has not always been seen as logical from the perspective of teaching and learning.

This theory/practice contradiction in teacher views about the reforms can be further illustrated by examining their comments on teaching and learning in the AS. The overwhelming message from teachers is that they have had to become more didactic in their approach to teaching. This is seen as a result of the amount of content in the AS specifications to be covered in just over two terms and the amount of time devoted to external examinations. Teachers are also concerned that they are not encouraging learners to develop the type of independent learning skills that are needed for advanced level and future study. Many have remarked that they felt that AS was all about teaching to the test to 'clock up the marks' rather than instilling a curiosity about and love of the subject. Some teachers also think that the AS has restricted time in such a way that they are not able to provide learners with opportunities to undertake vital practical work. In our site visits, we found Theatre Studies without performance, Biology without field trips and Chemistry without experiments. However, so far we have not encountered the same kind of concerns about the A2, probably because there is more teaching time for this award, more conceptual content and a greater sense of professional familiarity.

Teachers have been ambivalent about how far they think that the AS has facilitated a more accessible advanced level curriculum. By the beginning of the second year of *Curriculum 2000*, a UCAS/QCA national survey found that the majority of teachers thought that the AS enabled more learners to gain access to advanced level study than had previously been the case under the old A level system (QCA, 2002c). During the first year of implementation, teachers felt that the AS specifications were pitched more towards the A level than towards GCSE (QCA, 2002b; Savory *et al,* 2001a) and that they had responded by teaching the AS more to the A level standard. In the event, when the examination results were announced, they were pleasantly surprised by the grades many of their learners had gained. Over and above this, teachers report considerable differences in standards across different subjects. Mathematics, in particular, but also the Sciences and Modern Foreign Languages were perceived to be more difficult.

The concept of the A level specialist who taught motivated and dedicated learners and felt in control of her or his subject was challenged by *Curriculum 2000*. National surveys carried out for teacher and lecturer organizations (Savory *et al,* 2001a, 2002) and our interviews with teachers during site visits indicate that those teaching the AS found themselves with larger classes, often with less committed learners, limited resources, facing judgement on their examination results and feeling unsupported by QCA and the awarding bodies. During the first year of the reforms, in particular, A level teachers' sense of professionalism was thus severely undermined. However, this position has changed somewhat during the second year of *Curriculum 2000* implementation, both as a result of the more familiar-seeming A2 part of the course and the fact that teachers are coming to grips with the level of the AS, following the examination results of the first year. Nevertheless, most teachers are unhappy with the AS qualification because of its rushed nature and the way that it prevents them teaching in a creative manner. This concern about teaching and learning in the AS is echoed in OFSTED's review of the progress of the *Curriculum 2000* reforms (OFSTED, 2001).

Overall, the sense that emerges from analysing evidence about teacher views on *Curriculum 2000*, in particular the AS, is of an impoverished and rushed teaching and learning experience. Time and again, teachers we spoke to said that they were unhappy with the way they were teaching the AS. They admitted reverting to 'chalk and talk', because they felt that the more innovative pedagogy that they had previously employed in the first year of the old A level courses was too risky in the context of external tests at the end of the first year of advanced level study. While there is now evidence that many of the uncertainties of the first year of the reforms have been ironed out, our research suggests that the quality of the learning experience for advanced level learners taking the AS/A2 qualifications remains an issue. As we have seen, learner views on the AS were more positive. While they too echoed concerns about the quality of the learning experience, this was offset by the opportunities the new A levels offered for increased choice, flexibility, delayed specialization and grade attainment.

The new AS and A level – from review to crisis

What the evidence above suggests is that the new AS has only partially achieved its aims of broadening programmes of study and creating a more accessible advanced level curriculum. Moreover, both its design and the way it has been implemented has led to two major reviews in the first two years of implementation. The Hargreaves review was set up to look at the manageability of the new qualifications, in particular the examination timetable for the AS and how it impacted on schools and colleges at the end of 2001. The Tomlinson review, on the other hand, was established to restore confidence in the new qualifications following a public outcry about the apparent manipulation of A level grades in the summer of 2002. While the focus of the two reviews was different, we will argue that in both cases, the design of the AS/A2 played a major role.

It was the experience of the AS in the first year of the reforms which led to the Hargreaves review of *Curriculum 2000* announced in June 2001 by Estelle Morris, the new Secretary of State for Education and Skills. With the benefit of hindsight, the origins of the first 'summer crisis' of *Curriculum 2000,* which led to the review, are clear. They revolved principally around the assessment and examination problems associated with the AS. Prior to this point, the problems of the reforms being reported in the media had been more diffuse. They had been looming throughout the year and, apart from the major concern over key skills – which was already the subject of an 'unofficial review' – did not appear to be of crisis proportions. It was the AS examinations period that provoked uproar in the media. It was reported that teachers were unable to complete AS specifications, leaving little or no time for revision, schools' management faced dozens of examination clashes and there were well-publicized instances of learners taking eight or more hours of examinations in one day or having to be supervised overnight by teachers. This period happened to coincide with a general election when ministers and Labour Party candidates came under pressure from both teacher organizations and parents to do something (Hodgson and Spours, 2001b).

The first Hargreaves review of *Curriculum 2000* introduced some changes to the AS mainly in relation to its examination timetable

(Hargreaves, 2001a). The majority of AS subjects were to have one three-hour examination session rather than three shorter modular papers spread over a number of days. While learners objected to this change, because they find the length of the examination difficult and do not like having to move so swiftly from module to module, it has reduced the congestion of the examination timetable. This first review also resulted in an 'enquiry' into the AS in Mathematics to find out why the pass rate was so much lower than in other subjects. In his second review report, Hargreaves (2001b) recommended that no fundamental review of the AS/A2 should be undertaken before September 2003 to allow two cohorts of learners to experience and complete *Curriculum 2000*. Despite widespread opinion amongst practitioners that the AS was 'overloaded' in terms of its content, there was no indication that the Government intended to make any changes in this area as a result of the Hargreaves review.

However, the second summer crisis of *Curriculum 2000* occurred before the scheduled 2003 review of *Curriculum 2000* and led to a further investigation into the AS/A2 qualification. Again, it was examinations that lay at the centre of the controversy, but this time it was the examination process within the awarding bodies that was subject to scrutiny. One awarding body, in particular, was accused by a number of the heads associations of having manipulated A level results to lower the overall number of learners achieving high A level grades. It was also thought that political intervention had been brought to bear on the QCA and the awarding bodies in order to retain levels of attainment in the new A level at the level attained in the old A level and so avoid the accusation of 'dumbing down' in the new system. The row, stoked up by the media, quickly flared into a crisis of confidence in the new A levels with calls for a radical overhaul of *Curriculum 2000*. The crisis also saw major political casualties – Sir William Stubbs was forced to resign as Chair of the QCA, and Estelle Morris resigned as Secretary of State for Education and Skills.

Mike Tomlinson, the retired Chief Inspector for Schools, was asked to lead an inquiry into A level standards. In the autumn of 2002 he delivered two reports (Tomlinson, 2002a, 2002b). The first attempted to assess the scale of grade manipulation so that learners' grades could be reassessed in time for them to seek admission to the university of their choice. In this first report, Tomlinson informed the public that a total of nearly 10,000 candidate entries (less than 1 per cent of the total entries) had been affected as a result of grade manipulation and that the revisions required affected the overall A level grades of nearly 2,000 learners. The magnitude of the crisis at this particular point looked far smaller than the media furore had suggested. However, while the number of learners adversely affected was small in relation to all A level candidates, for those who were affected, the grade crisis in some cases made the difference between succeeding or failing to access the university of their choice.

The second report, published in December 2002, had a much broader remit including measures to avoid any repetition of the problems that had led to the crisis in summer 2002 and to 'secure the standards and integrity' (p5) of the following year's examinations. In the short term, Tomlinson recommended changes to the A level Code of Practice between QCA, as the regulator, and the awarding bodies, as the examiners; to the way A level boundaries are set; and to the way that the standards required for the AS and the A level are set. In the medium term, he proposed the professionalization of examining, a more transparent relationship between DfES, QCA and the awarding bodies, and simplification of the rules governing re-sits and the 'cashing in' of units towards the full A level. In the longer term, he recommended the decoupling of the AS and A2 to create two freestanding qualifications as part of future 14–19 policy developments, together with a reduction in the level of assessment.

What lay at the centre of the second crisis, in our view, was the attempt to retain the A level while trying to make the AS a more accessible qualification. This resulted in the congestion of AS specifications and their over-assessment, to complexities in the relationship between the value given to the AS and A2 components of the A level, and to a culture of re-sitting to maximize grade attainment in the A level. The net result was that learners and teachers were deflected from the aim of broadening the advanced level curriculum, the quality of learning was reduced, and the credibility of learners' actual achievements under the new system as a result of working harder and re-sitting was undermined.

Immediately following the publication of the second Tomlinson report, sections of the media heralded his recommendations for decoupling the AS/A2 as a return to traditional A levels. This, in our view, is to misread his report, because the creation of smaller freestanding qualifications blocks he recommends begs the question of how they are packaged together into coherent programmes of study. That process will now be debated as part of a longer-term reform of 14+ curriculum and qualifications arising from the Government's response to the 14–19 Green Paper (DfES, 2003).

Lessons from the AS/A2 experience

It is clear that the introduction of AS/A2 has fundamentally changed the experience of A levels. It is only in the second year of advanced level programmes when learners are typically taking three A2s that there are echoes of the old A level system. From our research it appears that the first year of study is more akin to GCSE because it is highly teacher-directed, content-driven, prescriptive and intellectually constrained. This is not to say that learners find it easy: it is difficult, but this is because of the amount of content to be covered and the pace of work rather than the intellectual challenge of the qualification. Overall, the AS experience is not perceived as enjoyable by either teachers or learners. It has been described as 'bloodless' and 'a grind'. The A2, on the other hand, appears to be a much more relaxed and enjoyable experience.

How then should we judge the AS/A2 at the end of its first two years of implementation; is it fulfilling the role that both Dearing and the Labour Government hoped? The AS was designed to boost advanced level participation rates and to reduce wastage inside the A level system by providing both a stand-alone qualification at the end of the first year of study and as a stage towards the full A level. It was also intended as a qualification that could be combined with others to provide broader programmes of study for advanced level learners. At the same time, the AS/A2 as a whole was designed to ensure that A level standards overall were retained. In this sense, it represents a halfway house to a new advanced level system by trying to combine, within the shell of an A level, features of the old and the new in an uncomfortable and unstable state. Our analysis suggests that the problems of the AS/A2 are not simply to do with over-assessment, real though these may be, but are to be found in deep-seated structural problems related to issues of standards resulting from the desire to retain the A level.

As we have indicated earlier in this chapter, there is a teacher perception that the AS has mildly boosted participation and has improved the work ethic in the first year of advanced level study. The role of the AS as a stand-alone qualification, however, has not been significant because only a small minority of advanced level learners has chosen to leave the system at the end of the first year. Moreover, the move to a high-stakes external examination system at the end of the first year of advanced level study has created considerable problems for the quality of the learning experience.

Similarly, the role that the AS has played in promoting broader advanced level programmes has only been partially realized. As we have seen in Chapter 3, it has allowed a slight majority of learners to take an additional subject in their first year, but the number of learners who combine AS and AVCE qualifications still remains small at just over 20 per cent of the advanced level cohort.

Arguably, the real impact of the AS is not to be found in these areas, but in the role that it has played in giving advanced level learners greater subject choice and flexibility and in boosting attainment rates. Learners have appreciated the possibility of changing their minds about which three subjects they want to take on to the second year of study, having had the opportunity of experiencing four in the first year. They have also liked the fact that they can re-sit modules in order to maximize their performance. However, there is a downside to this feature of open choice because, combined with the 'hunt for marks' and the increased cost of examinations, it has created clear subject winners and losers. Unfortunately, those subjects which learners have traditionally found hard and which governments have unsuccessfully been trying to promote (specifically, Mathematics, Sciences and Modern Foreign Languages) have suffered under the reforms, as learners are provided with additional opportunities to drop them.

In terms of the A level qualification as a whole and the issue of standards, superficially the AS/A2 combination has retained the A level standard because universities are still prepared to arrange entry to their courses via A level grades. However, if the concept of standards is viewed from the perspective of a high quality and skill-developing experience, the new qualifications do not measure up to their predecessors. The AS has encouraged a more instrumental and rote learning mentality in response to the pressures of prescription, too much content and over-assessment. In addition, there has been less time for enrichment or wider activities.

Given this analysis, what features of the AS/A2 qualification deserve to be taken forward into a future diploma or Baccalaureate system? We would suggest that the consistency of learner support for modularity, flexibility and choice together with the opportunity to check progress and change direction reflects the real strengths of the AS. We suggest that any future Baccalaureate system would, therefore, need to incorporate some or all of these features. At the same time, however, we would need to ensure that the learning experience in the first year of advanced level study was sufficiently intellectually satisfying and that it encouraged skill building and reflection. It is for these reasons that we argue for the AS to be reformed into a freestanding two-unit A1 block as part of a coherent and enhanced programme of advanced level study accredited within a Baccalaureate-style award. This approach could build on the strengths and address the most obvious weaknesses of the current AS. It might also tackle more successfully the issues of participation, progression and breadth of study, which were central aims of both the Dearing Report and *Qualifying for Success*.

Notes

1. Letter from DfEE official to one of the authors in October 1997.
2. Letter from authors to DfEE officials and Downing Street advisers in May 1998.
3. Correspondence between one of the authors and senior DfEE officials in June 1998.

5

The Advanced Vocational Certificate of Education – a general or vocational qualification?

This chapter tells the story of the Advanced Vocational Certificate of Education (AVCE) by examining both its origins and its role within the *Curriculum 2000* reforms. To do this we place the AVCE within the wider context of the reform of vocational qualifications since the mid-1980s and draw on the institutional experience of the award in IoE/Nuffield research sites, supplemented by national survey and evaluative data gathered by the Qualifications and Curriculum Authority (QCA), the University and Colleges Admissions Service (UCAS) and the Learning and Skills Development Agency (LSDA).

The media attention from the beginning of *Curriculum 2000* has been focused almost exclusively on problems with the AS/A2 qualification and its effects on learners in the academic track. However, it is our contention that the AVCE (and the Key Skills Qualification) suffer from far greater problems in purpose and design than the A level, but these have remained relatively invisible. Part of the function of this chapter is to redress the balance of attention towards the AVCE and the learners who have taken this award.

Our brief historical overview suggests that what has happened to vocational qualifications for full-time younger learners throughout the 1990s is a process of 'academic drift' as they have gravitated away from the workplace and vocational practices and towards school and college-based general education. AVCEs have thus emerged as 'applied' qualifications that are being used to broaden participation in full-time education. We will see that these qualifications have taken this trajectory as a result of successive government policies aimed at creating 'parity of esteem' between academic and vocational qualifications, but without requiring the fundamental reform of the academic track or the real involvement of employers in vocational education.

What recently gathered research data suggest, and we will argue, is that not only has the AVCE experienced a process of academic drift and become less vocational, but it has also proved difficult to deliver and is excluding many learners who, by the late 1990s, were being reasonably well served by the old Advanced GNVQs. The new AVCE (with the exception of IT) has not 'taken off' as a major player in the *Curriculum 2000* reforms, has a relatively low pass rate in comparison with A levels, and is unlikely to grow significantly in the future because of problems of purpose, design and status.

We conclude the chapter by suggesting that the AVCE, in its current form, does not appear to have a viable future and does not appear to be meeting the needs of the learners for whom it was designed. We suggest that important lessons can be drawn from the fate of the AVCE about similar qualifications reforms that are currently being introduced pre-16. We also argue that the AVCE can only function successfully as a way of broadening general education at advanced level. The proposed changes arising from the QCA review of the AVCE (QCA, 2002e) will aid it in this direction. In taking this trajectory, what the AVCE has not solved is the problem of low-status vocational qualifications in this country. This, in our view, needs to be addressed differently through the development of a range of vocationally focused grouped awards that form part of a unified curriculum and qualifications system from 14+.

The origins and creation of the AVCE

As we have seen in earlier chapters, until 1992 there was no single widely-recognized full-time general vocational qualification that could be easily delivered in both schools and colleges and could provide progression to both higher education and the workplace. The GNVQ was the first qualification of this type. Primarily introduced as a response to rising levels of full-time participation in the late 1980s, it was designed to provide a course of study for young people wanting to remain in full-time education but who were deemed unable to cope with the rigours of a three A level programme of study (Hodgson and Spours, 1997b). In its design, the GNVQ was a hybrid qualification with a style of assessment distinct from A levels (no external examinations), but containing a small element of general education through the inclusion of key skills and owing much to NVQ assessment methodology (a competence-based, evidence-gathering and portfolio-based approach).

During its first five years of implementation, GNVQ enjoyed a chequered reputation. On the positive side, our interviews show that the Advanced GNVQ managed to secure a niche in schools, in particular, as an alternative programme of study for learners who would have struggled on a full A level programme. Many of these learners went on to achieve high GNVQ grades and an opportunity to access the post-1992 universities. In addition, a progression route was established between Intermediate and

Advanced GNVQ. On the negative side, the award was difficult to deliver, not least because it contained key/core skills, there was always a question mark over its status, it had poor completion rates compared with BTEC awards, and OFSTED and the FEFC, albeit in different ways, were often unhappy with the way it was taught (Dearing, 1996; FEFC, 1994; OFSTED, 1994, 1996a). During its first five years, the GNVQ was constantly under review. In the main, reviews were focused on making the NVQ-style assessment more manageable and trying to raise the status of the award. Through all of this, Advanced GNVQ evolved as a minority, low status general education route into the post-1992 universities (FEDA/IoE/Nuffield, 1997). However, it essentially remained under the shadow of A levels and did not address the long-standing English problem of low status vocational education. The GNVQ also marked the beginnings of 'academic drift' in broad vocational qualifications (Ecclestone, 2000). This process of academic drift was to be taken further still with the AVCE.

The evolution of GNVQs into AVCEs started with the Capey (1996) and Dearing (1996) reviews in the mid-1990s and was carried through by *Qualifying for Success* (DfEE/DENI/WO, 1997). The Capey report suggested that the GNVQ become more unitized, externally assessed and more manageable. The Dearing report broadly supported these principles but further recommended that the title 'Applied A level' should replace Advanced GNVQ, that there should be a 12-, 6- and 3-unit Applied A level award and that key skills should be de-coupled from the main award. The 3-unit award was to be called the 'Applied AS'. Dearing's reasoning was that the size of the Advanced GNVQ as a grouped award had made it difficult both for many students to complete and also to combine with an A level qualification. The New Labour Government, which came into power one year after the publication of the Dearing report, accepted the main thrust of the Dearing recommendations, but with a central manifesto commitment to 'upgrade vocational qualifications' (Labour Party, 1997).

In the *Qualifying for Success* consultation exercise which took place in the autumn of 1997, the Government proposed building on the Dearing report and, in particular, focused on the introduction of a 6-unit Advanced GNVQ equivalent to one A level. However, it voiced concern about whether a proposed 3-unit award would have sufficient internal coherence or professional support. The main discussion around the 'new model GNVQ' was about its assessment regime – the desire being to develop an external and standardized approach to tests and set assignments. The emphasis in *Qualifying for Success* is on comparability with A levels and to this end it was suggested that the new model GNVQ should adopt the A–E grading scale associated with these qualifications.

In her response to QCA's advice on the *Qualifying for Success* consulta-tion, the Minister of State, Baroness Tessa Blackstone, endorsed the common grading scale for what was still referred to as the 'revised GNVQ', accepted that the 3-unit GNVQ could be developed in certain vocational areas, but rejected the term 'Applied A level' (Blackstone, 1998). The whole emphasis of her response was on standards and consistency, because these features were seen as the key to parity of esteem that would encourage learners to broaden their programmes of study by mixing academic and vocational qualifications. The direction had been set for the introduction of what was to become termed the AVCE.

The new AVCE, as originally conceived, was thus designed in 3-, 6- and 12-unit blocks and was graded A–E to align it with A levels; it was assessed by external examination as well as by portfolio; and the main award was decoupled from key skills. However, by the time the AVCE was introduced in September 2000, a political decision had been made to assess the award at the full A level standard throughout, on the grounds that this would raise its status – a key message from the Labour Party manifesto.

These design features represented a further shift away from vocational and towards general/applied education and the redesigned award became firmly hitched to the A level. As we will see from the evidence below, this was to have a powerful effect on the way that the AVCE was implemented by schools and colleges, taken up by learners and viewed by higher education providers.

The main features of the AVCE

The AVCE is available in 14 vocational areas in its 6- and 12-unit forms with the most popular subjects being Business, Health and Social Care, Leisure and Recreation, Travel and Tourism, ICT and Art and Design. The 3-unit AVCE is only offered currently in four vocational areas – Business, Engineering, Health and Social Care and ICT. According to the QCA Web site (www.qca.org.uk/14–19/vocational), the AVCE is designed:

> to be related to National Occupational Standards in relevant sectors and to equip students with up-to-date knowledge, skills and understanding of the underpinning principles and processes of those sectors. Learning is expected to be active and student-led, although directed by teachers and supported by professional and employer input.

The 3-unit AVCE was introduced primarily to provide enrichment for learner programmes and is normally completed within a year. The 6-unit award, which consists of at least three compulsory units and a maximum of three optional units, is the same size as a full A level and may be taken over one or two years. The 12-unit AVCE comprises a minimum of six and a maximum of eight compulsory units and maximum of six optional units, which makes it the same size as two A levels. It can be supplemented with additional units that are separately certificated and graded and which are normally offered in the same vocational subject area. The 12-unit award is normally taken over two years.

All AVCEs are assessed by both course-work and external tests (usually one third of the overall award). An aggregation of unit results provides the overall grade, although individual unit results are also available. The AVCE has a grading scale A–E like the AS/A2. However, unlike the AS/A2, all components of the AVCE are assessed at level 3 throughout. There is currently no AVCE equivalent of the AS in terms of level although the 3-unit AVCE is equal in volume.

While the acquisition of the three main key skills – Communication, Application of Number and IT – were a requirement for the achievement of the GNVQ at advanced level, this is not the case for the AVCE. Opportunities for assessing these key skills are sign-posted in AVCE specifications, but they are accredited separately through the new freestanding key skill awards.

The experience of the AVCE 2000–2002

In this section of the chapter, we draw extensively on data collected over the three years of the IoE/Nuffield research project (1999–2002). This allows us to compare data over time to help to determine what have been transitory issues linked to implementation and what might be more persistent and significant issues of purpose and design.

Over the three years of interviewing we have spoken each time to the curriculum manager for advanced level courses and to learners in groups of six. The results of analysing the 226 relevant interviews, in the 27 schools and colleges offering GNVQ/AVCE from our 50-site sample, are summarized in Table 5.1. All comments are derived from those made by teachers except where it is otherwise indicated. The themes we discuss are taken from this analysis, together with other national research data.

What emerges from Table 5.1 overall is the considerable consistency and continuity between responses over the period of our site visits, from the preparation for the *Curriculum 2000* reforms to their implementation in the first two years of their introduction. Below we draw some overarching conclusions from these data about the underlying issues of the AVCE cross-referenced, where appropriate, with data from other national research.

Patterns of AVCE provision – growth, decline or stasis?

Determining the uptake of the new AVCE compared with the old Advanced GNVQ has turned out to be a rather complex business. Data provided by UCAS, QCA and the Joint Council for General Qualifications (JCGQ) cross-referenced with the IoE/Nuffield site data suggest a number of different trends which taken together add up to a static or even declining picture for the AVCE in relation to Advanced GNVQ.

Table 5.1 The experience of the AVCE over time (1999–2002)

Themes	2000: Planning for *Curriculum 2000* programmes	2001: First year of implementation of *Curriculum 2000*	2002: Second year of implementation of *Curriculum 2000*
Patterns of GNVQ/AVCE provision in schools and delivery issues	• Anticipated decline of 12-unit AVCE • Planned reduction in time allotted – in order to mix with AS *Delivery concerns* • Duplication of courses between AS/AVCE (eg business and art) – harder to market AVCE as distinct • Mixed year groups (12/13) no longer possible • Expense of staffing vocational courses	• 6-unit ICT AVCE successful in some traditional academic sixth forms • 3- and 6-unit AVCEs useful for expanding curriculum offered in small sixth forms	• Drop in take up of 12-unit AVCE • Business, Science and ICT reported as areas of duplication with AS therefore schools more likely to choose AS *Delivery issues* • Problem of timetable constraints reducing time available for AVCE
Patterns of GNVQ/QVCE provision in colleges and delivery issues	• Anticipated continued strength of 12-unit AVCE as a full programme *Delivery concerns* • Duplication of courses between AS/AVCE/BTEC (eg Business and Art) – harder to market AVCE as distinct • AVCE seen as contrary to existing vocational culture • Organizational issues of new timetables	• Higher rate of funding for AVCE – positive incentive for colleges	• Strong move back to BTEC in some curriculum areas • Fewer students choosing 12-unit AVCE for 2003 *Delivery issues* • College timetable and traditions constrain mixing AVCE with AS • Business, Science and ICT reported as areas of duplication with AS
Breadth through mixing applied and academic learning	• Difficult to mix A levels and GNVQ because of different modes of assessment – why should the new system be any better? • Credit for AS more attractive than AVCE – therefore why will students mix? • Role of 6-unit AVCE in increasing breadth of offer approved by schools in particular	• Different modes of assessment still difficult to cope with in mixed programmes • Quantity of work, assessment burden and coursework deadlines with mixed programmes very demanding • Higher drop-out rate than previously – pressure of combining AVCE with AS – 12-unit AVCE + 2 AS just too hard	• Quantity of work on AVCE still high and assessment regime is still onerous • Less taught time for AVCE to enable mixing of AS and AVCE on timetable – learners not coping well

Table 5.1   *continued*

Themes	2000: Planning for Curriculum 2000 programmes	2001: First year of implementation of Curriculum 2000	2002: Second year of implementation of Curriculum 2000
Vocational coherence and relevance	• Concern about academic drift with new qualifications • Relevant vocational additionality in danger • Should have stuck with BTEC awards because of their vocational coherence and they are as good if not better for progression to HE	• GNVQ was not a broad experience but a rich one, students thrived on vocational courses – some students now just on 12-unit AVCE without even Key Skills	• Loss of benefits of vocational course as a full programme • AVCE no longer vocational in any meaningful way – academic drift • Creative Arts and Media already switching to BTEC in large numbers, also in Sports. Other subjects seriously considering possibility
Status of AVCE compared with GNVQ and AS/A2	• Students think GNVQ has lower status than A levels • GNVQ lower entry requirements than A level programme • Universities – will all accept AVCE?	• Students feel better about being on AVCE than GNVQ – it is an A level qualification • Aspirational parents still want students to do 4 AS, not anything with vocational in title	• Still residual lack of status with parents and students, AS/A2 students rarely choose AVCE • Entry requirements for AVCE levelled up to AS/A2 • No access problems reported from HE
Teaching, learning and assessment	*Positive* • Some support for new model of grading and assessment *Negative* • Loss of integrated Key Skills • Will students cope with new assessment requirements?	*Positive* • Standards raised through external assessment and 'fairer' assessment than GNVQ • AVCE not as rushed as AS *Negative* • Written exams put students under more pressure • Still too much box ticking – worst of both worlds • Idea of National Standards and assessment schemes still very unclear in AVCE • Lack of support from awarding bodies • Teaching for AVCE has become much more didactic than it was for GNVQ • Separation of Key Skills harder for students than when integrated	*Positive* • More rigorous than GNVQ *Negative* • Tests hard for the less academic students, but retakes in Jan 2002 gave much better results • System still suffering from NVQ legacy of box-ticking approach to assessment • Serious flaws in moderation process • Lack of support from awarding bodies and lack of published resources • Loss of positive aspects of GNVQ pedagogy

Table 5.1 *continued*

Themes	2000: Planning for Curriculum 2000 programmes	2001: First year of implementation of Curriculum 2000	2002: Second year of implementation of Curriculum 2000
Participation, progression and achievement	• Decline of Foundation and Intermediate GNVQ as a progression route • Loss of clear progression from Intermediate → Advanced because of level of AVCE • Concern over need for high entry requirements for AVCE • Levels of difficulty of AVCE – not 'stepped' like AS/A2	• Progression from Intermediate GNVQ → AVCE harder than with previous provision • No relevant courses for the GCSE '4–6 C grade' cohort – AVCE academically demanding – not serving old GNVQ constituency who used to often go on and prosper in HE • Higher level exams for AVCE than AS at first and poor exam result in January 2001 for AVCE	• Loss of progression from Intermediate GNVQ • Loss of option for the marginal A level students – students set up to fail again • Higher entry requirements for the AVCE compared with GNVQ • Foundation and Intermediate – the 'forgotten' students post-16 • Higher level exams for AVCE than AS at first

Overall, about 20 per cent of advanced level learners have been involved in AVCE in the first two years of implementation. This aggregate figure reflects different patterns in the first and second years of study, with more involved in the first year and fewer involved in the second year. The 20 per cent figure also masks sharp institutional differences, with about 35 per cent of *Curriculum 2000* learners in further education colleges taking AVCEs and as few as 2 per cent of those in independent or selective schools (QCA, 2002d).

Unlike the Advanced GNVQ, which could only be taken as a full award, the AVCE, as we have seen, comes in different sizes: 3-, 6- and 12-unit blocks. These have enjoyed different degrees of popularity and are being used in different ways. The GNVQ was normally taken as a full programme of applied or vocational study. The AVCE, on the other hand, is being used predominantly as a way of broadening programmes of study for those taking AS/A level (QCA, 2002d). This explains the relative popularity of the 3- and 6-unit blocks, particularly in IT. In this sense, the purpose of the AVCE is different from that of the Advanced GNVQ. It has moved from being an alternative vocational route for those unable to take A levels to being a means of mixing general and applied study for those taking A levels.

The other result of this pattern of take-up is that there has been a decline in the number of learners taking the 12-unit AVCE compared with Advanced GNVQ (JCGQ, 2002; see Appendix 2 in this book). In terms of the 6-unit AVCE, the fact that both AS and AVCE qualifications exist in the same subject area (eg Business), and given the deliverability and level of the AS, means that this qualification is likely to prove more popular than its applied counterpart. As a result of its design and location, therefore, the AVCE as a vocational award is now under pressure from a variety of directions – a general drift towards the AS as an easier step into advanced level study, a movement towards the 6-unit AVCE in schools as part of a mixed programme of study, and a shift towards BTEC National Diploma in colleges, as a full vocational programme.

Breadth through mixing applied and academic learning – a minority pattern

One of the main reasons for the design of the AVCE was to facilitate the mixing of general and vocational qualifications under *Curriculum 2000*. The highest aggregate figure for mixed patterns of study is recorded by the UCAS/QCA survey (QCA, 2002d), which indicates that about 22 per cent of advanced level learners in the first year combine different types of qualification including GCE AS/A2, AVCE, GCSEs, CLAIT and BTEC awards.

This figure indicates that more mixing of general and vocational qualifications is taking place than under the previous advanced level system and there is some professional agreement that growth in this type of programme has taken place (QCA, 2002d). However, as Table 5.1 indicates, growth in this area may already have plateaued because of the level of difficulty of the AVCE, the quantity of work it requires and the assessment burden a combined study programme entails. Moreover, we had no indication in the IoE/Nuffield site visits that higher education providers were encouraging learners to mix qualifications.

In addition, there are specific organizational factors affecting further education colleges, the most popular site for AVCEs, which militate against further mixing of study. The majority of further education colleges are organized into curriculum areas rather than having general education provision for 16–19-year-olds, so there is often very little opportunity for students on predominantly AVCE programmes to mix these qualifications with AS levels. AVCEs and AS levels are often delivered on different sites and timetabled separately according to curriculum rather than cross-college timetables. While LSDA has published examples of innovative approaches to *Curriculum 2000* provision (Tait *et al*, 2002), there is no overall evidence from the field that these islands of good practice have made a major impact on the general pattern of learner take-up of the AVCE and mixed programmes.

Vocational coherence and relevance – the process of academic drift

Where colleges have attempted to organize timetables to facilitate more mixed programmes of study they, like schools, have ended up with provision that cannot be organized so easily into coherent vocational programmes. It is not surprising, therefore, that a dominant theme throughout the three years of site visits has been teacher and lecturer concern about the loss of genuinely vocational advanced level provision. What they lament is the lack of a holistic vocational programme that gains its recognition and relevance from its relationship with the labour market. As the data in Table 5.1 reveal, learners on AVCE programmes not only have a much poorer diet in terms of hours of study than under GNVQ or BTEC, but they also do not experience the same degree of work-related learning. One of the strengths of earlier vocational qualifications was that they could be designed to prepare learners for working life or particular sectoral needs.

Prior to *Curriculum 2000*, learners in further education colleges following courses in particular vocational areas 'belonged' to that vocational department. This meant that pastoral and tutorial support was largely provided by staff in the vocational area. Learners were seen by staff, and indeed saw themselves, as being at the college to study Engineering, Tourism, Art and Design and so on. In order to make full programmes out of an Advanced GNVQ, many colleges encouraged, or required, learners to take relevant vocational qualifications, short courses and/or additional GNVQ units in the same subject area. The learner experience of these vocational programmes could not be described as broad, in the sense of combining study from a variety of separate subject areas, but they could provide what one college vice principal described as 'not a broad experience but a very rich one' in a particular vocational area (Savory *et al*, 2003 forthcoming).

Evidence from both the QCA evaluation report (QCA, 2002b) and the IOE/Nuffield site visits indicates that teachers consider the AVCE to be less distinctively vocational than even the Advanced GNVQ. This was put down to the emphasis on theoretical content and also the lack of connection with experience in the workplace. It is as a result of their search for vocational relevance and breadth that many colleges are reverting to the remodelled BTEC National Diplomas. The following comment from a teacher of Art and Design AVCE is typical:

> We have found the AVCE qualification in our subject, Art and Design, absolutely dreadful... we have opted out and are teaching BTEC National Diploma in September. (Savory *et al*, 2002, p24)

This loss of vocationally relevant study and experience is, arguably, the greatest failing of the AVCE.

Status of the AVCE compared with GNVQ and the AS/A2 – higher but still not equal

The problem of the academic/vocational divide and the low status of vocational qualifications in comparison with their academic counterparts in the

English education and training system is well known and commonly recognized. One of the major aims of the *Curriculum 2000* reforms was to create 'parity of esteem' between the A level and the AVCE – hence the effort to make the AVCE into a 'vocational' A level. In part, this mission is being achieved, mainly because of the take-up of the 6-unit and 3-unit AVCEs, particularly in ICT, as part of 'academic' advanced level programmes. However, the quest for parity of esteem is far from complete and has come at a price.

School and college managers, in particular, have welcomed the increased status and rigour of the AVCE. This view of the new award is, however, contested by teachers in the classroom who have to deliver what has become a less accessible and more demanding qualification. Two national surveys focusing on classroom teacher views of the reforms (Savory *et al,* 2001a, 2002) suggest that a sense of teacher professionalism has been undermined by seeing learners struggling and in some cases failing with the new qualifications:

> Increase in rigour in AVCE has led to poor motivation and high drop out rates. (Lecturer cited in Savory *et al,* 2002, p27)

It appears, too, that OFSTED inspectors have similar concerns about the design and function of the AVCE:

> Increased rigour in vocational subjects may not be best promoted by using criteria developed for use in academic courses. (OFSTED, 2001, p7)

Interestingly, a small-scale survey in Lancashire suggests that despite the changes to vocational qualifications brought in under *Curriculum 2000,* learners still see AVCEs and the learners who take them as second class (Garnett, 2002).

Initial responses from higher education providers, on the other hand, indicate that they are accepting the new award (UCAS, 2003), though it is difficult to tell at this stage whether the level of recognition is decisively different from that experienced by the old Advanced GNVQ. So far, there is little research evidence on the views of employers about AVCEs, but QCA data suggest that the AVCE is less well known and also less valued than traditional vocational qualifications or A levels (QCA, 2002f). However, the limited rise in status of the AVCE as a general qualification has, as we have seen above, done little for its vocational recognition or the overall position of the award vis-à-vis other qualifications. Furthermore, what little success it has enjoyed has been at the cost of a progression route for those learners who previously benefited from an applied programme of study at advanced level under GNVQ. Despite all the efforts to create parity of esteem between academic and vocational qualifications, in our view the AVCE has not achieved this. What this reform shows us, once again, is that esteem for vocational qualifications has to come principally from another quarter: their status and recognition by employers and the labour market.

Teaching, learning and assessment – the worst of both worlds

From the beginning of *Curriculum 2000*, teachers and lecturers were divided about the teaching, learning and assessment experience under the new AVCE. On the positive side, a minority thought that the specifications were clearer and that the external assessment was fairer and more rigorous than the type of assessment in GNVQ. On the negative side, the majority of teachers found that the AVCE combined the worst of both worlds – external tests that demotivated learners and put them under pressure, combined with echoes of an NVQ assessment methodology which insisted on coverage of grade-related criteria and extensive portfolio evidence. This dissatisfaction is summed up in the following quotation by a college vice principal in one of the IoE/Nuffield research sites:

> I think the AVCE is causing more problems... there is some feeling, I think, that they've got kind of the worst of both worlds, that the academic content has been raised, so there is actually more work to get through than there used to be on the old GNVQ, but they've retained the kind of competence-based box ticking approach to marking which means that again it seems that students are in danger of not passing the qualification if they haven't done one little thing.

Another problem according to practitioners in our sample sites is the grading approach in AVCEs, which requires learners to demonstrate mastery at Grade E in their portfolio work before they can achieve at higher grades. This is a remnant of the NVQ coverage approach to assessment, which was described by one senior manager as 'nit-picking and vindictive'. These difficulties were compounded by the early coursework deadline of 15 May compared with July under the old GNVQ regime. In addition, teachers and learners in both QCA and IoE/Nuffield research sites commented that the criteria for assessment were too specific and the language used in examination papers presented a problem for learners because of its ambiguity or lack of clarity. The overall effect of this approach to assessment was seen by some teachers as penalizing learners because the criteria were simply too specific and did not allow them to show what they had learnt (OFSTED, 2001;QCA, 2002b). As one teacher complained:

> I have a background in vocational teaching and I think it's a real tragedy that we are being squeezed through this mincer to produce work earlier, to be prescriptive, the flair and skills that students used to pick up, there's simply not the time.

This view has been supported by OFSTED:

> Many teachers believe that students following AVCE are not able to show what they know and can do by means of the assessment model now in place. (OFSTED, 2001, p7)

The concerns teachers felt about assessment were not helped by the continuing bureaucratic burden of the AVCE and, perhaps more important, by the perceived lack of support in this area from examining and awarding bodies:

> The exam boards have become so big that they are drowning and we find it almost impossible to find a real person to talk to about new specification problems. (Savory *et al,* 2002, p25)

In addition to the type of disruption that was caused by the late arrival of specifications and changes to information that might be expected in the first year of a reform, there were also complaints about the poor quality of learning materials, lack of feedback on marking standards and the loss of vital face-to-face contact with moderators. This was in marked contrast to the amount of contact teachers of vocational programmes had experienced with GNVQs.

The view of the learning experience in the AVCE from the learner perspective, however, was more positive. From our interviews with learners taking the 12-unit AVCE as their main programme of study, we have found a relatively high degree of satisfaction with the mode of learning because of the focus on course-work, applied and resource-based learning that was used in the old GNVQs. Learners felt more in control of their learning than their counterparts on predominantly AS programmes. These learners have also been more likely to engage with the Key Skills Qualification and have sometimes seen its relevance to their programme. The 6-unit AVCE was found to have worked well when learners wanted a particular course for specific progression purposes (QCA, 2002a). However, those learners who have taken a 6- or 3-unit AVCE as part of a predominantly AS programme have found juggling the demands of coursework for both types of qualifications difficult to manage. In addition, there were real concerns about failure rates.

Achievement and progression – high failure rates and a disrupted progression route

One of the central purposes of the *Curriculum 2000* reforms was to increase participation, progression and achievement in advanced level study by providing a stepping-stone between GCSE and A level through the creation of the AS. This design feature was not reproduced within AVCEs, however, and learners have had to move from GCSE to an award pitched at the full advanced level. Moreover, they are now confronted with a significant amount of external testing. These design features have changed the role of the AVCE in comparison with the Advanced GNVQ. The first two years of the AVCE have seen failure rates that are limiting the growth and scope of the award. Attainment data from the JCGQ shows that only 4 per cent of candidates taking AVCEs attained A grades compared with 20 per cent taking A levels. In addition, 22 per cent of AVCE candidates failed compared with 7 per cent in A levels (JCGQ, 2002).

Prior to *Curriculum 2000*, school sixth forms often relied upon the GNVQ to motivate and boost the attainment of their more marginal advanced level learners. The GNVQ was most successful when it was taught by a dedicated team as a full-time programme of up to 18 hours per week of taught time with extra independent study time built in for learners. It provided a progression pathway for Intermediate students and often considerable added-value in terms of advanced level point scores in areas with traditionally low points scores (Hodgson and Spours, 2002c). For some smaller, lower attaining schools, the GNVQ programme made up the main part of their advanced level offer. Schools fear that this world has disappeared under the new AVCE. As one head of sixth in our research sites reflected:

> We had excellent results under the old GNVQ, last year we got 60 per cent Distinction, and we used to timetable it so that those students were doing possibly 36 periods a fortnight, 36 hours out of 50 a fortnight of their GNVQ. What of course happens now is they're only doing 18 hours a fortnight and either it's that or the fact that the exams are completely different than they used to be, but you cannot ensure that kids coming through the intermediate route can progress to the AVCE route and get success whereas you could, you know, last year, we had a lot of students, well proportionately a lot of students, go from intermediate to advanced and often get Merit or Distinction and go onto university.

Concerns about the erosion of progression routes for both more marginal GCSE students and, in particular, students on Intermediate GNVQ programmes wanting to move on to advanced level programmes are noted in all the major evaluation reports on *Curriculum 2000* (OFSTED, 2001; QCA, 2002a, 2002b).

We would suggest that it is the effects of a more academic approach to study that has created these difficulties for progression from Intermediate GNVQ to AVCE provision, with colleges and schools in our sample sites remarking that many learners cannot successfully make this transition. What this means is that under *Curriculum 2000* there is currently no clear progression route beyond level 2 for learners on vocational programmes, a point made very directly by OFSTED:

> The three year route to Level 3 accreditation taken formerly by students via Intermediate and Advanced GNVQ has been disrupted by the changed demands of the AVCE. (OFSTED, 2001, p7)

One of the effects of these concerns at school and college level has been that institutions have been forced to think about the entry requirements for the AVCE. Traditionally, admission to a GNVQ Advanced Level programme was on the basis of four GCSE passes at Grades A*–C (FEDA/IoE/Nuffield Foundation, 1997). With the AVCE, however, this threshold may not be sufficient for learners to succeed in the qualification and, in part, explains high failure rates and low grades in the AVCE.

It may be that one of the effects of the initial reputation of the AVCE being difficult to achieve is that it is beginning to attract a different kind of learner than under the old Advanced GNVQ. As we have seen, it is learners on predominantly AS programmes who are taking advantage of the new smaller AVCE qualifications. While government may support this development, because it indicates a higher status for the AVCE, it does not answer the question for schools and colleges as to what they ought to be offering learners with marginal GCSE profiles. These are the learners who have appeared to have been left behind as a result of the *Curriculum 2000* reforms.

The review of the AVCE

As we have indicated earlier in the book, all aspects of the *Curriculum 2000* reforms were reviewed at the end of the first year of implementation and the AVCEs were no exception although, in fact, ministers had already asked for these latter qualifications to be reviewed in May 2001.

The first Hargreaves review report (2001a) focused on the lack of alignment between the AS/A2 qualification and the AVCE, which was considered a major concern because of lower learner pass rates in the latter – lower even than those for legacy GNVQs. The three other major issues raised were the vocational relevance of the specifications, the inflexibility and manageability of the assessment regime and the case for introducing 3-unit qualifications in more subjects. The only practical proposal in this report was the moving back by two weeks of the coursework deadline.

In the second review report in December 2001 (Hargreaves, 2001b), the concern about the difference in level of demand between AS/A2s and AVCEs was recognized and it was proposed that the latter should be revised by 2004 to include an AS level stage rather than remaining at level 3 throughout. The review report contained no such concrete proposals for changes to the assessment model, although it did indicate that it would be kept under review in order to maintain confidence in the AVCE.

The two Hargreaves reviews were followed in the summer of 2002 by a limited consultation exercise to revise the structure and assessment of the AVCE to align it more with the AS/A2 (QCA, 2002e). This exercise can be seen as creating out of the AVCE an applied AS and A2, responding not only to the protestations of teachers but also intended to provide a progression pathway from the new vocational GCSEs in September 2004. In our view, the attempts to give the AVCE an AS/A2 structure further confirm the process of academic drift and the AVCE's place as a general and applied qualification that forms part of A level provision. Our analysis suggests that this is the only sensible destination for the AVCE and that it cannot now be developed as a genuine vocational qualification. The Government, however, still clings to the hope that AVCE will remain vocational by suggesting that the restructured award should retain links with national occupational standards.

Conclusion – making sense of the AVCE within *Curriculum 2000*

It is worth reminding ourselves of the aim of the AVCE within *Curriculum 2000*. It was introduced to improve the status of full-time vocational qualifications so that more learners, who could not succeed with a full A level programme, would be attracted into full-time post-16 education. It was assumed that this aim could be achieved through learners taking the AVCE either as a main course of study or as part of a mixed academic and vocational programme. In these terms, has the AVCE achieved its aims?

Our overall assessment to date is that it is succeeding in fulfilling its political goal of achieving some sort of parity of esteem with the AS/A2, principally because it is being taken by a wider group of learners than the old Advanced GNVQ and appears to be becoming more widely recognized by universities. However, as the evidence above indicates, this recognition has come at a price and the political decision to make the first version of the AVCE less accessible than the AS/A2 qualification has already been judged to have been a mistake.

The way that the AVCE has been used in practice and its official revision in 2002 both confirm that it has become a general and applied qualification rather than a vocational one. It is being used as a means of broadening participation in general education, offering a wider range of subjects to learners in general education programmes and providing a limited form of breadth for a minority of learners.

At the same time, the emphasis of the AVCE on knowledge and theory rather than on practical learning and achievement has reduced its scope for succeeding in even this limited task. This, together with its assessment regime, makes the AVCE a difficult qualification to achieve and it is hard to imagine that learners will deliberately opt for this award rather than the AS/A2, particularly in a comparable subject area.

The policy direction of the AVCE (and the vocational GCSE) represents the formalization of academic drift. Despite the rhetoric of wanting to create a vocational ladder from 14+, the Government has failed to use AVCE for this purpose. Its concern to pursue the aim of parity of esteem via an assessment-led approach has made the AVCE neither fully vocational nor an accessible form of general education. The changes resulting from the current revision of the AVCE may address the latter issue of accessibility but certainly will not address the former of vocational relevance. In this sense, the AVCE suffers from fundamental problems of both purpose and design.

This policy direction opens up an enormous gap in vocational, technical and practical learning in the 14–19 phase. We would argue that more applied learning should form part of the curriculum for all young people from the age of 14. GCSEs in vocational subjects may only achieve this in a partial sense because they, like AVCEs, have been designed in the image of academic qualifications, hence the agonizing about their naming and whether to refer to the term 'vocational' at all. We, like others who write in this area (eg Wolf, 2002), believe that from the age of 16, on the other hand, there is a need for a solid programme of vocational and technical learning related to the workplace for those young people who are seeking more vocational relevance and access to vocational knowledge, skills and experience.

Some have argued that we should put the V (vocational) back into AVCEs. Offered as single or even double awards, we think that this is now impossible. Our view is that the V can only be brought back into learners' programmes if AVCEs are seen as part of a larger programme in the form of a grouped award that promotes a substantial degree of vocational special-ization. Moreover, what this would require is a more active involvement of employers in both the design and delivery of these new awards, so that they gather their esteem from their vocational relevance in the labour market. We argue throughout this book that such a goal would require accreditation through a progressive diploma framework from 14+ such as the one we describe in the final chapter. In the meantime, the desire by practitioners for such an approach is reflected in the growing popularity of BTEC National Diplomas and First Awards that aim to provide a more holistic and practical programme of vocational study for 16–19-year-olds. This trend is likely to be reinforced by the desire of the Government that schools and colleges become more distinctive, with the former involved primarily in general and applied education and the latter rediscovering their technical and vocational traditions (DfES, 2002b).

6

Developing key skills in the 14–19 curriculum: from an assessment-led to a curriculum-led approach

Introduction

The policy pursuit of key or core skills as part of post-16 education and training programmes over the last 20 years might be likened to the search for the Holy Grail.[1] There has been widespread professional and political support in this country, as in others, for all learners to develop broad transferable skills as part of their programmes of study but, to date, no effective model or strategy has been designed or implemented in England.

Furthermore, the most recent attempt at the development of key skills under *Curriculum 2000,* where for the first time they were brought out of the 'vocational ghetto' and into mainstream education, is perceived as having failed. We regard this failure as a tragedy because the development of key skills has the potential to enrich programmes of study and to create more effective learners. Lessons must therefore be learnt from what went wrong with key skills in *Curriculum 2000,* which was a brave but flawed attempt to make them part of all learner programmes. From our research evidence, we would suggest that the main problem stemmed from a focus on assessment and the acquisition of qualifications in key skills, rather than on the progressive development within the curriculum of the skills required for learning, progression and employment. An assessment and qualifications-led approach squandered professional and learner support for this form of broadening.

In this chapter, therefore, we argue for a fundamental rethink of how to foster these types of skills for all learners. We suggest that this development is more likely to be achieved through a three-fold approach within a new diploma/Baccalaureate system from 14+, which we discuss in the final chapter. Such an approach might involve the offer of stand-alone units in areas such as Mathematics and Numeracy, which require specialist teaching; the appropriate embedding of learning skills within subjects and specialist areas of study to broaden their scope; and the development of authentic 'vehicles' or 'platforms' for key skill acquisition and accreditation within the proposed diplomas.

One of the aims of the new strategy we propose is to galvanize learner, teacher, employer and higher education support for broad skill development for all learners. This will mean placing more emphasis on the 'use value' of key skills as an essential part of learner programmes, rather than focusing on vain attempts to develop 'exchange value' for stand-alone Key Skills Qualifications. We recognize the importance of 'exchange value' in what remains a very credentialist system, but we think that it is best achieved through the role that key skills play in a high-status diploma system.

In this chapter we begin by placing the approach taken to key skills in *Curriculum 2000* within its broader historical and policy context. This type of analysis allows us to focus on problems of purpose and design associated with the Key Skills Qualification as well as on problems of implementation. We then consider recent attempts by Government to review key skill developments within *Curriculum 2000*. This analysis and discussion informs our thinking on the alternative strategy for key skills indicated above, which is designed to improve both their use value and their exchange value.

The English approach to core/key skills: debates and developments

Since the late 1970s and the 'Great Debate' about the role and purpose of education, key/core skills have had an almost totemic significance for the English post-16 education and training system. Debates have raged over exactly what the key/core skills are or ought to be, how they should be developed, whether they can be transferred from one context to another and how they should be recognized and accredited. However, the belief that their absence in young people constitutes one of the major weaknesses of our education and training system and that their development would ensure a more highly skilled and competent workforce has continued for over 25 years. This section of the chapter provides a brief historical background to the development of the Key Skills Qualification in Application of Number, Communication and IT, as part of the *Curriculum 2000* reforms, why it experienced difficulties in this form and why changes were made to the Government's key skills policy following only one year of implementation.

While debates about the role of the education system in relation to the economy became highly public at the end of the 1970s with Prime Minister James Callaghan's speech at Ruskin College (Callaghan, 1976), as Green (1997) points out, the lack of a strong approach to technical and vocational education in this country had been seen as a problem throughout the 20th century. In comparison with other European countries, Green argues, this type of education in the UK tended to be narrow and to lack an element of general education. At the same time, general education, pre- and post-16, consisted largely of the study of academic disciplines with little attention paid to the application of skills and knowledge. Pressures for building more general education into technical and vocational education and more applied skills into academic education, in order to make both more responsive to the demands of the economy, thus began to grow towards the end of the 1970s and early 1980s. These demands became more pressing as rates of youth unemployment rose and the education and training system was increasingly criticized for failing to provide the work- force the UK needed to compete in the world economy. It was at this point that the first steps towards the process of developing core/key skills were taken and, since addressing the needs of unemployed or lower-achieving young people was the most pressing demand, it is here that development took place first.

The first steps towards core/key skill development – the origins of remedialism

During the early 1980s a series of pre-vocational and vocational qualifica- tions, courses and programmes, such as the Unified Vocational Preparation (UVP), the Youth Training Scheme (YTS) and the Certificate of Pre- Vocational Education (CPVE) were developed; all contained the type of core/key skills it was felt young people needed to make them more employ- able. Following an influential report by the Further Education Unit, *A Basis for Choice* (FEU, 1979), core/key skills were developed in each of these awards and programmes.

What was also common to all these developments was the fact that they were largely targeted at lower achieving young people. They were for those who did not have sufficient qualifications, skills or experience to enter the labour market directly or to continue on to academic post-compulsory study. In this first stage of their development, therefore, core/key skills were associated with an idea of remedial education, basic skill develop- ment and courses for lower achieving learners to develop flexible skills to cope with a context of high unemployment.

Key skills for all – a potential breakthrough at the end of the 1980s

From the mid-1980s to the beginning of the 1990s, however, there were a number of policy moves towards a more common approach to core/key skills involving learners with a range of abilities and on both academic and voca- tional programmes. The Extension Phase of the Technical and Vocational Education Initiative (TVEI) was introduced into all schools and colleges, which made the development of certain types of curricular experiences and processes focusing on core/key skill acquisition (eg work-related learning, careers education and guidance, IT and recording of achievement) a requirement for schools and colleges seeking funding from this initiative. Her Majesty's Inspectorate published a paper in support of core skills in 1989 (HMI, 1989). John McGregor, Secretary of State in 1989, taking his cue from his predecessor, Kenneth Baker, urged the curriculum and qualifications regulatory and advisory bodies – The Secondary Examinations and Assessment Council (SEAC), The National Council for Vocational Qualifications (NCVQ), The National Curriculum Council (NCC), The Further Education Unit (FEU) and the Training Agency – to report on which core skills could be incorporated into programmes of study for 16–19-year-olds following Advanced level (A level), Advanced Supplementary level and other courses (SEAC, 1991). The Confederation of British Industry published its influential document *Towards a Skills Revolution* (CBI, 1989), which recommended the development of core skills within all types of vocational education and training, and building skills as well as knowledge acquisition into the National Curriculum and, at the end of the decade, the NCC report on core skills in 16–19 programmes came out (NCC, 1990).

While there was still no absolute agreement about which specific core/key skills should be developed and supported in programmes for 16–19-year-olds, in the majority of reports there was a discussion of communication, problem solving, personal skills, numeracy, IT and, in many cases, a modern foreign language. More important, the idea that there were a number of generic skills that all post-16 learners needed to develop, regardless of their ability, qualifications and educational or training context, was manifested for the first time in concrete policy terms at the end of the 1980s.

Part of the political support for core/key skills at this time was fuelled by international studies on skills and qualifications acquisition in which the UK appeared to be doing badly in comparison with other developed countries (eg, DES, 1985; OECD, 1985). There was a commonly held assumption, supported by human capital theory, that raising the level of skills and qualifications within the population would contribute directly to increased productivity and economic competitiveness (eg CBI, 1989; DE, 1988, 1989). In addition, the arguments about the narrowness of the curriculum for 16–19-year-olds in relation to their counterparts in Europe continued to be used as part of the rationale for supporting core/key skills (Green, 1997).

Although the political argument around the necessity of all post-16 learners developing core/key skills was largely won by the beginning of the 1990s, the technical issues surrounding their development within all post-16 qualifications were far from being resolved (SEAC, 1991). These practical issues, together with the traditional fear of diluting A levels ensured that, despite the rhetorical commitment to the development of core/key skills in all post-16 programmes, in fact the main developments in this area continued to be taken forward in the vocational track throughout the 1990s.

Retreat from core skills and entitlement – GNVQs and key skills

We have argued elsewhere (Hodgson and Spours, 1997a) that the 1991 White Paper, *Education and Training for the 21st Century* (DfE/ED/WO, 1991) marked a policy move away from some of the arguments for a common entitlement for 14–19-year-olds which were prevalent at the end of the 1980s. Against a background of rising levels of full-time participation in post-16 education, the White Paper set the agenda for a much more sharply delineated triple-track post-16 qualifications system through the introduction of General National Vocational Qualifications (GNVQs).

The fact that it was exclusively in GNVQs that core/key skills became a requirement meant that once again in the early 1990s they became associated with vocational education rather than with the more prestigious academic track. This legacy, we will suggest later, has had a profound effect on how the current Key Skills Qualification is viewed by learners, teachers and higher education providers.

It might be wrong, however, to see the national policy drive for qualifications distinctiveness as the only reason for Government back-pedalling on the core skills entitlement agenda at the beginning of the 1990s. Numerous papers by NCVQ, SEAC and the Schools Curriculum and Assessment Authority (SCAA) throughout the 1990s bear witness to the significant technical and practical implementation difficulties of introducing core/key skills into A levels and National Vocational Qualifications (NVQs) or into post-16 programmes in general (eg, Oates, 1992, 1996; SEAC, 1991). Indeed these early concerns about the practicalities of introducing and assessing core/key skills within all post-16 programmes were borne out by the experience of GNVQ programmes, as several school and college inspection reports testify (eg, FEFC, 1994; HMI, 1996). The Government's cautious approach to core/key skills at this time may, therefore, also have had a very pedestrian underlying rationale – the simple difficulty of realizing the concept of core/key skills for all in practice. Again, we will return to this issue when we examine the policy of 'key skills for all', which became part of the New Labour administration's educational agenda in 1997.

The professional consensus and the debate about key skills – a search for breadth, skill development and remediation

While the national policy drive to develop core skills more broadly as an entitlement within all post-16 qualifications appeared to run out of steam during the early 1990s and was replaced by their development within GNVQs, there was still strong support for their development within the 16–19 curriculum from employers (eg, Institute of Directors, 1992) and particularly from education professionals. Numerous policy documents from academics, researchers and teacher professional associations put forward proposals for reforms to the 16–19 or 14–19 curriculum that included a common entitlement to core/key skills (eg, APVIC, 1991; Finegold *et al,* 1990; Royal Society, 1991; SHA, 1993). What united these documents and proposals was a critique of the narrow post-16 qualifications currently on offer (particularly A levels) and a desire to develop a broader, more flexible curriculum for 16–19-year-olds or, in some cases, 14–19-year-olds, which focused on application of knowledge and skills as well as on academic theory. The argument for an entitlement to develop core/key skills was seen as part of this broad preparation for further study and adult life, as well as a way of ensuring that all young people gained the basic skills needed for employment. Key skills were also seen as a way of linking separate qualifications tracks (Raffe *et al,* 1998).

Dearing and key skills – setting the agenda for the late 1990s and Curriculum 2000

During the mid-1990s, Gillian Shephard, the Conservative Secretary of State for Education and Employment at the time, recognizing that there were still substantial problems with the post-16 qualifications that had developed out of the 1991 White Paper, set in train a significant review agenda. This resulted in three major reports which all had an impact on the development of core/key skills – *Review of 100 NVQs and SVQs* (Beaumont, 1995); *The GNVQ Assessment Review* (Capey, 1995) and the *Review of Qualifications for 16–19 Year Olds* (Dearing, 1996). It was the third of these that had the greatest influence on the way that core/key skills developed in the late 1990s, effectively setting the agenda in this area for New Labour's *Qualifying for Success* (DfEE/DENI/WO, 1997) proposals and resulting in the development of a freestanding Key Skills Qualification in Communication, Application of Number and IT as part of the *Curriculum 2000* reforms introduced in September 2000.

In Section 7 of his report, entitled, *Improving skills for work and lifetime learning*, Lord Dearing, Chair of the National Review of Qualifications for 16–19-year-olds, stressed the need to improve standards in the skills of communication and application of number, which his evidence suggested had not been adequately developed within the National Curriculum. While recognizing the significance that end-users of education, and in particular employers, attached to these two skills, he also argued for the foregrounding of IT as a skill that would become increasingly important in the future. These three skills he then referred to as 'the key skills for all our young people' (Dearing, 1996, p46). Other skills that had previously been discussed as part of the core/key skills debate – team-working, interpersonal skills, problem solving and managing one's own learning – are referred to as 'wider skills'. The discussion that follows in the report is very much related to a basic skills approach to key skills and echoes some of the much earlier discussions about the problems of low standards in

English and Mathematics in this country (Bullock, 1975; Cockcroft, 1981).

Here already we can see two related lines of argument which were to prove so influential in the new Labour Government's thinking in its consultation document on reforms to 16–19 qualifications *Qualifying for Success*: the division between different types of core/key skills – the three main key skills and the wider key skills – and the confusion between the three main key skills and basic skills acquisition.

A third important strand of influence on the Government's policy in this area was undoubtedly Lord Dearing's suggestion of developing a freestanding qualification in the key skills of Communication, Application of Number and IT, but not making it mandatory for the award of advanced level qualifications. Rather, he suggested, and the Government took this line in *Qualifying for Success*, that key skills should be built into A level subject cores and syllabuses and that 'all schools, colleges and training bodies... should provide opportunities for young people to develop these skills and to have them assessed' (DfEE/DENI/WO, 1997, p54).

The two major differences between the Dearing approach to the Key Skills Qualification and the approach taken by the Labour Government in *Qualifying for Success* is that Lord Dearing recommended that the Key Skills Qualification should be developed as a new Advanced Subsidiary (AS) qualification and that it should be a requirement at level 3 for gaining the Advanced Level National Certificate or Diploma that he also proposed in his report. Neither of these recommendations, as we shall see below, was taken forward in the final *Curriculum 2000* qualifications reform process. The decision not to proceed with these particular recommendations could be seen as a movement away from real commitment to 'key skills for all'. In particular, the decision not to include any form of overarching certificate or diploma as part of the *Curriculum 2000* reforms has, arguably, removed one of the most effective ways of securing learner, teacher and higher education commitment to key skills at advanced level.

The purpose and design of the Key Skills Qualification within the context of Curriculum 2000

The Key Skills Qualification that emerged from the *Qualifying for Success* agenda and was initially implemented as part of *Curriculum 2000*, assessed achievement in the three main key skills of Communication, Application of Number and Information Technology. The so-called 'wider key skills' – Problem-Solving, Working with Others and Improving Own Learning and Performance – did not form part of the Key Skills Qualification, but could be accredited separately through individual wider key skill units. The units of the Key Skills Qualification could be achieved at different levels. Each unit was assessed by providing portfolio-based evidence and taking external tests. Much of this evidence was intended to be gathered from learners' main programmes of study and all Advanced Subsidiary (AS) and Advanced Certificate of Vocational Education (AVCE) specifications 'signpost' where there are opportunities to assess the six key skills (QCA, 1999b).

It was intended that the Key Skills Qualification should be offered to all 16–19-year-olds, although it was not mandatory for learners to take it or for schools and colleges to offer it. However, the Government put substantial resources into a Key Skills Support Programme delivered by the Learning and Skills Development Agency (LSDA) and offered to all schools and colleges free of charge. It also provided dedicated funding for general further education and sixth form colleges to offer the Key Skills Qualification as part of a *Curriculum 2000* entitlement programme for 16–19-year-olds.

This approach to core/key skills undoubtedly constituted a break with the past. It was an attempt to associate key skills with all types of programmes for 16–19-year-olds rather than exclusively with vocational qualifications. While key skills were signposted within AVCEs, successfully demonstrating competence in the three main key skills was not a requirement for gaining the award as it had been with GNVQ. There was also an attempt to indicate that curriculum breadth at advanced level could be provided through the acquisition of skills as well as through the more traditional means of taking additional academic subjects. These two approaches to core/key skills development might be seen as broadly progressive and even innovative. However, Dearing's recommendation to focus on the three key skills closely associated with employability marked a critical moment and, in our view, a mistake. In order to deliver 'key skills for all' at advanced level, Dearing could have broadened the range of key skills required to encompass those needed for progression to higher levels of study, so that key skills would be more likely to appeal to a wider range of learners, most of whom would be aiming for progression to higher education. Instead, the focus was narrowed to Communication, Application of Number and IT.

The Labour Government adopted Dearing's approach but with its own policy emphasis on national standards and inclusion (Hodgson and Spours, 1999a). A discrete qualification was designed to be part of the national qualifications framework, but at three levels of difficulty, not just at level 3. As a result, the focus on accrediting the main three key skills within the new Key Skills Qualification effectively played down the importance of the wider key skills. From the start, the qualification thus risked being associated with a basic skills agenda and remediation rather than with advanced level skills for further study or skills for the future. Moreover, in an attempt to ensure credibility and status for the new qualification, particularly in the eyes of employers, the Government opted for a strong external testing regime together with a demanding portfolio approach. This, as we shall see, created problems for embedding the key skills within learning programmes, for acquisition of the qualification and for authentic assessment in the workplace.

Finally, the Government also opted for a voluntarist approach to the whole *Curriculum 2000* agenda with regards to choices made by learners and recognition by end-users such as universities. At the same time, in April 2000, colleges were offered funding incentives directly tied to the different elements of *Curriculum 2000*. With this came the attendant risk of the Key Skills Qualification being seen as 'semi-compulsory' – something that was not necessarily valued but which institutions imposed on learners.

This historical analysis suggests that the Government's initial approach to core/key skills within the *Curriculum 2000* agenda was likely to be fundamentally flawed in three respects – the emphasis on remediation skills and a deficit agenda; the role of assessment in the search for credibility; and the issue of learner and external recognition in a voluntarist system. How these factors would be played out in practice has to be seen in the context of the whole *Curriculum 2000* reform process and its increased demands on learners and institutions.

The Key Skills Qualification in the context of *Curriculum 2000*

National surveys on *Curriculum 2000* undertaken during 1999 and 2000 suggested that there was a high level of support amongst schools and colleges for offering opportunities to achieve key skills in the post-14 curriculum. However, they also suggested that there was much lower support for offering the Key Skills Qualification to the majority of their learners. The Department for Education and Employment and Institute of Education survey, undertaken in the autumn of 1999, indicated that about 80 per cent of schools and colleges intended to offer some form of key skills provision under *Curriculum 2000* (DfEE/IoE, 2000). At the same time, however, it also suggested a lower level of commitment to offering accreditation, with 60 per cent intending to offer opportunities to achieve key skill units and as few as 22 per cent offering opportunities for most learners to achieve the full Key Skills Qualification.

The partial up-take of key skills – a step to universal participation?

The partial uptake of the Key Skills Qualification in the first year of implementation can be illuminated by responses from different types of institutions. The IoE/Nuffield telephone snapshot survey of its 50 case-study institutions (see Appendix 1) in October 2000 suggested that for general further education colleges and sixth form colleges there was likely to be a high registration rate for the Key Skills Qualification, principally as a result of funding. On the other hand, there was negligible interest from independent and selective schools, with not one of the eight schools of this type in the 50 sample sites indicating any engagement with the qualification. Maintained 11–18 comprehensives lay somewhere between these poles with some responding in the same way as colleges (albeit without the funding incentives) and others hanging back to see what might happen (Savory *et al,* 2001b). This institutionally variable approach was also confirmed by the UCAS survey undertaken in 2000 (UCAS, 2001), though the latter showed a small degree of engagement by selective and independent schools. The Key Skills Qualification, which was intended for all advanced level learners, thus started its period of implementation with support from those institutions that catered predominantly for the average to below average advanced level learners. The institutions containing the highest achieving learners, by and large, remained aloof.

Within this pattern of partial uptake, four other trends emerged during 2000/2001. The first was a progressive decline of learner participation within key skills provision as the year proceeded. Some colleges reported that they had all the provision in place but with a minority of learners involved and low numbers turning up for tests. In other institutions within our 50-site sample, learners themselves reported that a relatively small number of their peers persevered with key skills lessons and when key skill certification was achieved, learners did not bother to collect it. The second noticeable trend was poor early test results, particularly at level 3 Application of Number, with a small minority of learners passing and very high failure rates in other level 3 units. The third trend, and related to the second, is what might be termed 'a retreat from level 3'. Many schools and colleges originally anticipated that their learners would be registered for level 3 awards. However, in the light of their experience in the first term or two and seeing the early tests, they decided to enter advanced level learners at level 2, in particular in Application of Number (Hodgson *et al,* 2001). Finally, despite apparent widespread support in principle for the wider key skills, there was a very low uptake of these with fewer than 10 per cent of learners taking any of these units (UCAS, 2001).

These actions throughout the first year of implementation of the Key Skills Qualification, which was supposedly designed for all, can be interpreted as a retreat on a number of fronts. The result was that the Key Skills Qualification did not reach a position of 'take-off' after its first year of implementation.

Key skills in context – the demands of *Curriculum 2000* and issues of recognition

The learner response to the Key Skills Qualification in the first year of implementation was possibly the most decisive factor working against its success. Virtually all the practitioners we interviewed during 1999/2000 as part of the IoE/Nuffield Research Project foresaw difficulties with convincing learners to take the Key Skills Qualification, but no one really anticipated the scale and intensity of learner resistance and the support learners would receive from their parents. This comment from one school Head of Sixth serves to illustrate what was a very widespread problem:

> We had one classic conversation with parents of a very gifted, very able learner. He said, 'If you make him do key skills then I don't want him coming into your sixth form'.

The Key Skills Qualification was overwhelmingly viewed by learners and by practitioners as a 'hassle' without much 'currency' and with little 'use value' or 'exchange value'. Indeed, it is interesting to note that in every interview we had with learners as part of our visits to the 50 sites in 2000/2001, when we asked them what they were studying, none of them mentioned key skills. When we went on to ask whether they were following a key skills programme or were aware of key skills, they burst out laughing. It was at this point that learners invariably used words like 'pointless', 'a waste of time' and other less polite phrases!

Learner resistance to the Key Skills Qualification was exacerbated by its relationship with the other components of *Curriculum 2000*. Research from site visits suggested that the teacher and learner experience of the AS qualification in its first year – rushed, overloaded with content and often taught to the full A level standard – compounded the marginalization of key skills. Factors internal to *Curriculum 2000* – the concept of choice, more subjects and increased workloads – meant it was inevitable that learners would prioritize those elements that were more important to them and the Key Skills Qualification clearly was not.

A major negative factor for advanced level learners and teachers was the attitude of universities. The message about the Key Skills Qualification that gradually seeped out from higher education providers throughout the first year of *Curriculum 2000* was one of 'stand-off' and senior managers in schools and colleges were only too aware of the potential consequences of universities not providing clear incentives to recognize it. The following remark from a senior manager reflected widely held apprehensions:

> Key skills will be dead in the water unless universities recognize them, including selecting universities, which I have a fear they won't do.

There were several reasons for this position of 'stand-off'. First, the Key Skills Qualification was an unknown entity and it was highly likely that admissions tutors would take the same view as many schools in seeing the qualification as 'remedial' and associated with basic skills. Second, the preferred position of many universities was to require particular A level grades and, as we will see in Chapter 7, this position did not change radically as a result of

Curriculum 2000, despite the publication of the points-based UCAS tariff for admission to higher education. Third, and probably most important, was a fear of requiring a qualification that would not be universally taken by their pool of applicants. In the case of this last factor, both 'selector' and 'recruiter' universities would have needed to see a dramatic uptake of the Key Skills Qualification in all types of 16–19 institutions, including the independent sector, in order to feel safe in coming off the fence and asking for the Key Skills Qualification as part of their admissions requirements.

Purpose – the wrong key skills emphasis?

The focus of key skills development in the Key Skills Qualification was the result of two related policy trends. First, there was Dearing's assumption that the main role of key skills was to promote employability – hence the three main key skills of Communication, Application of Number and IT rather than the broader six core skills (Dearing, 1996). Second, these three main key skills were chosen because there was an assumption of skills deficits in these areas. This focus of the Key Skills Qualification thus contributed to the image among learners and many teachers that key skills were about something that should have been achieved in secondary education. Some learners went as far as labelling the qualification 'insulting'. The reminder of repetition of learning was also brought home to learners by the use of the 'proxies' of A*–C GCSE grades in Mathematics and English as substitutes for the external tests in Application of Number and Communication. Learners we interviewed overwhelmingly rejected the Key Skills Qualification on the grounds that they had 'done this before' and that it had little 'use value' or 'exchange value'. In our experience, the most sceptical were learners who intended to progress to higher education. Some of those who aimed to go straight to employment were less negative about the three main key skills, because they assumed that these were the skills employers would want, although research at the time suggested that this might not, in fact, have been the case (Henry, 2001; Unwin *et al,* 2000). This attitude by employers has been confirmed in recent research by QCA (QCA, 2002f), which shows that the current Key Skills Qualifications and units are generally not known or valued by employers.

Assessment-led problems – the cumulative effects of tests and the portfolio

Virtually every practitioner we talked to from 1999 to 2002 as part of the IoE/Nuffield Research Project remarked on the problems of assessing key skills. This is a long-standing issue, as the historical account earlier in this chapter has already highlighted, but one that became acute with the design of the Key Skills Qualification.

An awareness of this problem was already emerging during 1999. Mindful of the key skills pilots and the experience of GNVQs, practitioners pointed to the complexity of the assessment regime arising from mapping key skills opportunities across different A level and vocational subjects, to the potential pitfalls of the tests, and to the inevitable bureaucracy of recording associated with the portfolio. In the 1999/2000 DfEE/IoE survey of *Curriculum 2000*, even before the reforms were introduced, implementing key skills was identified by practitioners as the main practical problem looming for schools and colleges (DfEE/IoE, 2000).

Units of the Key Skills Qualification were assessed by both portfolio and by tests. What practitioners said was that it was the cumulative effect of these two approaches that led to problems of complexity, bureaucracy and non-achievement. The tests were assessed on a pass/fail basis with a 70 per cent mastery threshold that did not recognize partial achievement. In the case of the level 3 tests, the questions ranged from being relatively accessible at the beginning of the paper to extremely difficult at the end. The compilation of the portfolio was also seen as a major assessment hurdle due to the complexity of assessment criteria. The overall effect of these assessment requirements for key skills was to make the favoured 'embedded' delivery method (that is the delivery of key skills through learners' main chosen subjects) more difficult, if not impossible, to put into practice.

An assessment-led approach to taking evidence from subjects also failed to inspire. Learners commented on the meaningless drudgery of putting together their portfolios for the Key Skills Qualification. The transfer of written work from a subject file to a key skills file was labelled as 'pointless', particularly in the context of more subjects to study. For those institutions involved, the effects were noticeable, with the assessment demands triggering a new level of learner disaffection mid-way through the programme and more heart-searching among dedicated key skills staff who had to deal with growing disenchantment amongst their colleagues.

This process of growing disillusionment with the assessment requirements of the Key Skills Qualification as the year progressed was summed up for us by a single moment of defeat for a 'key skills champion' in one of our 50 sample sites. A Head of Sixth, keen to promote key skills, sent home a letter to some parents reminding them that their child was not up to date with her or his portfolio. He received a number of abusive letters and telephone calls in response and, as a result of the level of learner resistance and lack of parental support, he decided he was not able to go on. He then took up a job in a sixth form that did not deliver the Key Skills Qualification.

The first year of the Key Skills Qualification was one of initial professional commitment to key skills development, but also one of problems far greater than anticipated. While official evaluations of key skills reported evidence of islands of good practice amidst general difficulties of implementation and recognition (CEI, 2001; LSDA, 2001), learners resisted the reform on an unprecedented scale and key skills development did not make headway into subject areas. By the end of its first year of implementation, headteachers were threatening to boycott the Key Skills Qualification in 2001/2002 (Woodward, 2001). The qualification was thus not poised for 'take-off' with all advanced level learners. Rather, it had become ghettoized as a qualification for further education colleges and lower achieving learners, echoing the fate of earlier key skill developments. By the end of the first year of *Curriculum 2000*, the Key Skills Qualification could not simply be described as having 'teething problems' related to its implementation, as argued by official sources at the time (CEI, 2001; LSDA, 2001); it was suffering from more fundamental issues related to its context, purpose and design.

Although a low-key review of the Key Skills Qualification was set in train by Baroness Blackstone, the Minister of State for Further and Higher Education, in March 2001, it was not until the summer of 2001, and the review of *Curriculum 2000* as a whole, ordered by Estelle Morris, the new Secretary of State for the Department for Education and Skills, that the stage was set for the next development in the ongoing search for the Holy Grail of key skills.

Beyond the crisis of the Key Skills Qualification

The review of *Curriculum 2000*, which was led by Professor David Hargreaves, at that time the Chief Executive of the Qualifications and Curriculum Authority (QCA), was designed in two stages. The first stage reported in early July 2001 to 'provide short-term advice to schools and colleges' and was mainly focused on the AS examination system and key skills because these areas were perceived to be most problematic. The second stage, which considered 'the full range of issues including AS/A levels, vocational A levels and key skills' was completed by the end of the year.

QCA's review of key skills and new arrangements for 2001/2002

The largest single section of the Hargreaves report, and arguably the most radical, is the one on key skills. Having weighed up the balance of opinion on key skills (which varied from real hostility to the qualification to a passionate defence of it), QCA recommended four areas for change:

1. It was suggested that the assessment arrangements for the qualifications needed to be fundamentally reviewed as a matter of urgency. This would involve reducing the overall assessment burden in the key skills units and redesigning aspects of their portfolio requirements.
2. QCA recommended that 'schools and colleges need to have more flexibility and autonomy to shape their policy towards the (key skills) qualification, including the ability to match the qualification more closely to

individual student needs and aspirations' (p8). This meant that at level 3, the combined qualification for the three main key skills should be phased out. Schools and colleges would be encouraged to embed key skills into enrichment, support and guidance programmes. Such an approach, it was suggested, should also be supported by funding arrangements. To this end, QCA recommended that the National Learning and Skills Council made changes to the funding for key skills in further education and sixth form colleges.

3. The report noted that there was a 'potential basis for consensus that by the age of 19 all students should be able to demonstrate capability in the key skills of communication, application of number and ICT to at least level 2' (p9). It therefore recommended that all post-16 institutions should be encouraged to adopt this policy as part of a 14–19 curriculum entitlement approach.

4. QCA suggested a number of technical changes around the role of proxy qualifications in key skills accreditation and urged ministers to ensure that higher education providers recognized key skills certification.

Taken together, these recommendations can be seen to have had two major aims. First, they are intended to breathe life into key skills by suggesting that all students should pursue them to level 2 and by focusing on key skills development at advanced level, rather than expecting students to pursue yet more certification in the shape of the Key Skills Qualification. Second, they were intended to make the assessment of key skills more manageable for schools, colleges and learners.

The Government's response to the review

The Government's position on key skills was to accept QCA's advice on phasing out the combined Key Skills Qualification in Communication, Application of Number and IT. It also supported the recommendation of encouraging all young people who had not achieved good GCSEs in English, Maths and IT to pursue key skills awards at level 2 in these areas. All other learners would now be offered the opportunity to develop these three main key skills at level 3 and to gain accreditation in at least one of them. Both schools and colleges are also entitled to funding for key skills, tutorials and enrichment (DfES, 2001c).

What the Government did not accept was any major role for the wider key skills of Problem Solving, Improving Own Learning and Performance and Working with Others, because these 'key skill units are not externally assessed and are therefore not regarded as qualifications within the National Qualifications Framework' (DfES, 2001c, p10). The Government stated that learners should achieve all the other requirements for key skills before seeking formal assessment and certification in the wider key skills. This continued dogmatic insistence on the acquisition of Key Skills Qualifications, rather than on a consideration of how to develop learning skills in the curriculum, flies in the face of professional, learner and employer desire to see a much greater role for the wider key skills. It also showed how little the Government had learnt from the failure of the Key Skills Qualification in the first year of *Curriculum 2000*.

The result of the Government's narrow, qualifications-led key skills approach was that it legitimated a reduced level of engagement with key skills by schools. In the case of further education and sixth form colleges, which were funded to offer a key skills and enrichment package, the emphasis was on maximizing funding via the offer of provision and by focusing on qualifications outcomes. The evidence from our site visits in 2002 suggested that learner engagement in both schools and colleges was dramatically lower than the national survey data indicated. The view from the ground was that the Government's approach at that time was an attempt to make the totally unworkable more palatable by simply demanding less. Instead, what we argue for below is a re-engagement with the concept of key skills development and not Key Skills Qualifications. This is where a new and creative consensus could be forged to take forward what virtually every practitioner recognizes as an important area of learning and achievement.

The second review of key skills

A second and potentially more far-reaching review of key skills is now underway (QCA/ACCAC/CEA, 2002). It focuses on all six key skills, their specifications, their assessment, their take-up and the relationship between key skills and other qualifications. Consultation will continue until July 2003 and the new specifications are intended to be in use from September 2004. From discussions to date with officers involved in this review, it appears that there is a shift in thinking underway with a move towards considering all six key skills having equal status, less emphasis on external testing, more interest in the relationship between key skills and pedagogy, and a possible change of nomenclature. This could result in specifications which, in our view, have the potential for greater use value. However, these changes cannot be seen in isolation from other necessary short and longer-term changes to the 14–19 curriculum. For example, if the AS remains too content congested and learners are expected to take upward of 10 GCSEs, there will never be curriculum or learning space for key skills development, no matter how good the specifications might be.

The future of key/core skills within a coherent 14–19 phase

During our research on *Curriculum 2000*, both learners and teachers have repeatedly stated that they want key skills to aid teaching, learning and achievement at advanced level. Moreover, they have bemoaned the decline of enrichment activity under *Curriculum 2000*. However, they have also, as we have seen, roundly rejected the Key Skills Qualification and are less than enthusiastic about taking even a limited number of key skills units within *Curriculum 2000* as it stands. Above all, what *Curriculum 2000* demonstrated was that a freestanding qualification or even freestanding key skills units could not compete with learners' chosen qualifications. Despite all of the key skills development work offered by the LSDA, QCA and others, learners, teachers and higher education providers have remained largely unconvinced about the use or exchange value of key skills within the reformed advanced level curriculum.

What is needed is a fundamental rethink of the concept of key skills within 14–19 education and training. The current key skills review may take us some way forward in this respect. However, without the introduction of a curriculum and qualifications framework from 14+, within which key skills can be progressively developed over time, any changes to specifications will, in our view, not solve the fundamental problems of purpose and design that have bedevilled them within *Curriculum 2000*.

We can only see a future for key skills for younger learners as part of a coherent, inclusive and unified 14+ diploma system, in which key skills, designed to support learning, progression and employability, can be realized as an educational activity for all rather than a peripheral activity for some. This would require a number of changes:

- 'Key skills' would need to be renamed: the term now lacks credibility because it is associated with remediation and policy failure under *Curriculum 2000*. The term 'learning skills' or 'essential skills' might be more appropriate.
- There should be recognition of a wider range of these skills with the existing six forming a starting point.
- A new diploma system could utilize a three-fold approach to their delivery through stand-alone short courses (eg in Mathematics/Application of Number), embedding skills within the curriculum and the development of appropriate vehicles or platforms at each level of the diploma system. The aim would be primarily to help learners to develop these skills as a way of becoming more successful and confident in their main areas of study, rather than trying to certificate them independently to convince end-users of their presence and currency.
- Finally, in the movement towards such an approach it will be important to learn from other education systems that have developed more learning-led rather than assessment-led strategies (Wicht, 2002; Young, 2002).

Note

1. We use the term 'core/key skills' in the first part of the chapter as a generic term, even though we recognize that the term 'key skills' was first coined by Dearing in 1996.

7

Shaping *Curriculum 2000*: the role of higher education and other external incentives

Voluntarism and *Curriculum 2000*

The advanced level curriculum in England, Wales and Northern Ireland has traditionally been voluntarist, qualifications-focused and market-driven with no common requirements for all learners. There has been a notional idea of matriculation for university entrance – that is two A levels or equivalent – but this has been both implicit and flexibly applied (or ignored) according to market forces. The labour market has, by and large, not been based on 'licence to practice' and employers have recognized a range of criteria, only some of which are related to qualifications. In almost every sense, post-16 education has been seen as 'post-compulsory'.

Because of the voluntarist nature of post-16 education and training in England, Wales and Northern Ireland, incentives have been used by national government as a way of shaping the system. These incentives have ranged from exhortation and advice, at one end of the scale, through financial levers and quality assurance systems such as OFSTED and FEFC inspection, to legislation at the other end of the scale. Incentives can also be applied differentially to different actors in the system – learners, post-16 providers, higher education institutions and employers. Getting the balance of incentives right might mean the difference between the success or failure of a particular policy initiative.

Curriculum 2000 continued this tradition of voluntarism and incentives – it is not a compulsory curriculum. Learners are able to choose which qualifications (and combinations of qualifications) they take, schools and colleges have a free choice about what advanced level qualifications and programmes they offer, and higher education institutions and employers have freedom in what they demand for particular courses and occupations.

When *Curriculum 2000* was introduced as a voluntarist reform, it was not only underpinned by a set of positive assumptions by the Government but also by a feeling of constraint. In particular, ministers felt that they were not able to make demands of universities to recognize the new qualifications. Instead, as we have argued in earlier chapters, the underlying assumption was that a combination of three factors would drive the *Curriculum 2000* reforms. They assumed, to some degree correctly, that there was longstanding and widespread professional support for the principles of *Curriculum 2000* and that schools and colleges would do their best to put these into practice. Ministers and civil servants also thought that the power of competition between post-16 providers to attract the best students would encourage schools and colleges to offer a wide range of provision based on the new qualification blocks.[1] They assumed that no one would want to be left behind or to disadvantage their learners. The third factor which permeated *Qualifying for Success* was the Government's belief that bringing the Advanced Vocational Certificates of Education (AVCEs) and the Key Skills Qualification into the national qualifications framework alongside A levels would automatically give them status and make them attractive to learners.

By 1998, however, as a result of concerns about whether learners would take more than three AS/A2s and whether the AVCEs and particularly the Key Skills Qualification would be taken up, the Government began to talk about the use of three types of incentives to support the introduction of the reforms – funding, inspection and the UCAS tariff (Blackstone, 1998). This chapter, like the book as a whole, takes as its starting point that the success of a reform is not only determined by its content but also by its wider context (Raffe, 1984). In the first chapter we analysed the wider historical and system context for the reforms. In this chapter we focus primarily on the role of these three more immediate, direct and intended shaping factors and their impact on the decisions and actions of post-16 providers, learners and higher education institutions. We will argue that funding, inspection and the UCAS tariff have had an effect on the reform process, but that this effect has been partial and has not necessarily shaped the reforms in the way that the Government initially intended. This is partly because they were aimed primarily at providers, notably further education colleges, rather than at learners or end-users, but more important, in our view, because these incentives could not compensate for weaknesses in qualifications design and legitimacy.

We conclude the chapter by suggesting that the lesson to be learnt from this use of incentives is not simply to calibrate them or make them more powerful, but to ensure that the reforms themselves have intrinsic value and legitimacy. It is our contention that the use of incentives in relation to *Curriculum 2000* as a voluntarist reform has been a substitute for the introduction of a single, compulsory curriculum and qualifications system that would secure both breadth and depth of study at advanced level and the commitment of key stakeholders. In the final chapter we argue, therefore, for the establishment of such a system from 14+ in which incentives are used to support its implementation, rather than as a way of driving through badly designed qualifications reforms in a voluntarist context.

Higher education, *Curriculum 2000* and the UCAS tariff

For more than 50 years, since the introduction of A levels, higher education has been a dominant shaping influence on the advanced level curriculum because sixth form study has been seen primarily as a preparation for university. Universities have not only determined their own admissions criteria and thereby what post-16 providers should offer and what learners should study, they have also influenced the content of the curriculum through historical links with the examination boards. The fact that the English honours degree system has historically been based on a single-subject three-year programme of study, which is narrower and shorter than most other European degrees, has meant that universities have required considerable subject depth for entrance. In the 16–19 curriculum this led to a focus on two or three A levels; to a demand for high grades in subject-specific achievement rather than the acquisition of broader skills and knowledge, and a scepticism about the value of advanced qualifications other than A levels.

This position, as we saw in Chapter 1, changed somewhat during the 1990s through a mixture of expansion, marketization and regulation. University participation doubled from the mid-1980s to the mid-1990s; the number of institutions calling themselves universities increased as a result of the 1992 FHE Act; institutions were encouraged to compete for students; and new vocational qualifications, such as GNVQs, were introduced to meet the needs of the new post-16 participants. The whole post-16 education system, including higher education, expanded and became more complex, thus disrupting historical patterns. On the surface there was an expanded single university system including both the old universities and the rebadged polytechnics, which became known as the post-1992 universities. Underneath, however, the binary divide continued and universities fell broadly into two categories – 'selectors' (old universities) or 'recruiters' (post-1992 universities). As the 1990s proceeded, this new position was to frame the relationship between higher education institutions, schools and colleges and, thereby, the advanced level curriculum. Selector institutions, for the most part, continued to request three A levels with good grades, while recruiter universities were prepared to accept two A levels and a much broader range of other qualifications. In this sense, the recruiter universities found themselves more in touch with the Conservative Government's aim of developing an alternative full-time vocational route into higher education.

Over and above this, changes were also taking place elsewhere which affected the relationship between higher education and the advanced level curriculum. From the late 1980s, examination and validating bodies were going through a process of rationalization and by 1997, following the consultation paper *Guaranteeing Standards* (DfEE, 1997c), three new awarding bodies were formed – AQA, Edexcel and OCR. Their major relationship was not with the universities but with the new, powerful single regulator, the Qualifications and Curriculum Authority (QCA).

As a result, the advanced level curriculum and its relationship with higher education providers became more diverse, complex and divided, as new qualifications and new post-16 provider relationships co-existed alongside old established ones. However, as we will see, universities still had a strong shaping effect on post-16 provision because of the increasing demand for higher education and the effects of university offer-making on learner choices. The existence of a marketized and voluntarist post-16 system ensured that universities continued to exercise considerable influence over the shape of advanced level learner programmes, whether this was their intention or not.

This complex environment was the context into which the *Curriculum 2000* reforms were launched. The main mechanism for moulding the relationship between higher education institutions and post-16 provision was the reformed UCAS tariff (see Appendix 3 for the UCAS tariff table). The tariff was intended to be the basis of all university admissions offer-making. It is based on a common currency of points, covers all types of advanced level qualifications, including the new *Curriculum 2000* package and the new Scottish qualifications brought in under *Higher Still* (Scottish Office, 1994). Previously, only A levels had been recognized under the old tariff. The new UCAS tariff could thus be seen as a form of credit framework designed to establish parity of esteem between academic and vocational qualifications. The new tariff also altered the points-based relationship between the different grades at advanced level by reducing the level of differentiation between the A and E grades in such a way that it more closely represented the actual numerical relationship between these two grades.[2] The aim of this change in the tariff was to increase the value of the lower end of the A level grade scale in comparison with the previous system.

The Government hoped to use this new tariff in two major ways. First, it was intended to encourage learners to take up all three main new components of *Curriculum 2000* – the AS, AVCE and the Key Skills Qualification. Each was allocated points within the new UCAS tariff, although those for the Key Skills Qualification were part of a separate section of the tariff and were intended to be reported separately on the UCAS form. It was assumed (or hoped) that universities would make offers based on the tariff points, thereby recognizing the three new qualifications. Second, the UCAS tariff was seen as promoting and recognizing breadth and volume of study – the more qualifications learners achieved, the more points they would gain.

In this section of the chapter we describe the broad university response to *Curriculum 2000* at the end of the first two years of the reforms and examine how the UCAS tariff has been used in the higher education admissions process. Drawing on data from UCAS and from the IoE/Nuffield Project, we then discuss the role that higher education and the UCAS tariff have played in determining the shape of the *Curriculum 2000* reforms in the period 1999–2002.

Applying for university in this country is a long drawn out process because of the wide range of courses on offer and the fact that application and offer-making are based on predicted rather than on actual results. It is also complex because different courses and institutions make different requirements of applicants. Universities go through four major stages in the selection process – advertising their courses and entry requirements via their prospectus or Web site; sifting through the application forms of potential applicants and making individual offers of places based on their assessment of the candidate's potential suitability for a particular course; accepting or rejecting candidates when their actual examination results are known; and accepting individual applicants onto unfilled places during 'clearing'. This complex and long-winded process makes it difficult to establish exactly what higher education institutions' requirements for any particular course are – the kind of entry requirements advertised in the prospectus may vary significantly from the actual admissions criteria used at 'clearing'. Everything depends on the market and whether a course over- or under-recruits. So, for example, while University X may say in its prospectus that a candidate wanting to study an English Honours Degree needs to obtain three A grades at A level or 720 UCAS points to be accepted onto that course, if there are places left at the end of the applications process, then a candidate with two As and a B may well obtain a place.

However, there are some general patterns of offer-making which appear to be emerging during the first two years of the *Curriculum 2000* reforms and which, as we shall see, have had and are likely to have an important effect on learner and post-16 provider decision-making in relation to the reforms.

Use of the UCAS tariff

According to a UCAS analysis of offers involving *Curriculum 2000* qualifications for 2002 entry, the UCAS tariff was used in just under 41 per cent of offers (UCAS, 2003). However, in over 95 per cent of the cases where the tariff was used, the offer was qualified by the university requiring or excluding a particular qualification. Post-1992 universities were most likely to use the UCAS tariff system and made offers based on it in just over 70 per cent of cases. Old universities, however, only used the tariff in just under 15 per cent of cases.

Qualitative research undertaken as part of the IoE/Nuffield research project helps to explain possible reasons for this picture (Waring *et al*, 2003 forthcoming). The UCAS tariff, as we have seen, attempts to provide a common currency embracing different types of advanced level qualifications and, thereby, suggests an equivalence of status between them. It was controversial from its inception. This was not only because of the disagreements about equivalences between different qualifications and the complexity of the new points system, but also because of the increased weighting given to the lower grades. It is, therefore, unsurprising that only a minority of institutions is currently using the tariff fully.

The partial uptake of the tariff is also explained by the differing perceptions of central admissions tutors and subject specialists in universities. The former are much more likely to be in favour of its use, because they are primarily interested in stimulating the flow of suitable recruits. They are also more exposed to dialogue with UCAS. Subject specialists, on the other hand, are concerned above all with recruiting learners who have a depth of knowledge in their area and who are most likely to be committed and successful undergraduates. They are, therefore, less interested in breadth of knowledge or experience and are less prepared to accept the concept of qualification equivalences. The impact of the UCAS tariff is, therefore, likely to depend on how centralized or devolved the admissions process is in any particular university.

The explanation for the more common use of the UCAS tariff in the post-1992 universities is because these universities are in less demand and are more likely to need to fill their places and to attract as many applicants as possible. They are, therefore, more prepared to accept equivalent qualifications.

What both the UCAS statistics and the qualitative research show is that the role of the tariff as an incentive for breadth of study has been constrained by two deep-seated factors related to the English university system. The historical factor is the continued dominance of single-subject degrees and the persistence of the demand for depth and specialization. As we will see below, offer-making under *Curriculum 2000* in its first two years has followed a very similar pattern to what happened in previous years. The idea of all qualifications being equivalent and learners taking broad mixed programmes of study earning them recognized UCAS points only pertained, by and large, where the supply of places outstripped demand, typically in post-1992 universities.

The use of Curriculum 2000 qualifications in offer-making

While university prospectuses and Web sites often proclaimed support for the principles of breadth of study and experience, offer-making told a different story. From the UCAS data on offer-making for entrance to university in 2002, post-1992 universities commonly require 12 units (the equivalent of two A levels), whereas old universities commonly specify 18 units – the traditional three A level offer. Fewer than 1 per cent of post-1992 and only 6 per cent of old universities specified 21 units or more. What this indicates is that the volume of attainment required by universities was lower than that being offered in the majority of schools and colleges under *Curriculum 2000*. In other words, the fourth AS, taken by just over half of *Curriculum 2000* learners, was effectively not being recognized by universities. Learners, as we have seen in previous chapters, have used the fourth AS primarily as a way of ensuring that they are on the right course, to drop a weaker subject and then to concentrate on gaining three good A level grades. In the light of university offer-making, this appears to have been a very rational course of action. So far, we have no statistical evidence of how the AS has been used in offer-making; however, qualitative evidence suggests that there were very few if any instances of university places being made available on the sole basis of AS attainment. Recruiter institutions, on the other hand, by virtue of using a UCAS tariff points-based approach to offer-making were prepared to accept the AS as credit and as such appeared to be recognizing breadth as well as depth. On the other hand, this optimistic theory about their support for breadth is belied by their preparedness to accept learners who had taken relatively few advanced level qualifications and thus must have had a low volume programme of study. UCAS statistics show that offer-making based on 12 or fewer units was made in 50 per cent of post-1992 institutions, but only in 3 per cent of the old universities.

The traditional nature of offer-making under *Curriculum 2000* is also borne out by the fact that over 73 per cent of all offers were made in terms of A levels and this figure rose to 92 per cent in relation to old universities. Just under 80 per cent of all offers in old universities were made on the basis of three A levels. However, not all A levels were treated equally. General Studies, for example, was specifically excluded from either UCAS tariff point calculations or from satisfying A level requirements in nearly 46 per cent of cases, with old universities being the main excluders. Qualifications other than A levels fared even worse. There is some evidence on university Web sites that the AVCE 6-unit (or applied A level award) may be recognized so long as it is accompanied by other A level grades. However, UCAS data suggest that only 3 per cent of all offers explicitly required a 12-unit AVCE and 1 per cent a 6-unit award. Key skills were only specifically included in 6 per cent of offers by post-1992 universities. Not one old university specified key skills as part of an offer.

These figures graphically demonstrate the continued dominance of A levels in university admission requirements, particularly in relation to selector universities. The qualitative research suggests that the continuation of traditional patterns of offer-making was not simply influenced by the conservatism of admissions tutors in selector universities, but also by a concern to continue to attract a large flow of suitable candidates. Universities would only demand qualifications that they were confident were being taken by the learners they wished to attract. This, in particular, explains the very low demand for the Key Skills Qualification, which, as we have seen, was least likely to be taken in selective and independent schools. This pattern of offer-making could be interpreted in two ways –

either that selector universities dominated the relationship with schools and colleges and sent out signals about what they were prepared to accept, or that universities were, in fact, more dependent on what the provider institutions were offering to their potential applicants. Our qualitative research suggests that the second explanation is as powerful as the first.

What this research also shows is that, overall, the view of universities largely mirrors that of the teachers and lecturers involved in the delivery of *Curriculum 2000*. Universities are supportive of its principles, but critical of the new qualifications – for example, the perception of a rushed and superficial AS and that the practical and learner-centred content of the old GNVQ had been eroded with the introduction of the AVCE. Moreover, universities do not see *Curriculum 2000* as 'their' reform and, as a consequence, they do not believe that it is their role to drive through breadth of study at advanced level. It is not surprising, therefore, that these voluntarist qualifications have made very little difference to offer-making. Above all, higher education institutions have been concerned to ensure that they do not exclude the most suitable candidates by making offers that demand qualifications that they have not taken. In this sense, universities cannot be described as either villains or victims in the *Curriculum 2000* reform process. Their response might best be described as pragmatic. We conclude from this evidence that any voluntarist reform, due to its variability, is unlikely to change the way that higher education makes offers and thereby recognizes the reforms. The only alternative, it would seem, is to have a curriculum and qualifications reform that has breadth and depth built into it and is taken by all potential university applicants. Moreover, if higher education were involved in its design, it might then be viewed as 'their reform' in a way that *Curriculum 2000* never was.

Funding – a powerful, partial and distorting lever

Funding mechanisms promised to be a much more powerful lever than the UCAS tariff in driving the *Curriculum 2000* reforms. Governments have used funding mechanisms as a way of shaping the behaviour of autonomous institutions in a marketized education and training system from the late 1980s. From the provider perspective, funding mechanisms have the feel of compulsion. The most extensive experimentation with this form of 'arms length' regulation took place in the further education sector following incorporation and the creation of the Further Education Funding Council (FEFC) in 1993. Since its introduction in 1994, the FE funding mechanism has proved to be a very powerful driver of institutional behaviour in further education, particularly in relation to increasing participation and making efficiency gains. One of the major ways it achieved these aims was by changing the form in which learning was funded. While in schools learning was funded primarily according to the number of students on roll, in further education learning was funded according to qualifications up-take and outcomes – the more a learner studied and achieved, the more money the institution received. It was natural, therefore, to consider the use of funding as a means of securing *Curriculum 2000* as a voluntarist qualifications-led reform.

In practice, under *Curriculum 2000*, funding mechanisms were used unevenly across schools and colleges and were not used at all in relation to learners or higher education providers. Schools continued to receive funding for each sixth form student, regardless of what they studied, but were provided with some additional monies for supporting the introduction of the new qualifications. The amounts were not large and were channelled through LEAs (DfEE, 1999b). Many of the schools we visited during our research complained, however, that they did not receive a single penny. In interviews with senior DfEE officials and advisers it became clear that the Government considered that, as a result of research carried out before the publication of *Learning to Succeed* (DfEE, 1999a), many school sixth forms were relatively inefficient because of small class sizes and low volume programmes. *Curriculum 2000* could, therefore, be seen as a means of remedying these weaknesses. Moreover, there was a perception that schools were sufficiently supportive of the aims of the reforms and eager to attract high achieving students and that they would not, therefore, need financial incentives to introduce *Curriculum 2000*. In the event, the Government's assumptions were partially borne out by the response of schools to the reforms. Schools, as we have seen in Chapter 2, tended to follow their curriculum traditions and to introduce those aspects of the reforms which most supported their mission and ensured them a supply of learners for their sixth form. What they did not do, on the whole, was to develop new provision that went against the grain of their tradition. Selective institutions, for example, with an eye on higher education, did not immediately offer the Key Skills Qualification or five subjects.

General further education and sixth form colleges, on the other hand, continued to receive funding according to the number of qualifications learners took and, in addition, from April 2000, they also received specific funding for a curriculum package comprising the Key Skills Qualification, enrichment and guidance (FEFC, 1999). There were at least two reasons for this apparent generosity by the Government. First, there was a recognition that for some time further education providers had been under-funded in comparison with school sixth forms (DfEE, 1999a). Second, learners in general further education colleges had traditionally taken lower volume study programmes than those in school sixth forms or sixth form colleges (Savory *et al,* 2001b) and it was deemed necessary to incentivize the larger volume programmes of study intended under *Curriculum 2000*.

Our research suggests that this funding steer did indeed encourage both general further education colleges and sixth form colleges to offer higher volume study programmes and the Key Skills Qualification. However, there was a problem for colleges with this strategy because, in many cases, it meant that they had to force learners into taking programmes that learners did not want and did not value. Learners were thus being steered by colleges into decisions that were in the financial interests of the institution rather than in the interests of their own learning. The prime example of this is the Key Skills Qualification which, as Chapter 6 points out, was roundly rejected by learners. The process of incentivizing providers but not learners or end-users has led to what we term an 'imbalance of incentives', in which colleges offer provision but learners are reluctant or unwilling to take it up.

Furthermore, funding mechanisms have pressurized some education managers into taking unethical and unsound educational decisions. For example, under *Curriculum 2000* learners were encouraged *en masse* to take additional qualifications, such as RSA CLAIT, while at the same time the level of support offered in the qualifications that they had chosen to study was being reduced (Haines, 2002). This process of packing out a learner programme with qualifications but, at the same time, reducing support is known as 'nesting'. The result of this rather crude form of funding incentive was that learners were only superficially taking broader programmes. While on paper the number of weekly contact hours for AS and AVCE subjects appeared to be much the same in colleges as in schools, there is some evidence that senior managers in colleges deliberately blurred the boundaries between teacher contact hours and guided learning support. They thus reduced the actual classroom time to levels below those in schools (Haines, 2002).

The main problem with this use of funding mechanisms is that while they are powerful, they are also potentially distorting. Decisions are often made on economic rather than on educational grounds; the learner is treated as a commodity; funding replaces a curriculum conception; and other incentives, such as the role of end-users, are relegated in importance. Above all, funding mechanisms can be corrupting, as the education press has highlighted regularly over the last few years. Perry (2000) sees the real problem not as straightforward dishonesty, though there have been celebrated cases of this, but the tendency towards instrumental institutional behaviour. The elevation of economic decision-making also creates tensions between managers, teachers and learners (Haines, 2002), evident in the case of *Curriculum 2000*.

In the near future, the type of funding steers that have been used in further education will be applied to schools (DfEE, 2000). While this will create a more level playing field for the further development of *Curriculum 2000*, in our view it is still problematic, because funding is being used to drive the curriculum rather than the curriculum being supported by funding. Funding is, in effect, being used as a backdoor way of introducing a compulsory curriculum. The problem is that it is compulsory for maintained schools and colleges, but not for learners, for independent schools or for higher education providers. In this way, what has been seen as a powerful lever becomes a weak substitute for an educational consensus binding different parties in a common endeavour.

Inspection – a 'non-barking dog' for *Curriculum 2000?*

In a marketized system, inspection is also seen as a powerful regulatory lever. Governments see it as a way of controlling the behaviour of autonomous institutions and institutions see inspection as a factor in their own survival. A bad inspection report can mean a decline in demand for that institution along with all the associated financial penalties. On the other hand, a good inspection report can be a very effective marketing tool. Inspections in general can thus be seen as dogs that both bark and bite.

Our contention, however, is that in relation to *Curriculum 2000*, inspection to date has been a 'non-barking dog'. Below we explore why this may be the case, and why it may change in the future with inspection playing a very important role in post-14 institutional planning and decision-making.

First, it is important to point out the different role that inspection has played in relation to compulsory and post-compulsory education, because of the statutory difference between these two phases. Prior to the introduction of the Common Inspection Framework (OFSTED/ALI, 2000), when schools were inspected under OFSTED, it was the 11–16 part of the institution which formed the focus of attention and the sixth form was treated very much as an adjunct. There was, therefore, no strong tradition of inspection moulding the sixth form curriculum. In colleges, the FEFC Inspectorate worked in a different way, using a large measure of self-assessment and focusing more on college management and quality assurance systems than on the curriculum. Colleges certainly took note of the scores they were given by inspectors, but the dominant factor influencing college behaviour was funding rather than inspection. In this respect, in colleges inspection could be seen primarily as a way of correcting the worst excesses of funding-driven behaviour. Because of these factors, in both school sixth forms and colleges, inspection was not the major driver of curriculum decision-making.

By the time that *Curriculum 2000* was being implemented, the new Common Inspection Framework, which covered all post-16 provision outside of higher education, was only just being introduced. The new system focused primarily on the generic themes of the experience of the learner, appropriateness of provision, value-added and value for money. It did not, therefore, focus fundamentally on the advanced level curriculum offer. Moreover, it would have been difficult for inspectors to do so in the absence of a clear Government curriculum expectation. As we have indicated earlier, there was a general aim to broaden learner programmes at advanced level, but this was not expressed in terms of the number of subjects to be taken, how much mixing of qualifications should take place and whether there should be particular subject combinations. The only element of the *Curriculum 2000* package where the Government expressed any sense of expectation was, ironically, in relation to the Key Skills Qualification.

Furthermore, as an incentive, inspection essentially works retrospectively. It could not, therefore, play a strong role in the initial decision-making that schools and colleges took in the period preceding implementation in September 2000. This is important because once schools and colleges determined their curriculum offer in relation to the reforms, the pattern was to all intents and purposes set for at least the short-term future. Interviews we had with curriculum managers in school and colleges in the period 2000–2002 strongly supported this assertion. The guiding influences on early decision-making were market advantage and manageability because of the over-riding importance of ensuring institutional survival.

Finally, while Government had anticipated that the inspectorates would act as a lever driving institutional decision-making in relation to *Curriculum 2000*, the inspectorate did not see its role in this way. Interviews with senior members of OFSTED indicated that they saw their role nationally as commenting on the quality and function of the new qualifications, rather than as a reinforcement for the formation of learner programmes of study or as champions of the reforms. They saw the inspectorate's role as an independent commentator on the reforms as they were being implemented. In this sense, they were using a similar model of inspection for the new qualifications as they had done in the mid-1990s in relation to GNVQs and modular A levels (OFSTED, 1996b, 1999). In addition, the change in the leadership of OFSTED following the resignation of Chris Woodhead, altered the whole culture of the organization and its approach to inspection. Conflict, controversy and politicization, the hallmarks of the Chris Woodhead era, were replaced by the more consultative, independent, consensual and tentative style of Mike Tomlinson, which has been continued under David Bell.

All of these factors meant that both thematic and institutional inspections could not be a strong lever or an incentive for driving through the *Curriculum 2000* reforms in their initial implementation. However, this situation could change with the advent of the new Learning and Skills Council (LSC) and, in particular, with the introduction of area-wide reviews and inspections. Under this system, post-16 and now post-14 provision for the first time comes under the scrutiny of both OFSTED and the local LSCs. With the new arrangements, whole local areas are being scrutinized to assess their ability to offer a broad and relevant curriculum for all learners, with priority being given to inner-city areas. There will therefore be a focus on provision and the curriculum offer in a way that did not exist previously. Moreover, the post-16 inspection framework, which affects institutional inspection, will become more powerful because for the first time in schools, it will specifically focus on the sixth form. In this sense, inspection may become much more of a barking dog, particularly in urban neighbourhoods.

Lessons from *Curriculum 2000* – the relationship between voluntarism, incentives and compulsion

Our conclusion from the evidence to date is that the effects of the main external levers on *Curriculum 2000* – the UCAS tariff, funding and inspection – have been limited.

The UCAS tariff, while attempting to provide a framework of recognition for all aspects of *Curriculum 2000*, could not change the behaviour of higher education providers because other factors proved more powerful. Market forces, the voluntarist nature of the reforms and the continuation of specialist degree programmes ensured that universities did not actively seek to support the broadening principles of *Curriculum 2000* and were cautious about recognizing new qualifications that did not enjoy universal up-take. Moreover, the power of the UCAS tariff was limited from the start because it was voluntary and was only used when the higher education institution itself perceived an advantage. It is self-evident that it is, therefore, 'recruiter' courses or institutions that have used the tariff to attract more students. 'Selector' courses or institutions were simply able to continue making offers as they had done before *Curriculum 2000*. Far from being transformatory, the tariff has ended up largely reflecting the binary divide in the university system.

Funding, on the other hand, proved to be much more powerful but equally partial in its effects. Aimed at further education institutions only, it was able to drive decision-making by college managers to put on the broader programmes intended under *Curriculum 2000*. What it could not do was encourage learners to take these up or higher education providers to recognize them. Moreover, schools were not subjected to the same funding steers. It may be tempting for government to use funding mechanisms to pressurize schools in the same way as they have pressurized colleges. This, as we have observed, only incentivizes one of the major players in the reform process – the providers. The key skills experience suggests that funding mechanisms, by themselves, do nothing to raise the status of qualifications that lack legitimacy with either learners or end-users. In our view, such an imbalance of incentives does not work and cannot substitute for legitimacy and the concept of support and even compulsion that flows from this. The real risk of a reliance on funding mechanisms to drive reform is that they can distort decision-making and can work against educational aims and principles.

Inspection is a different kind of incentive with the potential to underpin educational aims and principles and to work overtly to improve provision for the learner. In order for inspection to play this role, its mission has to be recognized and supported by providers. In our view, the reason why inspection has not played a proactive role to date in *Curriculum 2000* is not simply due to lack of government leadership in making clear its expectations of the reforms, but also because inspection itself had become discredited. Under the leadership of Chris Woodhead, OFSTED had become associated with a politicized and punitive approach to inspection that appeared to be waging a war on teachers and providers, rather than supporting the profession in improving teaching, learning and the curriculum. Repairing the damage done to the legitimacy of inspection has taken time. As the relationship between schools, colleges and inspectors improves and as a more unified approach to quality emerges under the Common Inspection Framework, the constructive power of inspection to support curriculum change is more likely to be felt.

The limited, partial and unpredictable role that external incentives have played in shaping *Curriculum 2000* suggests two important lessons for the next stage of the reform process. One is that ostensibly powerful incentives, such as funding, only affect one set of players – the providers – and do not, therefore, bring about fundamental change. The second lesson is that any external incentives, on their own, are not powerful enough to combat the forces of the education market and the way that traditional and selective forces work within it. In particular, the value attached to A levels and subject specialism is so deep-rooted within the English education system that it will take more than incentives external to the qualifications system to bring about change.

As we have seen in previous chapters, the most powerful shaping factors for *Curriculum 2000* have been those internal to the reforms themselves – the design and assessment of the new qualifications and the way in which they have interacted with the market and the selective function of higher education.

What we draw from the above is that the purpose and design of the reform itself and the sense of educational legitimacy that it generates should be dominant. In the English system, this means that any curriculum and qualifications reform has to be well designed, consensual and binding on all parties. External incentives cannot substitute for weak or flawed design within a voluntarist framework. For us, the evidence suggests that what is required is a single, unified, inclusive and compulsory curriculum and qualifications system that can transform relations between learners, providers and end-users. Moreover, such a system has to actively include all stakeholders in its construction so that they see it as 'their' reform. Finally, external incentives are, in fact, required, but should be constructed to support widely-accepted curriculum aims rather than being bolted-on to weak qualifications to compensate for their lack of legitimacy and purpose.

Notes

1. This type of thinking was articulated by past and present senior DfEE/DfES officials in meetings and interviews undertaken as part of the IoE/Nuffield research project during the period 1999–2001.
2. Under the old UCAS points system an A grade had been allocated 10 points and an E grade 2 (a 5:1 ratio). Under the new UCAS tariff an A grade is allocated 240 point and an E grade 100 points (a 2.4:1 ratio).

8

Beyond A levels – a new approach to 14–19 curriculum and qualifications reform

Three major questions for *Curriculum 2000*

The *Curriculum 2000* reforms of advanced level qualifications are perhaps best known for their problems and weaknesses. From December 2000 onwards *Curriculum 2000* was barely out of the press, with students, teachers and parents complaining about workloads, examination stress and lack of guidance from examination and awarding bodies. At the end of its first year of implementation, in June 2001, the public concern over the first AS examinations led Estelle Morris, the new Secretary of State for Education and Skills, to instigate a review of the reforms. By the end of their second year of implementation, there was an even greater outcry, led largely by the independent school sector, about the 'manipulation' of A level grades. On this latter occasion, there were calls for the resignations of those involved and a radical overhaul of the whole examinations system.

If press reports to date were to be taken at their face value, *Curriculum 2000* might simply be seen as a bit of a disaster. The picture that emerges from our research between 1999 and 2002, however, while strongly supporting some of the concerns raised in the media, was one of positives as well as negatives. As we have seen from earlier chapters, the research of the IoE/Nuffield Project, together with that of other national agencies, suggests the need for a more textured analysis of the reforms. In this final chapter, therefore, we ask three related questions about the nature of *Curriculum 2000* and what its role and significance is for the future shape of the 14–19 education system in England:

1. What are the strengths and weaknesses of *Curriculum 2000*?
2. What lessons can be learnt from *Curriculum 2000* for future reform of 14–19 education?
3. What further reform is required for an inclusive and high quality 14–19 education system based on the principle of social justice?

In Chapter 2 we argued that there were two ways of judging *Curriculum 2000*: first, as the most recent attempt to modernize track-based A levels and second, as a stage towards a more unified 14+ curriculum and qualifications system. If the reforms are confined to 'broadening' A levels, then the criteria that should be used are its original aims outlined in *Qualifying for Success*. That is the primary approach we take here to assessing the reforms. However, the Government is now in the process of considering further reform of 14–19 education, which places the development of a more unified curriculum reform more firmly on the agenda (DfES, 2003). Moreover, because of the combination of its strengths and weaknesses, *Curriculum 2000* does not, arguably, constitute a stable resting place. In our view, these two factors suggest that it is legitimate also to consider the role and significance of *Curriculum 2000* as part of this broader reform agenda.

Our basic argument in this chapter, building on evidence from earlier chapters, is that the strengths of *Curriculum 2000* constitute an important step in reforming advanced level qualifications, but that its weaknesses and limitations create the need for further reform. *Curriculum 2000* introduced smaller qualification blocks, modularity and a new level of qualification between Intermediate and Advanced level, all of which, in our opinion, have the potential to play a role in a more coherent and unified 14–19 award structure. The weaknesses of the reform pertain largely to its limited scope and voluntarism, to design contradictions, the assessment burden it imposed on learners and teachers, and the manner in which the reform process was conceived and conducted.

We conclude the chapter by arguing for a more radical, long-term reform of the curriculum and qualifications system from 14+ through the gradual introduction of an English Baccalaureate System. In our view, this type of reform would not only remedy some of the weaknesses and limitations of *Curriculum 2000* and build on some of its strengths, but would also tackle some of the deeper-seated problems in the English education and training system which we outlined in the first chapter of this book and which *Curriculum 2000* was not designed to tackle. More importantly, such a system would support the wider purpose of creating what Coffield refers to as:

> a socially just society where all citizens acquire a high quality general education, appropriate vocational training and a job (or series of jobs) worthy of a human being while continuing to participate in education and training throughout their lives. (Coffield, 2002, p10)

An overall assessment of *Curriculum 2000*: strengths and weaknesses

Looking back on the consultation document, *Qualifying for Success*, which set out the reform of advanced level qualifications subsequently known as

Curriculum 2000, the eight discrete aims it contained could be grouped into four major types. The first set of aims was about achieving parity of esteem between academic and vocational qualifications; the second was about the need to achieve a balance between breadth and specialization in learner programmes; the third related to attainment in key skills and the fourth was about promoting participation, progression and attainment in lifelong learning. These aims were essentially an elaboration of the Labour Party manifesto commitments – to broaden A levels; to upgrade vocational qualifications and to introduce key skills for all. Fundamentally, what they were about was making the advanced level curriculum more accessible in order to increase participation, progression and achievement at this level and, at the same time, to broaden advanced level programmes of study because they were seen as too narrow.

The concept of breadth was thus seen from two standpoints. The first was the idea of broadening the A level route by the introduction of equivalent education-based vocational qualifications. It was assumed that if these awards achieved parity of esteem with A levels, they would attract more learners into advanced level study without the need to radically reform A levels themselves. The second concept of breadth was the idea of enriching what was seen as a narrow advanced level curriculum offered by the traditional two or three A level programme. This enrichment would be achieved by expecting all learners to take more subjects than they had done previously in their first year of study – some by mixing academic and vocational qualifications and all taking some form of key skills. The logic of the first approach to breadth was to increase participation, achievement and progression without fundamentally reforming qualifications from 14+. The logic of the second approach was primarily to enhance and enlarge advanced level programmes to bring them more into line with programmes of study in other European countries.

It is possible to see a contradiction between the aims of making the curriculum at this level more accessible and, at the same time, more demanding, and thus between these two concepts of breadth. A fundamental question was whether both these approaches to breadth could be achieved at the same time. Quite clearly government thought that, within its voluntarist approach, it could deliver both. One way of doing this would be to emphasize the accessibility of the Advanced Subsidiary (AS) level by making it easier than the old A level so that more students could access advanced level qualifications and more could also take more subjects in their first year of study. Another would be to design the Advanced Vocational Certificate of Education (AVCE), the new vocational A level, in such a way that it was more likely to acquire parity of esteem with the AS/A2 and would thus attract more learners to opt for the qualification alongside or in preference to the AS/A2. This would be achieved by ensuring that the AVCE had features in common with the AS/A2 – size, an element of external testing and the same type of grading system – and could be flexibly combined with AS/A2 qualifications in making up learners' advanced level programmes. The Key Skills Qualification was seen as the third way of achieving both accessibility and breadth by providing accreditation for the necessary skills required to progress within advanced level programmes and by introducing skill-based learning into what had traditionally been a content-based curriculum. In theory, one can see why the Government adopted these strategies in the absence of any specific demands of all learners, such as might be required by a Baccalaureate-style qualification. However, underpinning the reforms as a whole was the assumption that while A levels were being recast, maintaining the A level standard was politically essential.

In the light of this approach, what were the strengths and weaknesses of *Curriculum 2000*?

Accessibility, participation and achievement at advanced level

While there is no conclusive evidence yet about increased participation in advanced level study as a result of the *Curriculum 2000* reforms, there is a strong perception among teachers that more learners are now involved in advanced level study than were previously, principally due to the introduction of the AS. The AVCE and Key Skills Qualification, on the other hand, appear not to have attracted more learners to advanced level study. The number of learners taking the 12-unit AVCE is not significantly higher than the number previously taking Advanced GNVQs and key skills has, as Chapter 6 indicated, proved to be highly unpopular with students.

There is, however, strong evidence that learners have been able to achieve higher grades in the AS/A2 than with the legacy A levels. Because of the modular structure of the new A level, learners have had the opportunity to retake modules to improve overall grade achievement. In addition, the predominant pattern of taking four AS subjects in the first year of study and three A2s in the second year, has meant that learners have been able to focus on those subjects in which they feel confident and in which they are more likely to achieve higher grades in the full A level. Finally, the design of the AS/A2 qualification with a 50 per cent weighting for each element, allows learners to accumulate points related to the easier aspect of the A level and thus to achieve higher grades in the overall qualification.

On the other hand, the AVCE and the Key Skills Qualification have not been effective in making the advanced level curriculum more accessible. In the case of the AVCE, because it was designed at level 3 throughout and did not have an AS-type level in the first year of study, many learners found it difficult and there were high rates of failure in its first year. Moreover, as we have seen in Chapter 5, pass rates and grade achievement in AVCEs are considerably lower than those in A levels. Designed principally as a vehicle for mixing academic and vocational study, the AVCE has not proved to be a popular option for those learners who had traditionally chosen vocational qualifications at advanced level as an alternative to A levels. The idea that 'weaker' learners might access advanced level study through a combination of vocational and academic qualifications was thus effectively undermined by the design of the AVCE. It is here that the tensions between accessibility and parity of esteem can be seen most starkly.

The Key Skills Qualification, as Chapter 6 shows, was dogged by many design problems, which resulted in it being difficult to attain and perceived as of little value. It was thus broadly rejected by learners and teachers and was unable to play a constructive role in increasing accessibility, participation or achievement at advanced level.

The overall picture of *Curriculum 2000* from an accessibility, participation and achievement perspective is, therefore, very mixed, a conclusion QCA also shares (QCA, 2002g). The one clear success was the creation of a level between GCSE and the full A level – the AS – combined with a modular approach to study and assessment, with the opportunity to retake modules to improve personal performance. As previous chapters have shown, these positive features of the *Curriculum 2000* reforms were widely recognized by both teachers and learners in the first two years of the reforms, though even these were overshadowed by the growing burden of assessment.

Limited broadening of the advanced level curriculum

Although broadening the advanced level curriculum was a major aim of *Curriculum 2000*, there was no government requirement for learners to broaden their study programmes. In the event, during the first two years of the reforms a slight majority of 16–19-year-olds on advanced level programmes took four subjects (excluding General Studies) in their first year of study, with the most taking complementary rather than contrasting subjects. Only a fifth were on programmes containing a mix of AS and AVCE qualifications. A minority of learners was actively seeking certification of key skills although about half had had some experience of the new key skill units. Finally, the new broadening qualifications, such as Critical Thinking and Science for Public Understanding, had had very low take-up. At the same time, some forms of broadening had actually declined. There was a significant fall in the number of 16–19-year-olds on advanced level programmes taking General Studies and many of the schools and colleges in our research sites complained of the decline in learner take-up of extracurricular activities.

Moreover, as we have pointed out in earlier chapters, breadth in terms of the whole learning experience was compromised under *Curriculum 2000*. Our research suggests that the teaching and learning in the new AS was often considered by both learners and teachers to be rushed and superficial. Many teachers resented the fact that they were not able to build in the types of skills, exemplification and underpinning knowledge that they had found space for when teaching the old A levels and were concerned that learners were not being adequately equipped to tackle the demands of their subject at higher levels. Teachers of AVCE remarked that there was a loss of emphasis on the vocational and work-related aspects of the new qualifications in comparison with Advanced GNVQs and other full-time vocational courses such as BTEC National. They also commented that the emphasis on external testing left less time for development of learning and practical skills. With both the AS and AVCE, the design of the qualification arguably led to a narrowing of the learning experience inside programmes containing these awards. The Key Skills Qualification, which was intended to act as a broadening device for all advanced level learners, proved so cumbersome that it not only failed to achieve this goal, but also undermined other forms of broadening such as General Studies and extracurricular activities.

What our research into *Curriculum 2000* and the research of others in this area suggests is that the design of the new qualifications blocks, combined with the amount of assessment in the new system and the fact that there was no requirement on students to take particular numbers or combinations of subjects, resulted in only limited broadening in the first two years of the reforms. Broadening was largely confined to the taking of one extra subject in the first year of study, with other aspects of broadening, as indicated above, actually declining.

However, the take-up of this one extra subject should not be underestimated. From the learner's point of view, this limited broadening was popular in the majority of cases because they saw it as delaying specialization and keeping their options of university course or career open for longer. It also prevented many learners from ending up on a very narrow two A level programme, which was one of the particularly negative outcomes of the less flexible old A level system. From an education and training system perspective, too, the fourth subject has had an important impact because it has broken a long-standing pattern of learners taking three or fewer subjects at advanced level. In this sense, the AS has, arguably, provided a basis for creating a broader and higher volume advanced level system in the future.

The reform process – the problems of policy incrementalism, voluntarism and preservation of the A level

The strengths and weaknesses of any reform can be judged not only on its outcomes related to its aims but also on the way that the reform is introduced, because of the impact that this process has on its public image. In the case of *Curriculum 2000*, this has proved to be a very important issue. In our view, the way that the reforms were conceived and introduced led to many of the design faults as well as to implementation problems.

As we argued in earlier chapters, the problem started with the rejection by the Government of the Labour Party's pre-election document *Aiming Higher* with its two-stage and longer-term approach to the development of a diploma system from 14+ (Labour Party, 1996). Instead, the Government sought to implement its own version of the Dearing report, with its more limited and short-term approach to A level reform and its retention of a track-based qualifications system. The perceived political necessity to retain A levels was in many different ways to undermine the aims of *Curriculum 2000*. Our contention is that New Labour committed a fundamental political error in choosing the compromised, partial and short-term perspectives of Dearing rather than the more radical, comprehensive and longer-term approach of *Aiming Higher*.

This decision, which was deeply bound up with the Third Way politics of playing to both traditional and progressive educational opinion (Hodgson and Spours, 1999a), also meant that the new Government had to conduct a superficial consultation process in which the important decisions (and mistakes) were largely made behind closed doors. The designs of the new *Curriculum 2000* qualifications blocks were never seriously discussed with education professionals whose experience of delivery might have ground out some of the most obvious mistakes. *Qualifying for Success* was more about testing opinion in relation to New Labour's manifesto commitments on advanced level reform than a genuine act of consultation with the education profession. In fact, the period between the *Qualifying for Success* consultation process (autumn 1997 to spring 1998) was followed by a protracted period of silence of almost two years while ministers and the officials from the DfEE, QCA and awarding bodies discussed the designs of the new qualifications.

From the practitioner point of view, during this period there was uncertainty about whether any reform would take place and a reluctance to spend time planning for changes that were unclear and might not even happen. Thus a large amount of time was lost that could have been productively used for curriculum planning and informing parents, learners, higher education providers and employers about the future reforms. This was to have considerable ramifications when the reforms were finally introduced, because it appeared to those on the ground that they had been rushed. Many key stakeholders felt they had been kept in the dark and had not had sufficient time to prepare for change or to play their proper role in the reforms. Recent research by QCA strongly supports the view that the complexities of *Curriculum 2000* not only affected higher education but also employers. Employers had relatively little knowledge of the new qualifications and attributed a low value to them. In the absence of an engagement with *Curriculum 2000*, employers preferred to work with qualifications with which they were more familiar (eg NVQs and BTEC) and to base their recruitment on work experience and interviews rather than on qualifications (QCA, 2002f).

The underlying reason for limited consultation appeared to be political nervousness about A level reform. There was a sensitivity both to the opinions of traditionalists, who wanted to retain the 'gold standard', and to the demands of reformers who felt that *Curriculum 2000* did not go far enough and argued for a more comprehensive Baccalaureate-style reform. We would go so far as to say that from our direct experience of the policy process at the time, the run up to *Curriculum 2000* was deliberately kept low-key in order 'not to frighten the horses'. This is a feature of a reform approach that we term 'policy incrementalism', in which the Government seeks not to reveal its longer-term goal but attempts instead to work on reform bit by bit and at each stage to assess public opinion before moving forward. This approach, in our view, was a major contributor to the weaknesses of *Curriculum 2000*. Later we will contrast this approach with what we term 'strategic gradualism' in which the end-goal is made explicit so that all stakeholders can assess their progress towards it. Such an approach allows government and stakeholders together to plan key milestones in the reform process and to feel a sense of ownership of it.

A further factor confusing the reform process was the Government's voluntarist approach to *Curriculum 2000* with its dependence on market forces to determine which of the new qualifications blocks schools and colleges would offer, what learners would decide to take, and what higher education institutions and employers would recognize. *Curriculum 2000* was at its heart a qualifications rather than a curriculum reform and, as we have said earlier, could be more accurately termed 'Qualifications 2000'. In reality, no one knew for certain what was going to happen as a result of the changes or how best to respond to them. As we showed in Chapter 7, this uncertainty largely accounted for the cautious response of higher education. It appeared that the Government hoped there was enough grass-roots support for changes to the A level system to drive the reform process without the need to offer clear political leadership.

The areas adversely affected by policy incrementalism and voluntarism ranged, as we have seen, from the design of the qualifications blocks, in particular their assessment requirements, to the lack of clarity about breadth within the advanced level curriculum. Much has been said about the 'rushed nature' of the *Curriculum 2000* reform process (Hargreaves, 2001a, 2001b; Tomlinson, 2002b). Our major point is that the reform process appeared rushed and errors were committed because vital discussions (and disagreements) about design and implementation took place largely behind closed doors. From a practitioner perspective, the reform process certainly felt rushed and teachers found themselves unprepared – specifications, assessment requirements and support materials were not ready, there was no clear guidance on what should be offered or the standard to which they should teach. There was no time, for example, to calculate the accumulated effects of assessment on student programmes and workloads or to think through the consequences of design decisions on learner achievement. In fact, the assessment-led qualifications block features of the reforms actively prevented consideration of their overall effects on learner programmes and institutional timetables.

In our view, the combination of policy incrementalism, the desire to retain the A level and the market-led voluntarism associated with *Curriculum 2000* goes a long way towards explaining both the limited impact of the reforms and their constant state of instability and crisis.

Lessons from *Curriculum 2000*

As the Government embarks on the reform of 14–19 education, it is critical to learn lessons from *Curriculum 2000*. It will be evident from our analysis throughout this book that we see the main strength of *Curriculum 2000* arising from the AS. Its modular nature allowed learners to increase levels of achievement through the phasing of examinations, the accumulation of credit over time and the possibility of retaking modules to improve grade attainment. The existence of smaller qualification blocks has also enabled learners to keep their options open in the first year of advanced level study and to specialize in the second year in subjects that they know they will enjoy and in which they are most likely to succeed. Thirdly, and perhaps most important for any future system, the AS introduced the idea of a level between Intermediate and Advanced to facilitate progression between the two (traditionally a problem in the English system), as well as the idea of multi-level study to retain both breadth and depth.

In this sense, *Curriculum 2000* builds on well-established features of A level study – choice and specialization – while also introducing new features into the system to aid progression and achievement. In our view it is important, therefore, that any future qualifications and curriculum system embodies a degree of modularity, choice and specialization and includes both a new level between Intermediate and Advanced and the possibility of multi-level study. Making a system more flexible is, arguably, a precondition of making it more demanding in both breadth and depth of study.

The major lessons to be learnt from *Curriculum 2000*, however, result from its limitations – its closed and short-term focused reform process, its voluntarist nature and the fact that it was a partial reform with a narrow concept of academic standards linked to the old A level. The first and clearest message to emerge from the *Curriculum 2000* experience is that any future reform process needs to be long-term, open and transparent, and to involve stakeholders from its inception to its implementation. Only in this way will it be possible to iron out design problems and secure support from all parties. Second, there are evident limits to a voluntarist approach to reform because of its unpredictability and the possibility of division and inequity. Voluntarism also leads to complexity. As Chapter 7 indicated, higher education providers found *Curriculum 2000* confusing – it was not clear what schools and colleges would offer or what learners would study. Universities were not clear about the effects of the reforms on their supply of applicants. This implies that curriculum and qualifications reform demands a degree of consultation with both providers and learners in terms of what should be studied, achieved and recognized in order to secure equity, transparency, trust and predictability.

An important limitation of *Curriculum 2000* was the political insistence on maintaining a link with the past A level system. Elements of the new co-existed uneasily with earlier arrangements. The complexities of the 'semi-hooked' relationship between AS, A2 and A level bear eloquent testimony to this. No one fully understood this relationship or its implications. Moreover, partial reform of the A level system distorted the design of all the new qualifications. The attempt to make the advanced level system more accessible led to political demands to offset this with more external assessment to demonstrate publicly that the 'A level standard' had been retained. This not only had damaging effects on the AS/A2, but also had negative effects on vocational education, as Chapter 5 made clear. The inference of the change from GNVQ Advanced to AVCE was that high stan-dards could only be achieved by reference to academic study rather than by the qualification's relationship with the workplace. This was how the AVCE ended up becoming more academic and losing its vocational rele-vance. In doing so, it also lost its accessibility and distinctive role in 16–19 provision. This experience suggests two interrelated lessons for any future reform process – the need to value specialist vocational education and the need to have a broader and more forward-looking concept of rigour and standards that encompasses a range of learning outcomes and assessment approaches.

Finally, a major systemic weakness of *Curriculum 2000* was that it was essentially an 'island of reform' confined to full-time advanced level study and unrelated to other aspects of the education system. It was thus inher-ently unconnective and likely to cause tensions with areas of provision above and below it. It was this lack of connection that led, for example, to complaints about over-assessment, with learners, as a result of the reforms, ending up taking high-stakes examinations at the ages of 14, 16, 17 and 18. As an island of reform, *Curriculum 2000* was also unable on its own to address some of the more deep-seated problems in the English education and training system highlighted in earlier chapters of this book. The lesson we draw from this is that any future reform will have to be more system-wide and joined up in order to facilitate the kind of participation, progression and achievement for which the *Curriculum 2000* aims initially strove, but which were not achieved.

In terms of the criteria we set out in Chapter 2 for judging *Curriculum 2000*, our view is that the reforms have failed to modernize A levels – they have simply destabilized them. However, providing lessons can be learnt,

Curriculum 2000 has the potential to be seen as a stage in the transition towards a more unified and inclusive 14+ curriculum and qualifications system. For these reasons, we argue that there is a case for further and more fundamental curriculum and qualifications reform which builds on the gains of *Curriculum 2000* and the modular AS, but which also addresses the limitations and contradictions of this reform. We conclude this chapter by proposing a gradual but deliberate transition from *Curriculum 2000* to a more systemic and holistic transformation of the English education and training system through the introduction of an English Baccalaureate System from 14+.

What type of further reform is required?

Despite the fact that we consider *Curriculum 2000* to have been a strategic mistake overall, it has in some senses proved to be a catalyst for change. The question is how rigorous the process of 'policy learning' in the next few years will be.

The new context for curriculum and qualifications reform from 14+

It is possible to cast some light on the prospect of policy learning by looking at the Government's own agenda for the reform of 14–19 education. The main rationale for this agenda arose from the Government's own concept of 'policy sequence' – a political movement from a focus on nursery and primary education in the first Parliament to secondary education in this Parliament and the implementation of more fundamental changes to the 14–19 phase in a possible third term. The main aim of this policy sequence has been to raise standards of achievement within the public education system from nursery education upwards and to create a surge of attainment that would work its way through the different age groups right up to higher education. From this perspective, it is imperative to reform the system in different stages, so that the benefits of the achievements at lower levels can be sustained and realized at upper levels.

The Government's first policy document in this area, the Green Paper *14–19 Education: Extending opportunities: raising standards* was published in February 2002. This document stressed the gains of *Curriculum 2000,* but also began to recognize that there were deep-seated problems still to tackle in the English education and training system. However, it did not primarily focus on a curriculum solution to these problems and certainly shied away from radical systemic reform. The Green Paper's approach to reform, as we saw in Chapter 1, emphasized freedom of choice at Key Stage 4 of the National Curriculum, individualized learner pathways, acceleration of learning for the brightest, and vocational alternatives to GCSE to motivate the underachievers and the disaffected. At the same time, it avoided any criticism of *Curriculum 2000* or GCSE, and the Matriculation Diploma models trailed at the end of the document suggested that there was no need for provision below Intermediate level (GCSE equivalent). The answer was for learners to succeed in vocational GCSEs and, if necessary, to take longer to achieve Intermediate level.

As we have seen, these proposals were roundly criticized by the education profession during the consultation process on the Green Paper, although the freeing up of curriculum space at Key Stage 4 was welcomed because it was felt that the prescribed curriculum for 14–16-year-olds was too constraining. The main criticisms of the proposals were the lack of provision and recognition of achievement below Intermediate level, the negative effects of acceleration on breadth and quality of learning, the 'academic' nature of the new vocational GCSEs, the complacent approach to the assessment burden on learners at 16, 17 and 18, the voluntarism of *Curriculum 2000,* and the lack of value-added in the Matriculation Diploma models.

In its response to the Green Paper consultation, *14–19: Opportunity and excellence,* which came out early in 2003 after the A level crisis and the appointment of David Miliband as Schools Standards Minister, the Government signalled a new approach to reform of 14–19 education. As we said in Chapter 1, this second document represents, in our view, a sea-change in thinking about the 14–19 phase and provides some evidence of policy learning from consultation and reflection. The document is much more critical than the original Green Paper of existing qualification arrangements, including both GCSE and *Curriculum 2000,* and it accepts the need for a multi-level awarding system from at least Foundation level upwards.

The document talks about curriculum coherence and breadth as well as flexibility. Moreover, for the first time, there is a discussion of a Core of common learning for post-16 study. Significantly, the Government lays down a direction for long-term reform based on the exploration and development of a unified Baccalaureate-type award structure which, in due course, could replace existing qualifications for this age group. The document also attempts to integrate into this reform vision of a unified award structure a different approach to assessment based on validity and fitness for purpose. Moreover, vocational education is seen as a high status activity (referred to as 'specialist study') and not just as an alternative for the school-weary.

In addition, the document suggests a different approach to the reform process, which is based on consultation, open debate and a recognition of the importance of the opinions of education professionals as well as employers and higher education providers. The main mechanism for taking forward the long-term agenda is a 'Working Group for 14–19 Reform' to bring about 'the successful and lasting transformation of 14–19 learning' (DfES, 2003, p23).

The professional consensus – principles of reform

Despite the problems of the recent advanced level reforms, there is a recognition by the education profession, and now by some in Government, of the need for longer-term, sustainable curriculum and qualifications change, but with a reform process that is different from the experience of *Curriculum 2000*. It is important to understand the nature and extent of professional consensus in this area and where debates still need to take place, because, in our view, it is teachers, lecturers and trainers who hold the key to the success of any future reform. It is they who have to implement any changes and, as we have seen in earlier chapters, they also have a strong effect on the attitudes of both learners and higher education providers.

From our research on *Curriculum 2000* and our discussions with practitioners over several years about the future shape of the curriculum and qualifications system from 14+, there appear to be several areas of solid consensus on the basic principles of such a system and the required reform process to accompany it.

First, there is considerable agreement about a long-term policy strategy for 14–19 education based on the clear end-goal of an inclusive and coherent 14+ curriculum and qualifications system with a single transparent set of easily-recognizable qualifications products. They recognize that this type of reform process would facilitate the active involvement of all stakeholders in both the debate and design of any new system.

Second, with regards to the basic structure of a new 14–19 curriculum and qualifications system, there is also widespread agreement that it should be fully inclusive, embracing a number of levels from Entry to Advanced. As we have shown earlier, this was made clear in responses to the 14–19 Green Paper in which professionals argued very strongly that there needed to be recognized levels below Intermediate (the equivalent of A*–C at GCSE).

A third major area of consensus is around the need for a curriculum framework for the realization of learning entitlement for 14–19-year-olds and for the promotion of holistic programmes of study for all learners. While there is debate around the balance between flexibility, choice and prescription, there is support for some type of common Core of learning for all learners in the 14–19 phase. The nature of this Core at different levels and ages, however, as we shall see, could well be the subject of considerable discussion.

A fourth area of agreement, which has emerged particularly from the experience of *Curriculum 2000,* is the concern about over-assessment – year-on-year high-stakes external examinations – and its negative effects on the quality of the teaching and learning experience. There is, therefore, a desire that any new system should demonstrate how it will reduce the assessment burden for learners and teachers and provide more 'curriculum space' for innovative approaches to teaching and learning. In addition, there is very strong support for a concerted focus on using a wide range of assessment strategies based on their validity and fitness for purpose. In particular, there is consensus on the need to reduce the role of external examinations, but without this leading to a more bureaucratic and work-intensive approach to internal assessment.

The final area of consensus is that any new system should improve both general and vocational education. In particular, there is a desire to ensure that vocational education retains a strong connection with the workplace and working life and gains high status through this association. As we have indicated in Chapter 5, many practitioners are concerned that vocational qualifications have become too 'academic', thus undermining their attractiveness to learners and employers. There is considerable interest in the concept of vocational specialization and qualifications that support holistic programmes of study combining strong general education with strong vocational education and training.

Areas of debate – design and structure of a new system

There is, therefore, a strong consensus about the strategic direction of development and the basic principles of a new 14–19 curriculum and qualifications system that has arisen through a decade of debate and direct experience of piecemeal and partial reform. Moreover, there are few who would argue that the current 14–19 education system is either effective or sustainable. The areas of debate that are now taking place in the context of the Green Paper consultation and the desire for longer-term reform are not so much about basic purposes and principles, but more about system architecture. More specifically, the debates are about how a 14+ curriculum and qualifications system can be designed to become more inclusive and less divided, while promoting quality of learning, not least in relation to vocational education and training.

Prescriptive, open and combined approaches to design

First and foremost is the question of what type of awarding structure should be developed to raise levels of participation, achievement and progression in the English education and training system. The agreement on a multi-level approach to curriculum and qualifications from 14+ brings the Baccalaureate debates, which focused throughout the 1990s on advanced level and post-compulsory education, down the system into the lower levels and into compulsory education. This clearly expands the number of design and implementation issues to be considered, including the reform of GCSE.

Over the last decade, three interrelated approaches to the design of a new awarding structure have emerged – 'prescriptive', 'flexible' and 'combined':

- A *prescriptive and grouped* approach to qualifications architecture emphasizes curriculum frameworks, subject breadth and rules of combination. Awards of this type tend not to make use of existing qualifications blocks, but are made up of specific components which support the overall curriculum and qualifications package. Advocates of this more prescriptive approach tend to look to awards such as the International Baccalaureate and principles derived from a broad academic tradition, possibly accepting that vocational qualifications might be distinctive and part of a separate awarding structure. Because of the emphasis given to subject combination, particularly at advanced level, this approach can be seen to be more suited to some learners, but would not be appropriate for all.

- A *flexible and open* approach to a 14–19 awarding structure focuses on progression, learner choice, modular design, credit accumulation, key skills and overarching certification of current qualifications. Advocates of this approach question the academic language of Baccalaureate proposals and the way that prescriptive grouped systems contain hurdles that might prevent some learners from gaining recognition for their achievements. Supporters tend to be from further education and are concerned that Baccalaureates might undermine widening participation. Open systems can be more or less radical in their design. A cautious and possibly elitist example of this approach is contained in the 14–19 Green Paper *Matriculation Diploma*. A more radical approach is contained in the Association of College's proposals for a Learning and Skills Diploma (AoC, 2002b).

- A *combined* approach to qualifications architecture uses features of both of the above in combination in order to emphasize access and progression while also ensuring curriculum coherence. This is achieved through the use of a common Core for all learners, the prescription of breadth via the use of multi-level awards, a limited use of modularization and credit, and opportunities for learners to exercise choice. While using some current qualifications (eg A2s), this approach emphasizes the need to re-engineer existing qualifications and to design new ones to meet the demands of the envisaged new diploma awards. This particular fusion of features seeks to build on some of the strengths of the English system, while attempting to address its underlying weaknesses. It is this combined approach that underpins the proposals for an English Baccalaureate System laid out in the final part of this chapter.

Related to the type of model envisaged are professional debates about the use of the term 'Baccalaureate'. It is seen by some as an imported term and is associated with schools and broad academic education rather than with colleges and vocational education and training. While the term may not suffice on its own, for the reasons indicated above, the idea of an 'English Baccalaureate System' may be attractive, because it signals the development of our own inclusive national version of a highly-regarded approach to upper secondary education in other European countries. It also signals a new phase of fundamental reform. The only alternative term that has received widespread support from education professionals is 'Diploma', because this term already exists within the English awarding system, reflects solid achievement and is used in relation to both academic and vocational education.

The function and design of a 'Core' of common learning

While there are important differences between the three approaches outlined above, there is a concept of a Core of common learning in all three approaches. However, in the combined model the investment is greatest because of its emphasis on the Core providing the means of progression between and within different levels of learning and the need for added-value over and above that gained in the main areas of study. For different reasons both the open and prescriptive models pay less attention to this element of design. The prescribed approach devotes more attention to the role of subject combinations and the open model is more of an organizing mechanism for existing qualifications and units. However, there appears to be a degree of professional consensus about the role of a Core of common learning based on the need to develop wider learning skills beyond the requirements made by subjects or main areas of study.

In models which emphasize the role of a core, such as the Core and Specialization Diploma models within our proposed English Baccalaureate System, there are a number of important design and implementation questions raised by practitioners. At present, we identify three in particular. How can a Core be:

1. customized to meet individual learner needs, the needs of different levels and phases from 14+ so that 'unified learning' does not become 'uniform learning'?
2. delivered effectively and how is it related to chosen subjects/areas of study?
3. assessed so that it motivates learners and recognizes added-value achievement without contributing to the assessment burden?

Which aspects of work-based learning to include in any new system?

There is considerable agreement among the education profession and beyond that one of the most important and urgent roles of any future curriculum and qualifications system from 14+ is to improve the quality, visibility and status of vocational education and training. However, there are differences of opinion about which aspects of work-based learning should be accredited within such a system.

In all cases, there appears to be clear support for the inclusion of a strong strand of full-time vocational education to replace GNVQs, AVCEs and BTECs for younger learners. The aim of this approach would be to create holistic and clearly recognized programmes of study along the lines of earlier BTEC First and National Diplomas. Where there is more debate is how far and in what way the Modern Apprenticeship system and other forms of work-based training might be included and framed by a single awarding structure from 14+. The reason for this questioning is not because inclusion is undesirable, but because it may not be easily realizable within the current context of a varied and voluntarist apprenticeship system and a largely unregulated labour market. The inclusion of work-based learning for young people inside a diploma or Baccalaureate system would mean an acceptance that apprenticeship might become more educationally defined than at present.

Overall, at this stage of the debate about reform there appears to be a greater professional consensus about the direction, purposes and principles of a future inclusive and unified curriculum and qualifications system from 14+ than at any time in the past. Clearly, any reform process has to harness and build on this consensus. However, the debates about the architecture of the new system are also of fundamental importance and here there is less agreement. Openly debating design issues is thus a necessary first step in the reform process as a way of grinding out error and producing a feeling of policy inclusion. As we have seen, this stage didn't happen with *Curriculum 2000* because there was no open debate beyond an initial constrained and superficial consultation process. Moreover, the areas of debate outlined above do not necessarily represent mutually exclusive positions. Within them they contain the seeds of a pragmatic resolution of real problems and will form a useful basis of mutual learning as the debate proceeds.

In the final section of this chapter we lay out the broad principles and architecture of an English Baccalaureate System from 14+ that is based on Core/Specialization Diplomas which draw on the combined approach to design described above and thus borrow features of both open and prescriptive approaches. In our view, this type of Diploma model, which draws on different reform traditions, is most likely to provide the foundation of a fully inclusive and unified curriculum and qualifications system that meets the needs of all learners within the 14–19 phase. Moreover, we believe that this system is potentially flexible enough to build on the fragile gains of *Curriculum 2000*, while addressing some of its weaknesses and thereby remedying some of the deep-rooted problems in the English education and training system.

The English Baccalaureate System from 14+

The English Baccalaureate System outlined below aims to provide a transparent, flexible and rigorous system of education and training for all younger learners. It could also relate to adult learning, but for the purposes of this chapter we confine our attention to the education and training of 14–19-year-olds. A key principle underpinning the English Baccalaureate System is to build on strengths in the English education and training system – choice, flexibility, depth of study and innovative pedagogy – while addressing some of its long-standing weaknesses – low status vocational education, the lack of curriculum entitlement at 14–19 resulting in variability in learner programmes, inadequate curriculum breadth or space for skill-building, poor progression routes for many and over assessment for all.

As can be seen from Table 8.1, the English Baccalaureate System we propose is a unified curriculum and qualifications system that includes all types of study from general full-time education to occupationally-specific modern apprenticeship programmes. We believe that it is important to embrace all types of learning within a single framework that recognizes different forms of specialization in order to raise the status of vocational education. The System also extends from compulsory secondary education for 14–16-year-olds to post-compulsory education and training and covers five levels of study – Entry, Foundation, Intermediate, Advanced 1 and Advanced 2.

There would be four types of Diploma within this unified system – General; Specialist 1 (domain-based); Specialist 2 (broad vocational); and

Table 8.1 A unified English Baccalaureate System

Adv.2	Advanced (General)	Advanced Specialist (Domain)	Advanced Specialist (Vocational)	Advanced Specialist (Occupational)	**Advanced Diploma (The Bac)**
Adv.1					
Int.	Intermediate General (pre and post 16)	Intermediate (Domain)	Intermediate (Vocational)	Intermediate (Occupational)	**Intermediate Diploma**
Found.	Foundation General (pre and post 16)		Foundation (Vocational)		**Foundation Diploma**
Entry	Entry Level Provision (pre and post 16)				**Entry Diploma**

Specialist 3 (occupational) – and Diplomas would be awarded at four levels – Entry, Foundation, Intermediate and Advanced. However, Specialist Diplomas would only be offered post-16 and at Foundation, Intermediate and Advanced level. All Diplomas would contain elements of study at more than one level (like the International Baccalaureate) in order to ensure breadth as well as depth in learner programmes.

The main function of the Advanced level Diplomas (The Bacs) would be to provide broad programmes of study with enough specialization to prepare young people for higher education or for high-skilled employment. The role of the Foundation and Intermediate level Diplomas would be to mark a stage of development for the majority of learners and an exit quali-fication for a minority. These lower level Diplomas would be designed primarily to motivate learners to progress to the next stage of education, although for some they would be used as the basis of preparation for participation in the workplace. The intention would be to provide a balance of breadth and specialist study, to create the space for learning skill development and practical activities, to reduce the examination burden associated with GCSEs, and to promote progression and genuine employability. The Entry level Diploma would be the first level in the English Baccalaureate awarding structure at 14+ and would provide basic, practical and life skills alongside project work to motivate learners to progress to further learning.

All Diplomas would have a prescribed Core of learning, comprise credit-bearing qualifications units at specified levels and would be of a prescribed volume. Breadth would be assured at all levels through the requirements of the Core, the requirements of the Diploma as a whole and through multi-level study. Beyond this there would be considerable flexi-bility and the possibility of learner choice in terms of the subjects/areas studied and individualization of programmes of learning within the common Core itself.

It is important to stress that the English Baccalaureate System, illus-trated above, does not assume that all learners would move in the same way or at the same pace. There would be the facility for both vertical and horizontal progression and the possibility for learners working mainly within one level also to undertake units of learning at a higher level in areas in which they had particular aptitude or interest. Most learners would pass through Entry and Foundation levels as part of compulsory education and the majority would be expected to be working towards either an Intermediate or Foundation Diploma between the ages of 14 and 16. However, this would vary according to ability and interest. Beyond the age of 16 there would be the freedom to continue with a more general education programme, such as that offered within the General Diploma; to specialize in a particular combination of subjects (eg the natural sciences, the humanities) by working towards a Specialist 1 Diploma; to specialize in a broad vocational area (eg Business, Leisure and Tourism) by working towards a Specialist Diploma 2; or to enter the workplace as a Modern Apprentice and work towards a Specialist Diploma 3.

We refer to the learner's individual progression path within the unified system as their 'personal routeway'. This personal routeway represents the balance between compulsion, coherence and clarity of outcome, on the one hand, and individual flexibility and choice – a traditional hallmark of the English curriculum and qualifications system – on the other.

The concept of the Core

At the heart of all the Diplomas within the English Baccalaureate System lies the common Core of learning. This would comprise three components flexibly applied to all levels of Diplomas: a specialist research study; underpinning taught elements (eg at advanced level, critical thinking, theory of knowledge, people and organizations) and wider activities and experiences (eg experience of the world of work, Duke of Edinburgh Award, sport, drama and music). The Core would be supported by individual guidance, mentoring and supervision. If the Core, which would be compulsory, is to be accepted and valued by learners, it would need to contain an element of choice and specialization. This would mainly be achieved through the choice of specialist research study and wider activities and experiences, but could also be supported through the customization of the underpinning taught components by schools, colleges and employers/training providers.

Conceived in this way, the Core potentially supports six major principles within the English Baccalaureate System – breadth, progression, motivation, skill-building, pedagogical innovation and responsiveness to future demands of the education and training system.

It is possible to see the English Baccalaureate System, based on the type of combined Core/Specialist Diploma model described above, as recognizing both the importance of specialization and choice, traditionally associated with study in this country, and the need to introduce more breadth, common learning and skill-building into the curriculum. It would also allow the creation of a new concept of 'standards' based on a learner's whole programme of study rather than on individual qualifications, thereby reducing the examination and assessment burden associated with current modular qualifications. In addition, a unified structure of this type could provide the focus for the local and institutional collaboration and innovation envisaged under the new Learning and Skills Council system contributing to what we term 'inclusive and effective local learning systems (Coffield *et al,* 2002). Finally, it is our contention that because the English Baccalaureate System builds on the best of the current qualifications system and learns lessons from previous mistakes in this area, it would be capable of securing considerable consensus from the education profession and provides a clear vision or end goal for future curriculum and qualifications reform from 14+.

Key milestones towards an English Baccalaureate System

As we have commented earlier in this volume, a major feature of the consensus for reform of the English curriculum and qualifications system is being able to blend evolution of the existing system with radical structural change. The key to this conundrum in our view is time, transparency and political leadership building on professional experience. To support this we need a reform period of up to 10 years and the identification by Government of an end-goal or vision that will provide the education profession and all other stakeholders with a clear sense of the direction of reform and possible steps and stages to its achievement. This kind of reform process also requires a willingness and an ability to critically reflect upon reforms of the past. In other words, we have argued for strategic gradualism based on policy learning, rather than policy incrementalism based on policy amnesia. Our research with the education profession suggests that strategic gradualism is capable of gathering widespread and sustained support. Policy incrementalism, which led to the short-term and flawed approach of *Curriculum 2000* is, in our view, now discredited.

In moving towards an English Baccalaureate System, it is thus important to avoid two major mistakes – to tinker yet again in a complex and piece-meal way or to go for a 'big bang' approach overnight without adequate preparation. From the perspective of strategic gradualism and the concept of the 'long haul', there appear to be six major milestones in the transition from the current curriculum and qualifications system to a new English Baccalaureate System from 14+:

1. There would need to be an extended period of open and inclusive debate about the end goal of reform; steps and stages to its attainment; and the principles and design of the new system. Such a debate would not only cement the professional consensus for reform but would also raise awareness more widely among stakeholders about the new system and its implications.
2. The Government would need to commit itself in its next election manifesto to the building of an inclusive and coherent 14+ curriculum and qualifications system, such as that outlined above, in a third term of office. This action would be taken by all major stakeholders as a signal of genuine political will for change.
3. It would be necessary to set in train a process for designing the architecture of the new system involving all stakeholders. In the case of the English Baccalaureate System, this would mean creating a new level within the national qualifications framework (Advanced 1); designing new components of the diplomas (eg the Specialist Research Study, the taught underpinning elements of the Core); and the re-engineering of existing qualifications (eg a two-unit A1 qualification block and courses shorter than GCSE at Foundation and Intermediate level) to fit within the new architecture. Particular attention would need to be paid to the

assessment requirements of the new Diplomas in order to ensure that all forms of assessment were adequately exploited, that there was a reduction in the assessment burden for learners and teachers, and that validity and fitness of purpose became the underlying principles of design.

4. It would be important to establish a programme of piloting for the new Diplomas involving the testing of new components, re-engineered components and whole programmes of study. In all cases, the learners involved would need to be protected in terms of the quality of their learning programmes and the recognition of new awards by employers and universities.

5. As we saw in Chapter 7, no fundamental reform of this type could take place without consideration of key levers and drivers, as well as wider contextual and shaping factors in the education and training system. It would therefore be necessary to ensure that factors such as teacher recruitment, training and professional development, performance tables, funding arrangements and planning mechanisms were also reformed to support the establishment of the new system.

6. Finally, there would be a need to design a formative evaluation framework to underpin and inform the whole reform process and to facilitate a virtuous cycle of 'policy learning'.

Even with a 10-year reform programme, we do not underestimate the transformation that such a process would entail. At the same time, we are equally aware of how inadequate and unstable the current curriculum and qualifications arrangements for 14–19-year-olds are. We believe that a process of strategic gradualism could bring steady change without upheaval. The enduring message from *Curriculum 2000* is that piecemeal reform with no clear future direction has the potential to cause the greatest turbulence of all to the education system, because of the way in which it produces unpredictable complexity and lack of transparency. What is needed now is clarity of purpose and direction, beginning with an inclusive and open debate based on policy learning and vision so that we can get the policy process right over the next decade. It's time we stopped harking back to qualifications designed for a small elite in the 1950s, moved beyond A levels and focused instead on creating a modernized and inclusive curriculum and qualifications system for all 14–19-year-olds in the future.

Appendix 1

The Institute of Education/Nuffield Foundation Research Project (1999–2003)

The advanced level curriculum in this country has been extensively criticized for its narrowness. Following the *Qualifying for Success* consultation process in 1997, the Government announced qualifications reforms to broaden the advanced level curriculum. During its first three years (1999–2002), the Institute of Education (IoE)/Nuffield Foundation project examines how schools and colleges are responding to the *Curriculum 2000* reforms which were introduced in September 2000. The final year of the project (2003), to which we do not refer in this book, will be used to make comparisons between the qualification reforms in England, Scotland and Wales.

The project employs three interrelated research approaches:

1. *Desk research and interviews with key national agencies* were used to identify emerging issues as schools and colleges planned for the reforms during 1999/2000, and to examine how the reforms evolved throughout the academic years 2000/2002.
2. *Data from a number of national surveys on Curriculum 2000* were analysed to provide a quantitative picture of institutions' advanced level curriculum provision before and after the introduction of the qualifications changes and changes in learners' programmes of study as a result of the reforms.
3. *Further qualitative data have been collected from 50 schools and colleges across England* in order to examine in more detail changes to the advanced level curriculum offer in these institutions, how learner study programmes have been affected by the reforms and what major factors have affected both institutional and learner decision-making – these data have been collected through three sets of site visits during the academic years 1999/2000, 2000/2001 and 2001/2002.

The IoE/Nuffield research project sites

The central focus of the first three years of the IoE/Nuffield research project (1999/2001) was on schools and colleges' responses to the *Curriculum 2000* reforms in its planning and initial implementation phases. A total of 50 institutions were selected for half-day site visits. Each institution was visited three times during the first three years of the project

– in each case these visits took place in the spring and summer terms of the three consecutive academic years.

Each half-day visit involved interviews and discussions with a number of key actors within the institution. All the interviews and discussions were taped and transcribed for analysis.

During the first set of site visits, headteachers of schools or principals of colleges were interviewed to obtain an overview of the institution's response to *Curriculum 2000*. In addition, lengthier discussions took place with deputy heads/vice-principals/curriculum directors or heads of sixth form around the detail of their *Curriculum 2000* provision and implementation issues. In schools, Year 11 learners were interviewed to gain their views on the prospect of undertaking an expanded advanced level curriculum. In the case of general further education colleges and sixth form colleges, heads of department or faculties were questioned to find out their views on the effects of *Curriculum 2000* on their subject areas.

During the second set of site visits, carried out in the spring and summer terms of 2001, heads of sixth form/programme directors, Year 12/first year advanced level tutors and Year 12/first year advanced level learners were interviewed in order to focus on learner programmes of study and to capture the learner experience of *Curriculum 2000*.

The third set of visits involved interviews with curriculum managers, groups of learners in Years 12 and 13 and subject teachers. The focus of this third set of visits was on comparing the experience of the first and second years of the reforms to see if the issues that had emerged during the former had been resolved by the second year of implementation. Again learners' views were at the heart of the investigation but there was also a desire to gather more specific information from subject teachers on what was happening in the classroom as a result of the *Curriculum 2000* reforms.

The 50 institutions chosen for site visits represented a theoretical sample of schools and colleges. The sample was designed to reflect and exemplify the following characteristics which earlier work suggested were important in determining institutional responses to qualifications and curriculum reform (Hodgson and Spours, 1999b, 2000b).

Types of institution

All institutional types offering advanced level provision to 16–19-year-olds are represented in the sample: 11–18 comprehensive schools; selective schools; independent schools; sixth form colleges; and general further education colleges.

Size of sixth form

The 11–18 school sixth forms were chosen according to numbers of learners and thus represent the whole spectrum from 30 to 630.

Curriculum offer

The schools were also chosen according to their previous advanced level provision; they thus ranged from sixth forms offering only A levels through to those with more than 50 per cent GNVQ provision.

Geographical spread

Institutions are located in different parts of the country – the North West, the North East, the East Midlands, East Anglia, London, the Home Counties and the South West.

Locality

It was felt that institutions serving different localities might have different responses to *Curriculum 2000*. The sample thus includes schools and colleges in inner-city, urban, suburban, provincial and rural settings.

Competitive/non-competitive environment

Previous research had suggested that the level of competition among providers might make a difference to their response to *Curriculum 2000*. The sample of 50 schools and colleges therefore includes some institutions in highly competitive environments as well as those in non-competitive environments, with some schools involved in formal cooperation.

By using these criteria for selecting our sample we have also achieved a wide spread of learner intake in terms of average GCSE scores, average A level scores, and percentage of the cohort progressing onto higher education. In addition, we were careful not to approach any of the schools and colleges involved in either QCA or FEDA/LSDA projects on *Curriculum 2000* to avoid overburdening these institutions.

Appendix 2

The take-up of AGNVQ and AVCE, 1999–2002

Advanced GNVQ and AVCE entry and achievement, 1999–2002. All figures from JCGQ[1]

	1999 AGNVQ	2000 AGNVQ	2001 AGNVQ	2002 AVCE (12 unit)	2002 AVCE (6 unit)	2002 AVCE (3 unit)
Total entry[2] All subjects	83,402	80,290	70,717	42,291[4]	32,246[4]	12,411[4]
Achieve full award[3]	48,733	47,211	42,288	34,974	25,378	9,258
Full award as % of total	58	59	60	83	79	75

Notes

1. The Joint Council for General Qualifications is made up of representatives from the awarding bodies. These data are published each year and form the basis of the newspapers' league tables.
2. For the AGNVQ figures these numbers are labelled as 'active candidates', and are defined as someone who had either taken a test or who had reported unit completion, in the previous year.
3. In its conception, the GNVQ was meant to be a flexible, unitized qualification that could be completed over varying time scales. Although schools and colleges could not always easily accommodate this, it was not unusual for students to complete their award in the seventh term. The publication of exam result league tables could not reflect this ongoing completion, and so only students who had completed awards by the end of the summer term were included. Therefore, the actual completion rates for 1999–2001 are likely to be higher than the figures in the table.

4. The AGNVQ was seen as a whole programme, with some students taking a limited range of additional qualifications alongside. No one would have taken two full GNVQs at the same time. The AVCE has been designed to work as part of the student's programme, mixed with other qualifications in order to make up broader and fuller programmes of study. Therefore, the figures for AGNVQ entry represent different learners, whereas the AVCE entries contain an element of double counting, as a significant minority of learners have combined different AVCEs, which inflates the level of entries compared to the AGNVQ figures.

Appendix 3

THE UCAS TARIFF
A New Points Score System for Entry to Higher Education

WHAT IS THE NEW UCAS TARIFF?

- It is a completely new points score system to report achievement for entry to HE
- It gives numerical values to qualifications
- It establishes agreed equivalence between different types of qualifications
- It provides comparisons between applicants with different types of achievement

WHY DO WE NEED A NEW TARIFF?

- The current system was never intended for use in offer-making by HE
- The current GCE A level points scores (A=10 ➔ E=2) do not reflect the relative values of the levels of achievement
- The present system does not cover other qualifications such as Advanced GNVQ and Scottish qualifications – there is a need for a new Tariff capable of giving value to achievement in a range of qualifications in the new National Qualifications Frameworks in England, Wales and Northern Ireland, and Scotland

WHAT QUALIFICATIONS DOES IT COVER?

Initially it will cover:

- GCE Advanced and Advanced Subsidiary and stand-alone GCE Advanced units in Mathematics
- GNVQ Advanced (12-unit, 6-unit and 3-unit + units taken in addition to the 12-unit award)
- The three main Key Skills (Application of Number, Communication and IT) at levels 2, 3 and 4
- New Scottish Higher and Advanced Higher
- Intermediate 2 and Standard Grade Credit (Scotland)

The Tariff will be scheduled in due course to include other qualifications and entry routes.

HOW WILL HE USE THE TARIFF?

- The Tariff is a facility offered to HE to assist in expressing entrance requirements and making conditional offers
- It is not obligatory for HEIs to use the Tariff, although they will be encouraged to do so
- The current points score system will be discontinued
- Entry requirements expressed as a points score may be qualified to require a minimum level of depth and/or achievement in specified subjects

WHEN WILL IT TAKE EFFECT?

The new Tariff will be used for the first time for 2002 entry when the first cohort of applicants with the new post-16 qualifications will enter HE.

HOW DOES THE POINTS SCORE SYSTEM WORK?

The following chart indicates the agreed points scores:

UCAS TARIFF									
Single units		GCE A/AS and GNVQ Advanced				Scottish Qualifications			
Main Key Skills¹	1-unit award²	3-unit award³	6-unit award⁴	12-unit award⁵	Score	Advanced Higher	Higher	Intermediate 2	Standard Grade Credit
				A	240				
				B	200				
				C	160				
			A	D	120	A			
			B		100	B			
			C	E	80	C			
					72		A		
		A	D		60		B		
		B			50				
					48		C		
					42			A	
		C	E		40				
					38				Band 1
					35			B	
Level 4		D			30				
					28			C	Band 2
Level 3	A	E			20				
	B				17				
	C				13				
Level 2	D				10				
	E				7				

¹ The scores shown are for each unit – for the Key Skills qualification the individual scores are aggregated
² Covers stand-alone GCE Advanced Mathematics units, and GNVQ Advanced units over and above those required to achieve the 12-unit award
³ GCE Advanced Subsidiary and 3-unit GNVQ Advanced
⁴ GCE Advanced and 6-unit GNVQ Advanced
⁵ 12-unit GNVQ Advanced

- Points scores can be aggregated from different qualifications, eg GCE Advanced/Advanced Subsidiary and Advanced GNVQ
- There is no ceiling to the number of points which can be accumulated, thereby recognising the full breadth and depth of students' achievements
- There will be no double counting – students cannot count the same or similar qualifications twice
- GCE Advanced Subsidiary scores will be subsumed into a GCE Advanced score in the same subject. Similarly, Scottish Higher scores will be subsumed into Advanced Higher scores in the same subject
- Points scores for Key Skills achievement will be reported separately

ANY MORE QUESTIONS?

For further information, please consult the UCAS website (www.ucas.ac.uk) or contact UCAS' Curriculum & Development Department:

Tel: 01242 544862
Fax: 01242 544954
Email: h.wakefield@ucas.ac.uk

References

AoC – Association of Colleges (1997) *DfEE consultation document, Qualifying for Success: Response of the Association of Colleges*, AoC, London

AoC (2002a) *Response to 14–19 Green Paper,* AoC, London

AoC (2002b) *A Proposal for a Learning and Skills Diploma*, AoC, London

APVIC – Association of Principals of Sixth Form Colleges (1991) *A Framework for Growth: Improving the post-16 curriculum,* APVIC, Wigan

ATL – Association of Teachers and Lecturers (2002) *14–19: Extending opportunities, raising standards: ATL's response to the Green Paper,* ATL, London

Audit Commission/OFSTED (1993) *Unfinished Business: Full-time education courses for 16–19 year olds*, Stationery Office, Norwich

Ball, S J, Maguire, M and Macrae, S (2000) 'Worlds apart' – Education markets in the post-16 sector in one urban locale 1995–98, in ed F Coffield, *Differing Visions of the Learning Society,* The Policy Press, Bristol

Beaumont, G (1995) *Review of 100 NVQs and SVQs: A report submitted to the DfEE,* DfEE, London

Blackstone, T (1998) *Qualifying for Success: The response to the Qualifications and Curriculum Authority Advice,* 3 April, DfES, London

Blackstone, T (1999) *A Level Curriculum Will Guarantee Standards: Blackstone,* DFEE Press Release 125/99, 19 March

Blunkett, D (2000) *The Learning and Skills Council Remit Letter from the Secretary of State for Education and Employment,* DfEE, London

Broadfoot, P (ed) (1986) *Selection, Certification and Control,* Falmer Press, London

Bullock, A (1975) *A Language for Life: Report of The Committee of Inquiry into English Language Teaching,* The Stationery Office, Norwich

Callaghan, Rt Hon J (1976) 'Ruskin College Speech', *The Times Educational Supplement,* 22 October

Capey, J (1996) *GNVQ Assessment Review,* NCVQ, London

CEI – Centre for Education and Industry (2001) *Independent Reassert to Evaluate the Introduction of the Key Skills Qualification: Final report*, Centre for Education and Industry, University of Warwick

Cockcroft, W (1981) *Mathematics Counts: Report of the Committee of Inquiry into the Teaching of Mathematics in Schools*, Stationery Office, Norwich

Coffield, F (2002) *A New Strategy for Learning and Skills: Beyond 101 initiatives,* presented at the Institute of Education, University of London, 1 May

Coffield, F, Hodgson, A and Spours, K (2002) *Learning and Inclusion in the New Learning and Skills System: Research proposal to the ESRC Teaching and Learning Research Programme,* University of Newcastle and Institute of Education, University of London

Cohen, P (1984) Against the new vocationalism, in eds I Bates *et al, Schooling for the Dole? The New Vocationalism,* Macmillan, London

CBI – Confederation of British Industry (1989) *Towards a Skills Revolution: Report of the vocational education and training task force*, CBI, London

CBI (1993) *Routes for Success,* CBI, London

DE – Department of Employment (1988) *Employment for the 1990s*, Stationery Office, Norwich

DE (1989) *Training in Britain*, Stationery Office, Norwich

DE and DES (1986) *Working Together – Education and Training*, Stationery Office, Norwich

Dearing, Sir Ron (1995) *Review of 16–19 Qualifications: Interim report*, SCAA, London

Dearing, Sir Ron (1996) *Review of Qualifications for 16–19 Year Olds,* SCAA, London

DES – Department for Education and Science (1985) *International Statistical Comparisons of the Education and Training for 16–18 Year Olds*, Stationery Office, Norwich

DES (1988) *Advancing A Levels: Report of the Committee chaired by Professor Higginson,* Stationery Office, Norwich

DES/ED/WO (1991) *Education and Training for the 21st Century*, Stationery Office, Norwich

DfE/ED/WO – Department for Education/Employment Department/Welsh Office (1991) *Education and Training for the 21st Century*, Stationery Office, Norwich

DfEE – Department for Education and Employment (1997a) *Government defers A level and GNVQ reform,* DfEE Press Notice, 11 June

DfEE (1997b) *Building the Framework: A consultation paper on bringing together the work of the NCVQ and SCAA*, DfEE, London

DfEE (1997c) *Guaranteeing Standards: A consultation paper on the structure of awarding bodies*, DfEE, London

DfEE (1998) *The Learning Age: A renaissance for a New Britain*, DfEE, London

DfEE (1999a) *Learning to Succeed: A new framework for post-16 learning*, DfEE, London

DfEE (1999b) *Qualifying for Success: Post-16 curriculum reform,* Letter from Rob Hull, Director for Qualifications and Occupational Standards, to Heads of Secondary Schools and Principals of Colleges, 19 March, DfEE, London

DfEE (2000) *Learning to Succeed School Sixth Form Funding: Technical consultation paper,* December 2000, DfEE, London

DfEE/IoE (2000) Survey on the *Qualifying for Success Reforms*, DfEE, London

DfEE/DENI/WO – Department for Education and Employment/Department of Education Northern Ireland/Welsh Office (1997) *Qualifying for Success: A consultation paper on the future of post-16 qualifications,* DfEE, London

DfES – Department for Education and Skills (2001a) *Schools Achieving Success,* DfES, London

DfES (2001b) *Statistical Release SR30/2001,* DfES, London

DfES (2001c) *Government Response to QCA Report,* DfES, London

DfES (2002a) *14–19 Education: Extending opportunities, raising standards,* DfES, London

DfES (2002b) *Success for All,* DfES, London

DfES (2003) *14–19: Excellence and Opportunity: Government response to the 14–19 Green Paper,* DfES, London

Ecclestone, K (2000) Bewitched, bothered and bewildered: a policy analysis of the GNVQ assessment regime 1992–2000, *Journal of Education Policy,* **15,** 5, pp 539–58

Elsheikh, E and Leney, T (2002) *Work, Work, Work: Students' perceptions of study and work-life balance under Curriculum 2000,* ATL, London

FEDA/IoE – Further Education Development Agency/Institute of Education (1999) *Project Report: An overarching certificate at Advanced Level,* ACCAC/CCEA/QCA, London

FEDA/IoE/Nuffield Foundation (1997) *GNVQs 1993–1997: A national survey report,* FEDA, London

FEFC – Further Education Funding Council (1994) *General National Vocational Qualifications in the Further Education Sector in England: National survey report*, FEFC, Coventry

FEFC (1999) *Curriculum 2000: Funding for full-time 16–19 year olds*, Circular 99/33, FEFC, Coventry

FEU – Further Education Unit (1979) *A Basis for Choice: Report of a study group on post-16 pre-employment courses,* FEU, London

Finegold, D, Keep, E, Miliband, D, Raffe, D, Spours, K and Young, M (1990) *A British Baccalaureate: Overcoming divisions within education and training*, IPPR, London

Finn, D (1987) *Training Without Jobs: New deals and broken promises,* Macmillan, London

Fowler, Z, Hodgson, A and Spours, K (2002) *Strategies for Balancing Learning and Earning: Student, teacher and employer perspectives in the context of Curriculum 2000,* University of London Institute of Education, London

Fryer, R (1997) *Learning for the 21st Century: First report of the National Advisory Group for Continuing Education and Lifelong Learning,* NAGCELL, London

Garnett, J (2002) Advanced vocational courses: an examination of student choice and attitudes towards AVCE, in eds A Hodgson and K Spours, *The First Year of Curriculum 2000 in Lancashire: School-based research,* Lancashire County Council/IoE, Preston

Gray, J, Jesson, D and Tranmer, M (1993) *Boosting Post-16 Participation in Full-Time Education: A study of some key factors: England and Wales,* Youth Cohort Study No 20, Employment Department, Sheffield

Green, A (1986) The MSC and the three-tier structure of further education, in eds C Benn and J Fairley, *Challenging the MSC: On jobs, education and training,* Pluto Press, London

Green, A (1997) Core skills, general education and unification in post-16 education, in eds A Hodgson and K Spours, *Dearing and Beyond: 14–19 qualifications, frameworks and systems,* Kogan Page, London

Green, A and Lucas, N (eds) (1999) *FE and Lifelong Learning: Realigning the sector for the 21st century,* Institute of Education, London

Green, A and Steedman, H (1997) *Into the Twenty First Century: An assessment of British skills, profiles and prospects,* Centre for Economic Performance, London

Haines, A (2002) FEFC funding and curriculum decision-making, unpublished doctoral research, School of Lifelong Education and International Development, Institute of Education, University of London

Hargreaves, D (2001a) *Review of Curriculum 2000 – QCA's Report on Phase One,* QCA, London

Hargreaves, D (2001b) *Review of Curriculum 2000 – QCA's Report on Phase Two,* QCA, London

HEFCE – Higher Education Funding Council for England (2001) *Supply and Demand in Higher Education,* HEFCE, Bristol

Henry, J (2001) Schools hit the wrong key skills, *Times Education Supplement,* 25 May

Higham, J, Sharp, P and Yeomans, D (2002) *Changing the 14–19 School Curriculum in England: Lessons from successive reforms,* Research Report to the ESRC, University of Leeds

Hill, P (2001) *Selective Schools, Higher Education and Curriculum 2000,* MA Dissertation, School of Lifelong Learning, Institute of Education, University of London

HMC – Headmasters' and Headmistresses' Conference (2002) *Response of the Headmasters' and Headmistresses' Conference to the Government's 14–19 Green Paper,* HMC, Leicester

HMI – Her Majesty's Inspectorate (1989) *Post-16 Education and Training, Core Skills: An HMI Paper,* Stationery Office, Norwich

HMI (1996) *Assessment of General Vocational Qualifications in Schools 1995–96,* Stationery Office, Norwich

Hodgson, A and Spours, K (1997a) From the 1991 White Paper to the Dearing Report: a conceptual and historical framework for the 1990s, in eds A Hodgson and K Spours, *Dearing and Beyond: 14–19 qualifications, frameworks and systems,* Kogan Page, London

Hodgson, A and Spours, K (eds) (1997b) *Dearing and Beyond: 14–19 qualifications, frameworks and systems,* Kogan Page, London

Hodgson, A and Spours, K (1999a) *New Labour's Educational Agenda: Issues and policies for education and training from 14+,* Kogan Page, London

Hodgson, A and Spours, K (1999b) *Planning for the New 16–19 Qualifications Era,* an Institute of Education and Essex LEA Research and Development Project, Essex LEA/Institute of Education, University of London

Hodgson, A and Spours, K (2000a) Expanding higher education in the UK: from 'system slowdown' to 'system acceleration', *Higher Education Quarterly,* **54**, 4, pp 295–322

Hodgson, A and Spours, K (2000b) *Qualifying for Success: Towards a framework of understanding,* Broadening the Advanced Level Curriculum, IoE/Nuffield Series, No. 1, Lifelong Learning Group, Institute of Education, University of London

Hodgson, A and Spours, K (2001a) Part-time work and full-time education in the UK: the emergence of a curriculum and policy issue, *Journal of Education and Work,* **14**, 3, pp 373–88

Hodgson, A and Spours, K (2001b) *Evaluating Stage 1 of the Hargreaves Review of Curriculum 2000,* Broadening the Advanced Level Curriculum IoE/Nuffield Series, No. 2, Institute of Education, University of London

Hodgson, A and Spours, K (2002a) Increasing demand for higher education in the longer term: the role of 14+ qualifications and curriculum reform, in eds A Hayton and A Paczuska, *Access, Participation and Higher Education: Policy and practice,* Kogan Page, London

Hodgson, A and Spours, K (2002b) *Developing an English Baccalaureate System from 14+,* Institute of Education, University of London

Hodgson, A and Spours, K (2002c) *Raising Achievement in Advanced Level Provision in Tower Hamlets: A statistical baseline paper,* Institute of Education, University of London

Hodgson, A, Spours, K and Savory, C (2001) *Improving the 'Use' and 'Exchange' Value of Key Skills: Debating the role of the Key Skills Qualification within Curriculum 2000,* Broadening the Advanced Level Curriculum IoE/Nuffield Series, No. 4, Lifelong Learning Group, Institute of Education, University of London

Hodgson, A, Spours, K and Young, M (1998) Broader and broader still in post-16 education, *Times Educational Supplement,* 16 May

Hodkinson, P and Mattinson, K (1994) A bridge too far: the problems facing GNVQs, *The Curriculum Journal,* **5**, 3

Hyland, T (1994) *Competence, Education and NVQs: Dissenting perspectives,* Cassell, London

Institute of Directors (1992) *Performance and Potential: Education and training for a market economy,* IOD, London

Institute of Education (1997) *Response to the DfEE Consultation Paper Qualifying for Success,* Institute of Education, University of London

JACG – Joint Associations Curriculum Group (1997) *The Next Step Towards a New Curriculum Framework Post-16,* JACG, Wigan

JACG (2002) *The Proposal for a Baccalaureate-Style Diploma,* JACG, Haywards Heath

JCGQ – Joint Council for General Qualifications (2002) *National Provisional GCE A Level Results June 2002,* JCGQ, London

Kennedy, H (1997) *Learning Works: Widening participation in further education,* FEFC, Coventry

Kingdon, M (1991) *The Reform of Advanced Level,* Hodder and Stoughton, London

Labour Party (1996) *Aiming Higher: Labour's plans for reform of the 14–19 curriculum*, Labour Party, London

Labour Party (1997) *Labour Party General Election Manifesto 1997: Because Britain deserves better*, Labour Party, London

Leney, T, Lucas, N and Taubman, D (1998) *Learning Funding: The impact of FEFC funding, evidence from twelve FE colleges,* NATFHE/Institute of Education, University of London

LSDA – Learning and Skills Development Agency (2001) *Response to QCA from the Key Skills Support Programme*, LSDA, London

Lumby, J and Briggs, A with Wilson, D, Glover, D and Pell, T (2002) *Sixth Form Colleges: Policy, purpose and practice,* University of Leicester, Leicester

Miliband, D (2002) *Speech to Annual Meeting of QCA*, November, DfES, London

Morris, E (Secretary of State for Education and Skills) (2001) *Morris Points Forward on A Level Reform,* DfES Press Release, 2001/0304, 11 July

Morris, E (2002) *Foreword to the consultation document '14–19: Extending opportunities, raising standards',* DfES, London

MSC – Manpower Services Commission (1981) *A New Training Initiative – A Consultative Document,* MSC, London

NACETT – National Advisory Council for Education and Training Targets (1994) *Report on Progress,* NACETT, London

NAHT – National Association of Head Teachers (1997) *Qualifying for Success: NAHT paper to accompany consultation questionnaire,* NAHT, Haywards Heath

NAHT (2002) *14–19 Green Paper: Extending opportunities, raising standards: The proposal for a Matriculation Diploma,* NAHT, Haywards Heath

NATFHE – National Association of Teachers in Further and Higher Education (2002) *NATFHE Response to the Green Paper 14–19: Extending opportunities, raising standards*, NATFHE, London

NCC – National Curriculum Council (1990) *Core Skills 16–19*, NCC, York

NCIHE – National Committee of Inquiry into Higher Education (1997) *Higher Education in the Learning Society* (The Dearing Report), NCIHE, London

NEDO/MSC (1984) *Competence and Competition: Training in the Federal Republic of Germany, the United States and Japan*, NEDO/MSC, London

NUT – National Union of Teachers (2002) *Submission from the NUT to the DfES Consultation on the Green Paper 14–19: Extending opportunities, raising standards*, NUT, London

Oates, T (1992) *Developing and Piloting the NCVQ Core Skill Units*, NCVQ, London

Oates, T (1996) *The Development and Implementation of Key Skills in England*, NCVQ, London

OECD – Organization for Economic Cooperation and Development (1985) *Education and Training After Basic Schooling,* OECD, Paris

OFSTED – Office for Standards in Education (1994) *GNVQs in Schools 1993/94: Quality and standards of General National Vocational Qualifications,* Stationery Office, Norwich

OFSTED (1996a) *Assessment of General National Vocational Qualifications in Schools in 1995/96,* Stationery Office, Norwich

OFSTED (1996b) *Modular A Levels*, OFSTED, London

OFSTED (1999) *Modular GCE AS and A Level Examinations 1996–98,* Stationery Office, Norwich

OFSTED (2001) *Curriculum 2000: The first year of implementation,* OFSTED, London

OFSTED/ALI (2000) *The Common Inspection Framework for Inspecting Post-16 Education and Training*, OFSTED, London

Oppenheim, C (1998) (ed) *An Inclusive Society: Strategies for tackling poverty*, IPPR, London

Payne, J (2001) *Post-16 Students and Part-Time Jobs: Patterns and Effects: A report based on the England and Wales Youth Cohort Study,* DfES Research Report 323, DfES, Nottingham

Pearce, N and Hillman, J (1998) *Wasted Youth: Raising achievement and tackling social exclusion,* IPPR, London

Perry, A (2000) Performance indicators: measure for measure or a comedy of errors?, in C Mager *et al, The New Learning Market*, FEDA, London

Piatt, W and Robinson, P (2001) *Opportunity for Whom? Options for Funding and Structure of Post-16 Education,* IPPR, London

Pratley, B (1988) Who's driving the curriculum now?, in eds B Kedney and D Parkes, *Planning the FE Curriculum*, FEU, London

Pring, R (1986) In defence of TVEI, *Forum,* **28**, 1, pp 14–18

Pring, R, White, R and Brockington, D (1988) *The 14–18 Curriculum: integrating CPVE, YTS and TVEI?,* Youth Education Service, Bristol

QCA – Qualifications and Curriculum Authority (1998) *The Future of Post-16 Qualifications: The response of the Qualifications and Curriculum Authority to the Government's consultation on Qualifying for Success,* QCA, London

QCA (1999a) *Unitisation and Credit in the National Qualifications Framework: A position paper*, QCA, London

QCA (1999b) *Qualifications 16–19: A guide to the changes resulting from the 'Qualifying for Success' consultation,* QCA, London

QCA (2002a) *Curriculum 2000 Case-Study Centre Visits: November – December 2001*, QCA, London

QCA (2002b) *Report of the Evaluation of the First Year of Curriculum 2000: September 2000 – July 2001*, QCA, London

QCA (2002c) *UCAS/QCA Report on Curriculum 2000 Provision in Schools and Colleges, November 2001, Weighted Results*, QCA, London

QCA (2002d) *Report on Curriculum 2000 Provision in Schools and Colleges, June 2002, Weighted Results*, QCA, London

QCA (2002e) *Consultation on the Redevelopment of Vocational A Levels*, QCA, London

QCA (2002f) *Employers' Perceptions of Curriculum 2000*, QCA, London

QCA (2002g) *The Second Year of Curriculum 2000: Experience compared with objectives*, QCA, London

QCA/ACCAC/CEA (2002) *Reviewing the Key Skills*, QCA, London

QCA/CCEA/ACCAC (1998) *An Overarching Certificate at Advanced Level: Research specification*, QCA, London

Raffe, D (1984) The content and context of educational reform, in ed D Raffe, *Fourteen to Eighteen,* Aberdeen University Press, Aberdeen

Raffe, D, Howieson, C, Spours, K and Young, M (1998) The unification of post-compulsory education: towards a conceptual framework, *British Journal of Educational Studies, 46*, 2, pp 169–87

Rainbow, R (1993) Modular A and AS Levels: The Wessex Project, in eds W Richardson, J Woolhouse and D Finegold, *The Reform of Post-16 Education and Training in England and Wales,* Longman, Harlow

Ranson, S (1985) Towards a tertiary tripartism: new codes of social control and the 17+, in eds P Raggatt and G Weiner, *Curriculum and Assessment: Some policy issues,* Open University Press, Buckingham

Richardson, W, Woolhouse, J and Finegold, D (eds) (1993) *The Reform of Post-16 Education and Training in England and Wales,* Longman, Harlow

Royal Society (1991) *Beyond GCSE: A report by a working group of the Royal Society's Education Committee*, The Royal Society, London

Savory, C, Hodgson, A and Spours, K (2001a) *Teachers' Views on the Changes to A Levels and GNVQs Resulting from Curriculum 2000,* A Research Report of a Survey by the National Union of Teachers in Collaboration with the Institute of Education, NUT, London

Savory, C, Hodgson, A and Spours, K (2001b) *Planning and Implementing Curriculum 2000: Institutional approaches,* Broadening the Advanced Level Curriculum Research Series, No. 3, Institute of Education, University of London

Savory, C, Hodgson, A and Spours, K (2002) *Colleges and Curriculum 2000: Research for NATHFE and the School of Lifelong Learning and International Development of the Institute of Education*, NATHFE/IoE, London

Savory, C, Hodgson, A and Spours, K (2003 forthcoming) *The Advanced Certificate of Vocational Education (AVCE): A general or vocational qualification?* Broadening the Advanced Level Curriculum IoE/Nuffield Series, No. 7, Institute of Education, University of London

SCAA – Schools Curriculum and Assessment Authority (1997) *Post-16 Briefing Notes*, SCAA, London

Scottish Office (1994) *Higher Still: Opportunity for all,* Stationery Office, Edinburgh

SEAC – School Examinations and Assessment Council (1991) *Core Skills and A/AS Examinations: Report by the School Examinations and Assessment Council on the 1991 Exemplification Exercise*, SEAC, London

SEU – Social Exclusion Unit (1999) *Bridging the Gap: New opportunities for 16–18 year olds not in education, employment or training*, SEU, London

SHA – Secondary Heads Association (1993) *14–19 Pathways to Achievement: A discussion paper,* SHA, Leicester

Smithers, A (1993) *All Our Futures: Britain's education revolution,* A Dispatches Report on Education, Channel 4 Television

Spours, K (1993) The reform of qualifications within a divided system, in eds W Richardson, J Woolhouse and D Finegold, *The Reform of Post-16 Education and Training in England and Wales,* Longman, Harlow

Spours, K (2000) Developing a national qualifications framework for lifelong learning: England's unfinished business, in ed A Hodgson, *Policies, Politics and the Future of Lifelong Learning,* Kogan Page, London

Spours, K, Savory, C and Hodgson, A (2000) *Current Advanced Level Provision in England and Wales: An institutional response to Curriculum 2000,* Broadening the Advanced Level Curriculum IoE/Nuffield Series, No. 2, Institute of Education, University of London

Tait, T, Frankland, G, Smith, D and Moore, S (2002) *Curriculum 2000+ 2: Tracking institutions' and learners' experiences,* LSDA, London

Tomlinson, M (2002a) *Report on Outcomes of Review of A Level Grading,* DfES, London

Tomlinson, M (2002b) *Inquiry into A Level Standards: Final report,* DfES, London

UCAS (2001) *Report on Survey of Provision and Take-up of Curriculum 2000 in Schools and Colleges – November 2000,* UCAS, Cheltenham

UCAS (2003) *Analysis of Offers involving Curriculum 2000 Qualifications for 2002 Entry, NJCC/02/13,* UCAS, Cheltenham

Unwin, L (2002) Young people, transitions and progression, in *14–19 Education,* Papers Arising from a Seminar Series held at the Nuffield Foundation, London

Unwin, L, Wellington, J, Fuller, A and Cole, P (2000) *Effective Delivery of Key Skills in Schools, Colleges and Workplaces,* Centre for Research in Post-Compulsory Education and Training, University of Sheffield, DfEE, Sheffield

Waring, M, Hodgson, A, Savory, C and Spours, K (2003 forthcoming) *Higher Education and Curriculum 2000,* Broadening the Advanced Level Curriculum Research Series, No. 7, Institute of Education, University of London

Welsh Department of Education and Training (2002) *Learning Pathways 14–19: Consultation document,* Welsh Department of Education and Training, Cardiff

WJEC – Welsh Joint Education Committee and National Assembly for Wales (2001) *The Welsh Baccalaureate Qualification,* WJEC, Cardiff

Wicht, M (2002) A comparative study on the development of 'Key Skills' in England and Key Qualifications in Germany: is there a process of convergence around the issue of the quality of learning?, MA Dissertation, Institute of Education, University of London

Wolf, A (2002) *Does Education Matter? Myths about education and economic growth,* Penguin, Harmondsworth

Woodward, W (2001) New exams for sixth formers condemned as shambolic, *The Guardian,* 31 May

Young, M (1997) The Dearing review of 16–19 qualifications: A step towards a unified system?, in eds A Hodgson and K Spours, *Dearing and Beyond: 14–19 qualifications, frameworks and systems,* Kogan Page, London

Young, M (2002) Key Skills and the Post-Compulsory Curriculum, paper delivered at the Key Skills for All? Conference, Institute of Education, University of London, 17 May

Young, M and Leney, T (1997) From A-Levels to an Advanced Level Curriculum of the future, in eds A Hodgson and K Spours, *Dearing and Beyond: 14–19 qualifications, frameworks and systems,* Kogan Page, London

Index